HISTORICAL OUTLINES OF ENGLISH
SOUNDS AND INFLECTIONS

Historical Outlines of English Sounds and Inflections

By

SAMUEL MOORE

Late Professor of English at the University of Michigan

Revised by

ALBERT H. MARCKWARDT

Professor of English Linguistics, Princeton University

GEORGE WAHR PUBLISHING COMPANY

ANN ARBOR, MICHIGAN

1969

2/63 6.95

PREFACE

It is now seventeen years since the untimely death of Professor Samuel Moore and thirty-two since the first appearance of this textbook under its original title, *Historical Outlines of English Phonology and Middle English Grammar*. The passage of time has lessened neither the usefulness of nor the demand for the volume which presented with such clarity and concision the broad experience and profound learning of its author. The *Historical Outlines* has introduced many generations of graduate students to the language of Chaucer, guided them in their analysis of Middle English texts, and provided them with a synthesis of the development of the sounds and inflections of the English language. The present revision of this book has been undertaken in order that it may continue its long career of service.

Instructors and students will find in this revised edition a thoroughgoing alteration of the scheme of organization, some changes in presentation, but, except in one instance, no essential difference in the factual content or the conclusions which have been derived from these facts. The changes in organization have been made as a result of my knowledge of the way in which the book is used in various graduate and undergraduate courses in a number of institutions throughout the country. They may be summarized as follows: (1) Whereas in the earlier editions the sounds, inflections, and dialects of Old English served mainly as a point of departure for the treatment of Middle English, they are here treated fully, though concisely, as subjects in their own right. (2) All materials pertaining to Middle English have been placed in juxtaposition, including the appendix of the previous volume, devoted to Middle English spelling, which has been added to the chapter on Middle English sounds. (3) The section on Middle English is followed by a treatment of the transition from Middle to Modern English. (4) The chapter on the language of Chaucer is so placed that it may be employed as an introduction to Middle English in general, or as an auxiliary to literary study.

Changes in presentation involve chiefly a complete revision of the phonetic alphabet which is employed. When Professor Moore wrote the first version of this text, the use of phonetic symbols in language textbooks was still in a chaotic state. Many similar books used confusing systems of diacritics with little uniformity among them. There was an International Phonetic Alphabet, but it had not yet been satisfactorily adapted to the purpose of indicating English, particularly American English, pronunciation. Moore saw the virtues of the International

v

Phonetic Alphabet, but he was forced to compensate for its shortcomings by devising certain auxiliary symbols himself.

Since that time, largely owing to the efforts of Moore's close friends and associates, Professors John S. Kenyon and Thomas A. Knott, the International Phonetic Alphabet has become the principal medium for indicating pronunciation in works of a scholarly nature in this country. New symbols have been supplied to fill in the gaps which existed thirty years ago. These, however, have generally taken the form of unmodified characters, such as small capitals, reversed or inverted letters, and borrowings from alphabets other than the Roman. The hooked symbols, devised at that time by Professor Moore, have not found general acceptance, particularly in the face of the more recent philosophy that diacritical additions should appropriately be employed only for non-qualitative modifications of sounds. Consequently it seemed that the usefulness of Professor Moore's work might be increased if the phonetic transcriptions in it were made to agree with the use of the International Phonetic Alphabet in Knott and Kenyon, *Pronouncing Dictionary of American English,* which provides the widest present dissemination of this alphabet in a form adapted to the sounds of American English.

In order to reinforce the treatments of the Old and Middle English dialects, maps and illustrative selections have been introduced in this revision. Likewise a chart of the Old English inflectional system has been included to aid the student in his review.

The greatest difference between this and the preceding editions will be found in the treatment of Middle English dialects. At the time of his death, Professor Moore was engaged in editing the Middle English Dictionary. The regional differences in the English language during the Middle English period was always a subject which held the greatest fascination for him, and almost the first task which he and his associates, Professors Sanford B. Meech and Harold Whitehall, undertook in connection with their editorial work was a re-examination of dialect evidence. The results of this study appeared shortly after Professor Moore's death in Volume XIII of the University of Michigan series, *Essays and Studies in English and Comparative Literature,* under the title, "Middle English Dialect Characteristics and Dialect Boundaries." Since the conclusions which were reached in this study represent a considerable advance both in content and method over the treatment of Middle English dialects even in the 1929 revision of the *Historical Outlines,* it would have been unjust to Professor Moore's work and to his reputation to have omitted them from the present edition.

Albert H. Marckwardt

Ann Arbor, Michigan
August 1, 1951

CONTENTS

I. The Elements of Phonetics................................ 1

II. Modern English Sounds................................ 8

III. Old English Sounds, Inflections, and Dialects.............. 19

IV. The Language of Chaucer............................. 36

V. The Development of Middle English Sounds.............. 64

VI. The Development of Middle English Inflections........... 79

VII. Middle English Dialects.............................. 110

VIII. The Development of Modern English Sounds.............. 130

IX. The Development of Modern English Inflections.......... 141

CHAPTER I

THE ELEMENTS OF PHONETICS

1. Organs of Speech. The primary condition for the production of speech-sounds is the passage of a stream of breath through the mouth passage or through the nasal passage or through both. This stream of breath is modified in various ways by movements of the organs of speech. The principal movable organs concerned in the production of English speech-sounds are the vocal lips or folds,[1] situated in the larynx; the soft palate or velum; the tongue; the lips; and the lower jaw. The velum (which terminates below in the uvula) forms the back part of the roof of the mouth, the hard palate forming the front part.

2. Voiced and Voiceless Sounds. With reference to the action of the vocal lips, sounds are either voiced or voiceless. In the production of a voiceless sound, the stream of air passes freely through the larynx; the vocal lips are separated, so that they offer no impediment to the stream of air and therefore do not vibrate. But in the production of a voiced sound, the vocal lips are drawn into contact or close together so that they are caused to vibrate by the stream of air which passes between them. This vibration can be felt by placing the first two fingers upon the larynx or "Adam's apple" while one is pronouncing a vowel sound, or such a consonant as **v.** All vowel sounds are ordinarily voiced, but some consonants are voiced and some are voiceless.[2] It is chiefly voice that distinguishes **g** (as in **get**) from **k** (as in **kept**), **d** from **t**, **b** from **p**, **v** from **f**, **z** (as in **zoo**) from **s** (as in **soon**), and the sound of **th** in **then** from the sound of **th** in **thin.**[3]

[1] The common term *vocal cords* is not employed here because it is misleading. The vibrating mechanism consists of two muscular and tendinous ledges projecting from the side walls of the larynx. Seen at rest they appear to be lip-like projections; when set in vibration by the pressure of the out-going breath stream they are characterized by a rolling or folding type of movement.

[2] Vowels and the consonants that are ordinarily voiced can also be whispered. In whispering the breath stream passes between the arytenoid cartilages rather than the vocal lips in a way that causes friction but not those regular vibrations that characterize voice. Speakers of English very commonly whisper the last of two voiced fricatives that terminate a word followed by a pause (e.g. in **leaves**). Voiceless consonants are probably not modified when we whisper, but are made with the glottis open as in ordinary speech.

[3] By practice one may soon learn to distinguish voiced sounds from voiceless ones. A good exercise for practice is to pronounce alternately **s** and **z**, **f** and **v**, and the two

1

3.   Stops and Fricatives. With reference to the manner of their articulation, consonants are distinguished as stopped consonants (or plosives) and fricatives (or spirants).   In the production of stopped consonants, the breath stream is stopped at some point by the complete closing of the mouth passage.   If (as is usually the case) it is the outgoing breath stream that is stopped, the density of the air behind the stoppage becomes greater than the density of the outer air, so that when the stop is opened an explosion occurs.   In the production of fricatives, however, the breath stream is not completely stopped but is made to pass through an opening so narrow that the friction causes a buzzing or hissing noise.   Stopped consonants are Modern English **g** (as in **go**), **k, d, t, b, p;** fricatives are **z, s, th** (as in **then**), **th** (as in **thin**), **v, f.**   The **ch** in **chill** and the **g** in **gin** are combinations of a stop consonant with a fricative (approximately **t** with **sh** and **d** with **s** as in **measure**).   In these combinations the closure for the stop and for the fricative is made at the same or nearly the same point, and when the stop is opened the explosion occurs through the narrow opening of the fricative; such combinations are called **affricates.**

4.   The complete or partial closure required to produce stops and fricatives is usually made by means of the tongue of lips, and the quality of the various sounds is determined by the place where the closure is made.   Modern English **g** (as in **go**) and **c** (as in **comb**) are produced by contact of the tongue against the soft palate; **y** (as in **yield**) is made with an incomplete closure between the tongue and the hard palate; **d** and **t** are made by contact of the tongue against the ridge above the upper front teeth (alveolar ridge) or against the teeth themselves; **z** and **s** are made with an incomplete closure at the same point; **b** and **p** are produced by a closure of the two lips; **v** and **f** are produced with an incomplete closure between the lower lip and the upper front teeth; **th** as in **then** and **th** as in **thin** are produced by causing air to pass between the tongue and the backs or edges of the upper front teeth.

According to the place of their formation, these consonants are there-

---

sounds of **th,** taking care to pronounce the consonant sound **alone** without the aid of a vowel. The sounds of **t** and **d, p** and **b,** etc., when pronounced without a vowel, will also be felt and heard to be very different in character. It will also be observed that voiced sounds, whether vowels or consonants, are capable of being uttered with variations of musical pitch without changing the shape of the mouth cavity, whereas voiceless sounds are not.

fore classified as velar consonants (**g** as in **go, c** as in **comb**); palatal consonants (**y**); alveolar consonants (**d, t, z, s**) interdental consonants (**th** in **then, th** in **thin**); labiodental consonants (**v, f**); labial consonants (**b, p**).

5. Nasal and Oral Sounds. All of the consonants mentioned in the preceding paragraph are oral consonants. Nasal consonants are **m, n, ng** (as in **thing**). In the articulation of the oral consonants, the velum is retracted until it makes contact with the back wall of the throat, which at the same time moves forward so as to close the passage from the throat to the nasal cavity, forcing the breath stream to issue through the mouth. In the articulation of nasal consonants, however, the velum is in the position it occupies in ordinary breathing, and the mouth passage is stopped by the lips or tongue, the closure being made for **m, n,** and **ng**, precisely as for **b, d,** and **g,** respectively, the breath stream issuing through the nose.

Vowels are normally oral sounds, but they become nasalized if the velum is not completely retracted and the passage to the nasal cavity is partly open. Consonants are also nasalized when they are pronounced with incomplete retraction of the velum. The nasalized vowels of Modern French are pronounced with no retraction of the velum and with the passage from the throat to the nasal cavity wide open.

6. Vowels. Vowel sounds are more open than fricatives. In the formation of a fricative, a stream of air is made to pass through an opening so narrow that the passage of the air causes friction and therefore noise. In the formation of a vowel, however, the mouth opening is so wide that the friction of the air against the sides of the opening causes very little noise or none at all.

7. Open and Close Vowels. But the vowels are not all equally open in their formation. If one pronounces in order the vowel sounds of the words **hat, hate, heat,** he will observe that in pronouncing each of these successive sounds the tongue is closer to the roof of the mouth. When we pronounce the series, the tongue starts from a position considerably below the roof of the mouth and ends in a position quite close to the roof of the mouth. This can be felt, and it can also be seen by pronouncing the sounds before a mirror. The same thing can be observed in regard to the vowels of the words **law, low, loot.** As we pronounce this series of vowels, we can feel the tongue going higher in the mouth, and we can see it indirectly by watching the upward movement of the lower jaw as we pronounce the three sounds before a mirror.

8. This difference in openness or height is the basis of one of the most important classifications of vowel sounds. We distinguish at least three degrees in the height of vowel sounds. If the tongue is quite close to the roof of the mouth, we call the vowel a **high** vowel. If the tongue occupies a low position in the mouth, we call the vowel a **low** vowel. If the tongue is in a position about midway between its extreme high position and its extreme low position, we call the vowel a **mid** vowel. So the vowels of **law** and **hat** are **low** vowels, the vowels of **low** and **hate** are **mid** vowels, and the vowels of **loot** and **heat** are **high** vowels.

9. Back and Front Vowels. When we pronounce in succession the two series of vowels heard in **law, low, loot,** and **hat, hate, heat,** we can perceive that the tongue lies differently as we utter the two series. When we pronounce the vowels of **law, low, loot,** the tongue is closest to the **back** part of the roof of the mouth. When we pronounce the vowels of **hat, hate, heat,** the tongue is closest to the **front** part of the roof of the mouth. This can be felt, and it can also be seen to a certain extent by looking into the mouth as we pronounce the two series of sounds before a mirror. We therefore call the vowels of **law, low, loot, back** vowels, and the vowels of **hat, hate, heat, front** vowels. This is the second basis of the classification of vowel sounds.

10. Combining the two classifications of vowel sounds, we say that the vowel of **hat** is a **low front** vowel, that the vowel of **hate** is a **mid front** vowel, that the vowel of **heat** is a **high front** vowel, that the vowel of **law** is a **low back** vowel, that the vowel of **low** is a **mid back** vowel, and that the vowel of **loot** is a **high back** vowel.[4]

11. Round and Unround Vowels. If one pronounces before a mirror the two series of vowel sounds heard in **hat, hate, heat,** and **law, low, loot,** he will see that the action of the lips in pronouncing the two series is not the same. In pronouncing the first series, the lips are either in the neutral position which they occupy when they are in a position of rest with the mouth slightly open, or else the lip opening is enlarged by a slight depression of the lower lip or by drawing apart the corners of the mouth. But in pronouncing the latter series the lip opening is modified by bringing together the corners of the mouth, with or without raising the lower

---

[4] Some vowels, for example **a** in English **Cuba, e** in German **gabe, e** in French **je,** are neither front vowels nor back vowels. They occur chiefly in unstressed syllables and are generally termed **central** vowels.

lip. On the basis of this difference in the action of the lips we make the distinction between **round** and **unround** vowels, and call the vowel of **law** a **low back round** vowel, the vowel of **low** a **mid back round** vowel, and the vowel of **loot** a **high back round** vowel. The vowels of **hat, hate, heat,** on the other hand, are **unround** vowels.

Round vowels differ considerably in the degree of their rounding. The vowel of **loot** is more rounded than the vowel of **low,** and the vowel of **low** is more rounded than the vowel of **law;** in fact some speakers of English pronounce the vowel of **law** with very little rounding or none at all.

12. All of the English front vowels are unround, but front round vowels occur in French and German. The vowels of French **une** and German **kühn** and **müssen** are high front round vowels. The vowels of French **peu** and German **schön** and **hölle** are mid front round vowels. The vowels of **une** and **kühn** may be roughly described as formed with the tongue position of the vowel of English **heat** and the lip rounding of the vowel of English **loot**. The vowel of **müssen** may be described as formed with the tongue position of the vowel of English **hit** and the lip rounding of the vowel of English **full.** The vowels of **peu** and **schön** may be described as formed with the tongue position of the vowel of English **hate** and the lip rounding of the vowel of English **note.** And the vowel of **hölle** may be described as formed with the tongue position of the vowel of English **bet** and the lip rounding of the vowel of English **law.**

13. Tense and Lax Vowels. If we pronounce the vowel of **loot** and then the vowel of **look,** the vowel of **beat** and then the vowel of **bit,** we can feel in pronouncing the first vowel of each pair a degree of tenseness in the tongue that we do not feel in pronouncing the second vowel of the pair. The first pair of vowels are both high back round vowels, the second pair are both high front unround vowels, yet the acoustic quality of the first member of each pair is distinctly different from that of the second member. This difference of acoustic quality is chiefly the result of the difference that we observe in the tenseness of the tongue. Therefore, the vowels of **loot** and **beat** are called **tense** vowels and the vowels of **look** and **bit** are called **lax** vowels. The distinction between tense and lax vowels is most clearly perceptible and most distinct in its acoustic effect in the high vowels, but we find the same difference, though in a less degree, in the mid and low vowels. The vowel of **bait** differs from the vowel of **bet** chiefly in being more tense, at least in American English.

The vowel of **earth** is tense, and the vowel of the second syllable of **Cuba,** though made with nearly the same tongue position, is lax. The vowel of **note** is tense, and sometimes that of **naught** as well. The vowel of the first syllable of **fairy** is tense in the speech of some persons and lax in the speech of others. The other vowels of English are all lax.

The distinction between tenseness and laxness in vowels is often accompanied by certain other differences in the mechanism of their formation. Generally a tense vowel is slightly higher in jaw position than the corresponding lax vowel. Some phoneticians, notably Jones and Kenyon, recognize this as the basic difference between such a pair of sounds as the stressed vowels of **seat** and **sit,** defining the former as a high front vowel, and the latter as a lower high-front vowel. Tense vowels are commonly longer in duration than lax vowels and are more likely to be slightly diphthongized.

We should understand, moreover, that this distinction between tense and lax vowels is highly relative. All the English vowels are lax as compared with the stressed vowels of French, which are all very tense. The German short vowels are lax, and the long vowels are tense, though less tense than those of French. And the English tense vowels are less tense than the German tense vowels.

14.　Quantity of Vowels. The foregoing classification of vowel sounds has reference only to the **quality** of vowels. But vowels differ from each other not only in quality but also in **quantity** or length of duration. With regard to quantity, vowels are commonly distinguished as **long** and **short.** But the student must be on his guard against the phonetically incorrect use of the terms long and short that he will encounter in naive or unscientific treatments and discussions of speech sounds, even in some dictionaries. The vowel of **bite,** for example, is sometimes called "long i" and the vowel of **bit** "short i," but the first is really a diphthong and the second a simple vowel; the vowel of **mate** may be called "long a" and the vowel of **mat** "short a," but the two vowels differ in quality as well as quantity, for the first is a mid front unround vowel and the second is a low front unround vowel; the vowel of **loot** is called "long oo" and the vowel of **look** "short oo," but though they are both high back round vowels they are not a longer and shorter variety of the same vowel, for the first vowel is tense and the second is lax. Differences of mere quantity or duration in vowels of the same quality do occur, however, in Modern English. The vowel of **gnaw** is longer than the vowel of **gnawed** and the vowel of **gnawed** is longer than the vowel of **naught,** though the quality of the vowel is the same in the three words. But this variation depends on the phonetic environment of the vowel; a vowel is longer when it is final than when it is followed by almost any single consonant, and longer when it is followed by a voiced consonant than when it is followed by a voiceless consonant. This adaptation of vowel quantity to the phonetic environment of the vowel is made automatically by speakers of English.

In the speech of some persons who do not pronounce **r** before consonants the words **heart** and **hot, hard** and **hod, part** and **pot,** etc., differ only in the fact that the vowel of the first word of each pair is of longer duration than the vowel of the second word of the pair. And in the speech of perhaps the majority of Americans the words **balm** and **bomb** differ only in the fact that the vowel of the first word is longer than the vowel of the second. With these exceptions, however, differences in vowel quantity are not in themselves significant for the expression of meaning in Modern English, but are either dependent on the phonetic environment of the vowel or are combined with differences in vowel quality.

15. Diphthongs. A diphthong consists of two vowel sounds pronounced in a single syllable. In Modern English we have diphthongs in the words **foil, foul,** and **file.**[5] In these diphthongs the first element is more strongly stressed than the second; such diphthongs are called **falling** diphthongs. Diphthongs in which the second element is more strongly stressed than the first as in **fuel** are called **rising** diphthongs.

[5] For the diphthongization of certain long vowels in Modern English see Section **17** below.

CHAPTER II

16. Phonetic Alphabet. In order to discuss or refer to the sounds of human speech in a reasonably accurate fashion, it is necessary to employ an alphabet which has a consistent set of values for its characters or letters. Such consistency can be attained only if each letter indicates one and no more than one sound, and conversely, if every sound is indicated by one and only one symbol. A moment's reflection will be sufficient to convince anyone that the ordinary system of English spelling does not maintain such a one-to-one correspondence of sound and symbol. Consequently students of language have been forced to devise phonetic alphabets which do maintain this general principle. The one most frequently employed is the International Phonetic Alphabet, a form of which, particularly adapted to the English language, is presented here.

The first of the three columns below gives the IPA symbol for each of the distinctive sounds of English, the second contains a key word which indicates the value of the sound in question, and the third column shows how the key word would be transcribed in phonetic notation.

SYMBOL	KEY WORD	TRANSCRIPTION
ɑ	calm	kɑm[6]
æ	hat	hæt[7]
b	bat	bæt
d	doom	dum
e	hate	het[8]
ɛ	met	mɛt[9]

[6] The vowel written o in *fodder, hot, not*, etc., is in most parts of the United States the same sound as that which is written with **a** in *father* or *calm* but shorter in duration. In eastern New England and Great Britain, however, the o in *fodder, hot, not*, etc., is a vowel which may be represented in this notation by [ɒ]. (Here and elsewhere the brackets indicate that the spellings they enclose are phonetic spellings.)

[7] A sound intermediate between [ɑ] and [æ], representing the vowel sound of French **la,** may be indicated by the symbol [a]. No satisfactory English keyword can be given for this sound because, though it occurs in a number of varieties of English, there is no word or group of words in which it occurs in *all* varieties of English. It is the vowel which some persons use as a compromise between [ɑ] and [æ] in words like *past, laugh, half,* etc.

[8] See Section **17.**

[9] In those dialects where the vowel of *fairy* differs from that of *ferry*, the stressed vowel of the first word may often appropriately be represented by [æː]. No special

8

SYMBOL	KEY WORD	TRANSCRIPTION
f	fate	fet
g	gate	get
h	hate	het
i	feet	fit[10]
ɪ	hit	hɪt
ɪ	pretty	prɪtɪ[11]
j	yield	jild
k	keep	kip
l	let	lɛt
m	mate	met
n	need	nid
ŋ	sang	sæŋ
o	note	not[10]
ɔ	law, fork	lɔ, fɔɚk
p	pet	pɛt
r	rat, merry	ræt, mɛrɪ
s	sit	sɪt
ʃ	shape	ʃep
ʒ	vision	vɪʒən
t	take	tek
θ	thin	θɪn
ð	then	ðɛn
u	boot	but[10]
ʊ	full	fʊl
ʌ	hut	hʌt
ɝ	hurt, earth, bird, berth, word (General American pronunciation)	hɝt, ɝθ, bɝd, bɝθ, wɝd[12]

symbol has been employed for this sound because the low ront tense vowel which it would represent is replaced in some varieties of English by the mid front tense vowel [e] and at times even by the low front lax vowel [æ]. The vowel [æ:] seems to prevail more widely in *fairy* than in any other word. The symbol [æ:] is used here to represent any front tense vowel that is lower than [e]. For the use of the modifier [:], see Section **18.**

[10] See Section **17.**

[11] This vowel occurs only in unstressed syllables. See note 36 below.

[12] The sound represented by **u, ea, i, e,** and **o** plus **r** in these words is a single sound which may be represented phonetically by the character ɝ alone, e.g. [hɝt], [ɝθ], etc. In that it constitutes the crest of the syllable it does not differ materially from the ʌ of [hʌt], [bʌd], etc.

SYMBOL	KEY WORD	TRANSCRIPTION
3	hurt, earth, bird, etc. (Southern British and eastern New England pronunciation)	h3t, 3θ, b3d, b3θ, w3d[13]
ə	above	əbʌv[14]
ɚ	further, perverse	fɝˑðɚ, pɚvɝˑs[15]
v	vat	væt
w	win	wɪn
z	zest	zɛst
Diphthongs:		
ɑɪ	find	fɑɪnd[16]
ɑʊ	found	fɑʊnd[16]
ɔɪ	boy	bɔɪ[16]
ɪu	mute	mɪut[17]
Consonant combinations:		
tʃ[18]	choose	tʃuz
dʒ	jaw, cage	dʒɔ, kedʒ
hw	wheat	hwit[19]

[13] This sound differs from [ɝ] chiefly in that the tongue is flat in the mouth, not in a retroflex position (turned upward) when it is uttered. It closely resembles [ə] and is tense instead of lax (see Section **13** above). It occurs only in varieties of English in which **r** is not pronounced before consonants.

[14] This vowel occurs only in unstressed syllables.

[15] This vowel occurs only in unstressed syllables and in varieties of English in which **r** is pronounced before consonants. In the so-called **r**-less varieties of English, [ɚ] normally appears as [ə]: **better** [bɛtə], **perverse** [pəvɝs].

[16] The symbols [ɑɪ], [ɔɪ], and [ɑʊ] are used for practical convenience to represent diphthongs which vary considerably in different varieties of English. In cultivated speech the first elements of [ɑɪ] and [ɑʊ] vary between [ɑ] and [a]. The second element of these diphthongs sometimes approaches [i] and [u] in quality.

[17] In American English both [ju] and [ɪu] occur in such words. The combinations are composed of nearly the same elements but in the production of [ju] the second element is more strongly stressed than the first and in the production of [ɪu] the two elements have equal stress or the first is more strongly stressed than the second.

[18] The transcription [tʃ] is only an approximation of the **ch** sound. Actually, a combination of [t] followed by [ʃ] as in *white shirt* is not identical with the initial sound of *choose*. In *white shirt* the [t] is alveolar, but the closure for [ʃ] is slightly farther back, in an alveolo-palatal position. In *choose* there is but a single point of contact, namely alveolo-palatal. Consequently, it would be logical to employ a unit or single character for the **ch** sound, but one that is satisfactory in every respect has not been devised. The same conclusions also apply to the [dʒ] sound and symbol.

[19] This sound consists of [w] preceded by a voiceless fricative made while the tongue and lips are approaching the position for [w]. In southern British English *what, which, why*, etc., are usually pronounced with [w] instead of [hw] and this pronunciation is very common also in American English.

For the representation of certain sounds that occurred in Old English and Middle English, but which do not occur in Modern English, the following additional characters are needed:

y   pronounced as **üh** in German **kühn; u** in French **une**

Y   pronounced as **ü** in German **müssen**

œ   pronounced as **ö** in German **hören, wörter; eu** in French **peu, peur**

ɣ   pronounced as **g** in North German **sagen**[20]

x   pronounced as **ch** in German **nicht, nacht**[21]

17. Diphthongization. In stressed syllables Modern English [e], [i], [o], and [u] tend to be diphthongs, not simple vowels. But the degree of diphthongization varies greatly according to circumstances. Diphthongization is most pronounced when the vowel is final and is followed by a pause. Such words as *hay, key, hoe,* and *coo* when they are followed by a pause could be written [hɛe] or [heɪ], [kɪi] or [kij], [hɔo] or [hou], and [kʊu] or [kuw]. The quality of the vowels composing these diphthongs varies more or less with different individuals and in different localities. There is a considerable amount of diphthongization when the vowel is final but is not followed by a pause or when the vowel is followed by a voiced consonant. In such words as *fade, feed, load,* and *food* the vowels may be transcribed either as diphthongs or as [e], [i], [o], and [u]. When these vowels are followed by voiceless consonants there is little or no diphthongization. The reason for this variation in amount of diphthongization according to the phonetic environment of the vowel is that the longer the vowel is the more it is diphthongized, and Modern English vowels are longest when they are final and followed by a pause and are shortest when they are followed by voiceless consonants. See section **18** below. When [e], [o], and [u] occur in unstressed syllables, as in *vacation, donation,* and unstressed [hu], they are simple vowels.

18. Vowel Quantity. The vowels [e], [i], [o], [u], [ɝ], and [ɜ], when fully stressed, are always long or "half-long." The vowels [æ], [ɛ], [ɪ], [ɪ], [ʊ], [ʌ], and [ə] are nearly always short.[22] The vowel [ɑ] when fully

---

[20] See note **70** below.

[21] Strictly speaking the symbol [x] represents only the voiceless velar fricative, that is the **ch** of German *nacht*. The **ch** in German *nicht* is a voiceless palatal fricative, for which some phonetic alphabets provide the symbol [ç]. Yet [k] and [g] undergo a similar differentiation on the basis of the kind of vowel which follows (see note 29) but are represented by only a single symbol each. Therefore in the interests of simplicity, the symbol [x] will be employed here for both velar and palatal fricatives.

[22] The chief exceptions to this statement are that [ɪ] and [ʊ] are long before **r** (as in *hearing* and *poorer*) and that [æ] occurs as a long vowel in some varieties of English under the conditions stated in **120.3** below (see also note 9 above).

stressed is always long in some varieties of English, but in others it occurs both as a long and as a short vowel, as does [ɔ].

Long vowels may be marked by the modifier ː placed after the vowel, and half-long vowels may be marked (if it seems desirable to indicate two degrees of length) by the modifier ˑ; for example, *fade* and *feed* may be transcribed [feːd] and [fiːd] and *fate* and *feet* may be transcribed [feˑt] and [fiˑt]. But since (as was stated above in section 14) differences in vowel quantity in Modern English are nearly always either dependent on the phonetic environment of the vowel or are combined with differences in vowel quality, it is not necessary for most purposes to mark long vowels in the phonetic transcription of Modern English. In the subsequent chapters, all long vowels are marked as such in the transcription of Old and Middle English but not in the representation of Modern English.

19. Accentuation. In almost all Modern English words of two or more syllables, one syllable is pronounced with decidedly stronger stress than the others.[23] Stress is indicated when necessary by prefixing to the stressed syllable the symbol ˈ, as in [ˈhæpɪ]. In words of two or more syllables there is frequently a secondary stress on one of the syllables, as in [ˈɪndɪˌket], [ˈdɛzɪgˌnetəd], [ˌɪntɚˈmidɪət]. And in a group of words constituting a short sentence or an element of a longer sentence we find a similar distribution of syllables uttered with varying degrees of stress. In the sentence "Did he find the book he was looking for?", for example, *find, book*, the first syllable of *looking*, and *for* are uttered with decidedly stronger stress than the other syllables.[24] And of the weakly stressed syllables, *did* has a slightly stronger stress than *he* which follows it. But if we utter the sentence in the way that is suggested by printing it "*Did* he find the book he was looking for?", we notice that *did* has become a strongly stressed word. And when we utter the sentence as is suggested by printing it "Did *he* find the book he was looking for?", we notice that the first *he* has become a strongly stressed word, though the second *he* is still unstressed. The preponderance of stress on one or more syllables of a single word is called **word-stress,** and the preponderance of stress on certain syllables of a syntactical group of words is called **sentence-stress.**

[23] "Level" stress occurs in such words as *undo* and in such an expression as *black bird* as compared with *blackbird*.

[24] The distribution of primary and secondary stresses among the four strongly stressed syllables of the sentence would depend on the particular situation in which the sentence was uttered, but *for* would always probably have secondary stress.

20. Gradation. "Perhaps the most characteristic feature of English phonology is the extreme sensitiveness of its sounds to variations in the degree of stress, giving rise to the varied phenomena of gradation."[25] Gradation is illustrated by the changes in vowel quality when derivative suffixes are added as follows:

aristocrat	æˈrɪstəˌkræt	aristocracy	ˌæˌrɪsˈtɑkrəsɪ
illustrate	ˈɪləˌstret	illustrative	ɪˈlʌstrəˌtɪv
superior	səˈpɪrjɚ	superiority	səˌpɪrɪˈɔrətɪ

In these examples it will be noticed that when the syllables containing [æ], [ɪ], [ʌ], [ɛ], and [ɔ] are pronounced without stress the quality of the vowel changes to [ə] or [ɪ]. But gradation also occurs in correlation with differences in sentence-stress. If we listen closely to the sentence "Did *he* find the book he was looking for?" as uttered colloquially, we notice that the first *he* is the "strong" form [hi] which is used when the word is emphatic and therefore stressed, and that the second *he* is the "weak" form which is used when the word is unstressed; this weak form is [hɪ] at the beginning of a sentence or after a pause, but usually [ɪ] in other situations. In the sentence "Did ͺhe find the book *I* was looking for?" the word *I* has the strong form [ɑɪ], but when the word is unstressed it has the weak form [əɪ], which in very rapid colloquial speech is reduced to [ə]. Many examples of weak forms of pronouns, auxiliary verbs, prepositions, conjunctions, etc., may be found in the phonetic transcription given in section **22.**[26]

21. Syllabic Consonants. The sounds [n] and [l] frequently form a syllable even when not accompanied by a vowel, for example in *written* [rɪtn], *saddle* [sædl]. These syllabic consonants may be represented by the symbols [n̩] and [l̩]. It is unnecessary in the examples just given to mark the consonants as syllabic because in such words as these they can scarcely be pronounced at all without being syllabic. The special designation for syllabic consonants is used only where there is a possibility of the sound being either syllabic or nonsyllabic, as in *gluttony* [glʌtn̩ɪ] and *apple* [æpl̩].[27]

[25] Sweet, *The Sounds of English*, p. 65.

[26] For a detailed treatment of gradation see J. S. Kenyon's *American Pronunciation*, 6th edition, pp. 90–110; also *Webster's New International Dictionary*, Guide to Pronunciation, pp. xxxvii–xxxix.

[27] Syllabic [m] may also occur in *prism* [prɪzm̩], or in combinations such as *stop 'em* [stɑpm̩], *keep 'em* [kipm̩].

22. Modern English in Phonetic Notation. The pronunciation represented in the paragraphs printed below is the natural pronunciation of the transcriber (who is a native of southeastern Pennsylvania) when speaking at a rate about midway between slow, formal speech and rapid, conversational speech. In the transcriber's dialect the vowel [ə] is extremely frequent and occurs in many situations where speakers from some other localities would use [ɪ], for example in [klæsəz] and [kʌltəvetəd], line 1. In the transcriber's dialect also the vowel [æː] occurs in certain words which have [æ] or [ɑ] in some other varieties of English, for example [kəntræːst], line 43. In the conventional spelling the first paragraph of the text transcribed below is as follows:

In every cultivated language there are two great classes of words which, taken together, comprise the whole vocabulary. First, there are those words with which we become acquainted in ordinary conversation,—which we learn, that is to say, from the members of our own family and from our familiar associates, and which we should know and use even if we could not read or write. They concern the common things of life and are the stock in trade of all who speak the language. Such words may be called "popular," since they belong to the people at large and are not the exclusive possession of a limited class.

ɪn ɛvrɨ kʌltəvetəd læŋgwɪdʒ ðɛr ɚ tu gret klæsəz əv wɝdz hwɪtʃ tekn təgɛðɚ, kəmpraɪz ðə hol vəkæbjələrɨ. fɝst, ðɛɚ ɚ ðoz wɝdz wɪð wɪtʃ wɨ bɨkʌm əkwentəd ɨn ɔɚdənɛrɨ kanvɚseʃn—hwɪtʃ wɨ lɝn, ðæt ɪz tə sei, frəm ðə mɛmbɚz əv aɚ on fæmlɨ ən frəm ar fəmɪljɚ
5 əsoʃɨəts, ənd wɪtʃ wɨ ʃəd no ən juz ivən ɪf wɨ kʊd nat rɪd ɚ raɪt. ðe kənsɝn ðə kamən θɪŋz əv laɪf, ənd ɚ ðə stak ɪn tred əv ɔl hu spik ðə læŋgwɪdʒ. sʌtʃ wɝdz me bɨ kɔld²⁸ "papjəlɚ" sɪns ðe bəlɔŋ tə ðə pipl ət laɚdʒ ənd ɚ nat ðɨ ɪkskluzɪv pəzɛʃn əv ə lɪmɪtəd klæs.

ɔn ðɨ ʌðɚ hæɪnd, aɚ læŋgwɪdʒ ɪnkludʒ ə mʌltɪtud əv wɝdz wɪtʃ
10 ɚ kəmpærətɪvlɨ sɛldəm juzd ɪn ɔɚdənɛrɨ kanvɚseʃn. ðɛɚ minɪŋz ɚ non tu ɛvrɨ ɛdʒəketəd pɝsn, bət ðɚ ɨz lɪtl əkeʒn tu ɪmplɔɪ ðəm ət hom ɔɚ ɪn ðə maɚkət-ples. ar fɝst əkwentəns wɪð ðəm kʌmz nat frəm aɚ mʌðɚz lɪps ɔɚ frəm ðə tɔk əv ar skulmets, bʌt frəm bʊks ðət wɨ

²⁸ In the phrase "called popular," line 7, the closure for [d] is made and is then held while the lips make the closure for [p]; there is only one explosion, that of the [p]. In the phrase "called learned" the [d] of *called* can only be exploded if one speaks very slowly; in more rapid speech we are likely to omit the stop altogether. If this is done the [l] of *called* may be prolonged, and this prolongation may be indicated if desired by transcribing it [lː].

rid, lɛktʃɚz ðət wɨ hɪɚ, ɔɚ ðə mɔɚ fɔɚml kɑnvɚˈseʃn əv haɪlɨ ɛdʒəketəd
15 spikɚz, hʊ ɚ dɪskʌsɪŋ sʌm pɚtɪkjələ tapɪk ɪn ə staɪl əˈpropriɑtlɨ
ɛləvetəd əbʌv ði əbɪtʃuəl lɛvl əv ɛvrɨde laɪf. sʌtʃ wɝdz ɚ kɔl²⁸
"lɝnəd," ən ðə dɪstɪŋkʃn bɨtwin ðɛm ən "papjələ" wɝdz ɪz əv gret
ɪmpɔɚtns tʊ ə raɪt ʌndɚˈstæ:ndɪŋ əv lɪŋgwɪstɪk prɑsɛs.

ðə dɪfɚns bɨtwin papjələ ən lɝnəd wɝdz me bɨ izəlɨ sin ɪn ə fju
20 əgzæmplz. wɨ me dɪskraɪb ə gɝl əz "laɪvlɨ" ɔɚ əz "vɪveʃəs." ɪn ðə
fɝst kes, wɨ ɚ juzɪŋ ə netɪv ɪŋglɪʃ fɔɚmeʃn frəm ðə fəmɪljɚ naʊn
"laɪf." ɪn ðə lætɚ, wɨ ɚ juzɪŋ ə lætn dərɪvətɪv hwɪtʃ həz prɨsaɪslɨ ðə
sem minɪŋ. jɛt ði ætməsfɪɚ əv ðə tu wɝdz ɪz kwaɪt dɪfɚnt. no wʌn
ɛvɚ gat ði ædʒɪktɪv "laɪvlɨ" aʊt əv ə bʊk. ɪt əz ə paɚt əv ɛvrɨbadɨz
25 vəkæbjələrɨ. wɨ kænət rɨmɛmbɚ ə taɪm wɛn wɨ dɪd nat no ɪt, ən wɨ
fil ʃuɚ ðət wɨ lɝnd ɪt lɔŋ bɨfɔɚ wɨ wɚ ebl tə rid. ɔn ði ʌðɚ hæɪnd, wɨ
mʌst əv pæst sɛvrəl jiɚz əv aɚ laɪvz bɨfɔɚ lɝnɪŋ ðə wɝd "vɪveʃəs."
wɨ me ivən rɨmɛmbɚ ðə fɝst taɪm wɨ sɔ ɪt ɪn prɪnt ɚ hɝd ɪt frəm sʌm
gronʌp frɛnd hu wəz təkɪŋ ovɚ aɚ tʃaɪldɪʃ hɛdz. boθ "laɪvlɨ" ən
30 "vɪveʃəs" ɚ gʊd ɪŋglɪʃ wɝdz, bət "laɪvlɨ" ɪz "papjələ" ən "vɪveʃəs"
ɪz "lɝnəd."

. . . .

ɛvrɨ ɛdʒəketəd pɝsən hæz ət list tu wez əv spikɪŋ ɪz mʌðɚ tʌŋ.
ðə fɝst ɪz ðæt hwɪtʃ ɨ ɪmplɔɪz ɪn ɪz fæmlɨ, əmʌŋ ɪz fəmɪljɚ frɛndz,
ənd ɔn ɔɚdnɛrɨ əkeʒnz. ðə sɛkənd ɪz ðæt hwɪtʃ ɨ juzəz ɪn dɪskɔɚsɪŋ
35 ɔn mɔɚ kamplɪketəd sʌbdʒɪkts, ænd ɪn ədrɛsɪŋ pɝsnz wɪð hum ɨ
ɪz lɛs ɪntəmətlɨ əkwentəd. ɪt ɪz, ɪn ʃɔɚt, ðə læŋgwɪdʒ wɪtʃ ɨ ɪmplɔɪz
wən ɨ ɪz "ɔn ɪz dɪgnɪtɨ," æz ɨ pʊts ɔn ɪvnɪŋ drɛs wən ɨ ɪz goɪŋ aʊt tə
daɪn. ðə dɪfɚns bɨtwin ðiz tu fɔɚmz əv læŋgwɪdʒ kənsɪsts, ɪn gret
mɛʒɚ, ɪn ə dɪfɚns əv vəkæbjələrɨ. ðə besəs əv fəmɪljɚ wɝdz məst bi
40 ðə sem ɪn boθ, bət ðə vəkæbjələrɨ əˈproprɨət tʊ ðə mɔɚ fɔɚml əkeʒn
wɪl ɪnklud mɛnɨ tɝmz hwɪtʃ wəd bi stɪltəd ɚ əfɛktəd ɪn ɔɚdnɛrɨ tɔk.
ðɚ ɪz ɔlso kənsɪdrəbl dɪfɚns bɨtwin fəmɪljɚ ən dɪgnɪfaɪd læŋgwɪdʒ ɪn
ðə mænɚ əv ʌtərəns. kəntræːɪst ðə ræpɪd ʌtərəns əv aɚ ɛvrɨde daɪə-
lɛkt, ful əv kəntrækʃnz ən klɪpt fɔɚmz, wɪð ðə mɔɚ dɪstɪŋkt ɪnʌnsɨeʃn
45 əv ðə pulpət ɚ ðə plætfɔɚm. ðʌs, ɪn kanvɚˈseʃn, wɨ əbɪtʃuəlɨ ɪmplɔɪ
sʌtʃ kəntrækʃnz əz "aɪl," "dont," "wont," "ɪts," "wid," "hid," ən
ðə laɪk, hwɪtʃ wɨ ʃəd nɛvr juz ɪn pʌblɪk spikɪŋ, ʌnlɛs əv sɛt pɝpəs,
tə gɪv ə maɚkədlɨ kəlokwɨəl tɪndʒ tə wat wɨ hæv tə sei.

(Transcribed from Greenough and Kittredge's *Words and their
Ways in English Speech*, pp. 19, 20, 27, 28.)

23. Phonetic Classification of Modern English Sounds. The following diagram shows the vowels of Modern English, classified, as in Sections **7-13,** according to the positions assumed by the jaw, tongue, and lips in pronouncing them.

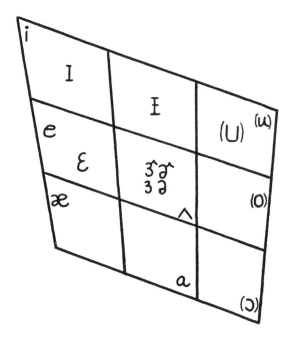

A quadrilateral rather than a rectangle has been employed to illustrate the various vowel positions because experimental evidence has demonstrated the relativity of the several terms of classification: *high* in respect to the front vowels is higher than with the back vowels; *back* is more retarded for the low vowels than for the high, etc. The rounded vowels are shown enclosed in parentheses. The vowels [i, e, u, o, 3, 3˟] are always tense; the others are generally lax, although there are tense varieties of [ɔ] and [æ]. The sounds [3˟] and [ɚ] are made with the tongue turned upward (retroflex). The sound [ɨ] is variable in position, ranging from a vowel close to [i] to one that may resemble [ɪ] or even [ɛ], but it is usually produced with the tongue decidedly more centralized than any of these.

The classification of the consonant sounds, according to the principles explained above in **1-5,** is as follows:

		Labial	Labio-dental	Inter-dental	Alveo-lar	Alveolo-Palatal	Velar
Stops	Voiceless	p			t		k[29]
	Voiced	b			d		g
Fricatives	Voiceless		f	θ	s	ʃ	
	Voiced		v	ð	z	ʒ	
Affricates	Voiceless					tʃ	
	Voiced					dʒ	
Nasals		m			n		ŋ

[h] is a voiceless sound made with the tongue and lips in the position, or approaching the position, which they will occupy in producing the vowel that follows. It is classified sometimes as a voiceless glottal fricative.

[j] is usually a voiced frictionless "glide" sound produced with the tongue moving from the [i] position to the position which it is to occupy in the formation of the vowel that follows it. It is a fricative only when it is produced with the tongue so close to the hard palate that the passage of air through the narrow opening causes audible friction; this is the case when [j] is followed by a high front vowel, as in *yield*.

[l] is a "divided" or "lateral" consonant; it is formed by placing the point of the tongue against the alveolar ridge and allowing the air from the lungs to escape at the sides. A "unilateral" [l] is produced when the tongue is so placed that the air can escape at one side only. When the point of the tongue is in the position that is essential for the production of the [l] sound, the back of the tongue may be in various positions which modify more or less the quality of the sound. [l] is usually voiced but may be partly or wholly voiceless after voiceless stops, as in *play*.

[r] is produced in a variety of ways in English. In northern British

[29] Although [k] and [g] are classified here as velar stops, they are actually palatal or velar according to the nature of the vowel that precedes or follows. (The term *palatal* implies contact with the hard palate, *velar* with the soft palate.) The closure is made farther forward when a front vowel follows, as in *key* and *gate*, than when a back vowel follows, as in *coo* and *go*.

English it is trilled with the tip of the tongue when a vowel follows. In southern British English, the [r] consists of a single flap of the tongue when it occurs between vowels, as in **very,** but this is very exceptional in American English. In both British and American English there is some tendency to trill the [r] after [θ], as in *three.*

All types of untrilled [r] are produced by turning the tip of the tongue up towards the ridge behind the upper front teeth or towards the hard palate and then gliding or moving the tongue to the position for the following sound. If the tip of the tongue is very close to the roof of the mouth, a certain amount of friction accompanies the production of the sound, but most types of [r] are vowel-like sounds produced with little or no friction. Initial [r] and intervocalic [r] are often made with some rounding of the lips. [r] is usually voiced but may be partly or wholly voiceless after voiceless stops, as in *pray.*

[w] is usually a voiced frictionless glide produced with the lips rounded and with the tongue moving from the [u] position to the position which it is to occupy during the production of the vowel that follows it. But when [w] is followed by a high back vowel, as in *woo,* the tongue is so close to the roof of the mouth that the passage of air through the narrow opening causes audible friction; in this situation [w] may be described as a voiced velar spirant made with decided rounding of the lips.

For a description of [hw] see note 19.

CHAPTER III

OLD ENGLISH SOUNDS, INFLECTIONS, AND DIALECTS

24. Pronunciation of Old English. For purposes of convenience, three periods in the development of the English language are usually recognized. The first, Old English, extends from the beginnings of recorded English to 1050. Middle English covers the period from 1050 to 1450. The language after 1450 is considered Modern English, although at times the period from 1450 to 1700 is called Early Modern English.

The pronunciation of the Old English vowels and diphthongs is shown in the following table:

OE Spelling	Pronunciation	Examples	Transcription
ā	[ɑː]	stān, *stone*	[stɑːn]
a	[ɑ]	man, *man*	[mɑn]
ǣ	[æː]	hǣþ, *heath*	[hæːθ]
æ	[æ]	þæt, *that*	[θæt]
ē	[eː]	swēte, *sweet*	[sweːtɛ]
e	[ɛ]	helpan, *help*	[hɛlpɑn]
ī	[iː]	rīdan, *ride*	[riːdɑn]
i	[ɪ]	drincan, *drink*	[drɪŋkɑn]
ō	[oː]	dōn, *do*	[doːn]
o	[ɔ]	crop, *crop*	[krɔp]
ū	[uː]	hūs, *house*	[huːs]
u	[ʊ]	sunu, *son*	[sʊnʊ]
ȳ	[yː]	fȳr, *fire*	[fyːr]
y	[ʏ]	þynne, *thin*	[θʏnːɛ]
ēa	[æːə]	strēam, *stream*	[stræːəm]
ea[30]	[æə]	hearpe, *harp*	[hæərpɛ]
ēo	[eːo]	bēon, *be*	[beːon]
eo[30]	[ɛo]	weorc, *work*	[wɛork]
īe	[iːə]	hīeran, *hear*	[hiːərɑn]
ie[30]	[ɪə]	ieldra, *elder*	[ɪəldrɑ]

[30] Some recent authorities have questioned the diphthongal value of the **ea, eo,** and **ie** spellings, maintaining that they were devised by Anglo-Saxon scribes to indicate the velar nature of following **l, r,** and **h,** and the palatal character of preceding **ċ** and **ġ** sounds. This applies to the short diphthongs only. In this connection, see M. Daunt, "Old English Sound-Changes Reconsidered in Relation to Scribal Tradition and Practice," Transactions of the Philological Society, 1939, pp. 108–137. However, because the traditional view of their diphthongal value was implicit in Professor Moore's subsequent treatment, I have hesitated to modify his opinions to this extent. The suggestion is one which deserves further consideration. A.H.M.

The pronunciation of the Old English consonants is shown in the following table:

OE Spelling	Pronunciation	Examples
c	[k]	cēpan, *keep* [keːpɑn]
ċ³¹	[tʃ]	ċīdan, *chide* [tʃiːdɑn]
cg	[dʒ]	brycg, *bridge* [brʏdʒ]
ġ	[ɣ]	boga, *bow* [bɔɣɑ]
ġ³²	[j]	ġiefan, *give* [jɪəvɑn]
ng	[ŋg]	singan, *sing* [sɪŋgɑn]
sc	[ʃ]	scip, *ship* [ʃɪp]

h before consonants or after vowels is pronounced like ch in German ich, nacht; e.g., niht [nɪxt], *night*, sōhte [soːxtɛ] *sought*.

f and s are pronounced like [v] and [z] when they occur between voiced sounds, as in ġiefan, *give*, and rīsan, *rise*; like [f] and [s] when initial or final, and when they precede voiceless sounds or are doubled, as in fæder, *father*, stæf, *staff*, sunu, *son*, wæs, *was*, hæft, *haft*, cyssan, *kiss*.

þ and ð are used without distinction for the sounds [θ] and [ð]. They are pronounced like [ð] when they occur between voiced sounds, as in cūðe, *knew*; like [θ] when they are initial or final, as in þæt, *that*, cūþ, *known*.

r is strongly trilled with the tip of the tongue.

The other Old English consonants are pronounced as in Modern English. But double consonants were pronounced lengthened, as in Modern English *pen-knife*, *book-case*, e. g. sunne, sittan [sʊnːɛ, sɪtːɑn].

25. Old English in Phonetic Notation. The Old English version of the parable of the Good Samaritan, Luke 10:30-35, in the Old English spelling and accompanied by a literal translation, is as follows:

Sum   man ferde fram Hierusalem tō Hiericho and becōm on
A-certain man went from Jerusalem to Jericho and fell   among

þā scaðan, þā   hine bereafodon and tintregodon hine and forlēton
the thieves, who him robbed   and tortured   him and left

hine samcwicne. þā   ġebyrede hit þæt sum   sācerd ferde on
him half-alive. Then happened it   that a-certain priest went on

---

³¹ The Old English manuscripts do not distinguish ċ from c or ġ from g; the dot is added by modern editors and is not used in the standard Old English dictionaries.

³² See note 30 above.

þām ilcan weġe; and þā   hē þæt ġeseah, hē hine   forbēah.
the same way; and when he that saw,   he from-him turned-away.

And eal swā sē dīacon, þā   hē wæs wið þā stōwe and þæt ġeseah,
And also   the deacon, when he was by the place and that saw,

hē hine   ēac forbēah.   þā   fērde sum   Samaritanisc
he from-him also turned-away.   Then went a-certain Samaritan

man wið   hine; þā   hē hine ġeseah, ðā   wearð hē mid
man opposite him; when he him saw,   then became he with

mildheortnesse ofer hine āstyred.   þā   ġenēalæhte hē and wrāð
pity   over him moved.   Then approached he and bound

his wunda and on āġēat   ele and wīn and hine on his nīeten sette
his wounds and in poured oil and wine and him on his beast set

and ġelædde on   his læċehūs and hine lācnode; and brōhte   ōþrum
and took   into his hospital and him treated; and brought the-next

dæġe twēġen peningas and sealde þām   læċe   and þus cwæð,
day two   pennies and gave to-the physician and thus said,

"Beġīem   his; and swā hwæt swā þū   māre tō   ġedēst,
"Take-care-of him; and whatever thou more in-addition doest,

þonne iċ cume, iċ hit forġielde   þē."
when I come, I it will-repay thee."

Transcribed in phonetic notation the Old English passage just given is
as follows:

sʊm man feɪrdɛ³³ fram hɪərʊzalɛm toː hɪərɪkɔ and bɛˈkoɪm³⁴ ɔn θɑː ʃaðan
θɑː hɪnɛ bɛˈræɪəvɔdɔn and tɪntrɛɣɔdɔn hɪnɛ and fɔrˈleɪtɔn hɪnɛ sam-
kwɪknɛ. θɑː jɛˈbʏrɛdɛ hɪt θæt sʊm saɪkɛrd feɪrdɛ ɔn θɑɪm ɪlkan weɪjɛ; and
θɑː heɪ θæt jɛˈsæəx, heː hɪnɛ fɔrˈbæɪəx. and æəl swaː seː diɪakɔn, θɑː heɪ
wæs wɪθ θɑː stoɪwɛ and θæt jɛˈsæəx, heː hɪnɛ æɪək fɔrˈbæɪəx. θɑː feɪrdɛ
sʊm samarɪtanɪʃ man wɪθ hɪnɛ; θɑː heɪ hɪnɛ jɛˈsæəx, θɑː wæərθ heɪ mɪd

---

³³ In keeping with the transcription practice employed at present by Kenyon and
others, I have altered Professor Moore's original transcriptions of Modern English by
limiting consonantal **r** to pre-vocalic positions and transcribing the post-vocalic sound
as [ɚ]. If OE **r** was, as is generally assumed, an alveolar trill, it could have occurred
post-vocalically as well as pre-vocalically. Consequently it is so employed in the transcriptions of Old and Middle English in this revision.

³⁴ The stress is on the first syllable unless otherwise indicated.

NOUNS

	STRONG DECLENSION					WEAK DECLENSION		
	Stems in -a-			Stems in -ō-		Stems in -n		
	Masc.	Neuter		Feminine		M.	N.	F.
		(short)	(long)	(short)	(long)			
Sg. N.	bāt	scip	horn	scinu	glōf	oxa	ēare	heorte
G.	bātes	scipes	hornes	scine	glōfe	oxan	ēaran	heartan
D.	bāte	scipe	horne	scine	glōfe	oxan	ēaran	heortan
A.	bāt	scip	horn	scine	glōfe	oxan	ēare	heortan
Pl. N.A.	bātas	scipu	horn	scina, -e	glōfa, -e	oxan	ēaran	heortan
G.	bāta	scipa	horna	scina	glōfa	oxena	ēarena	heortena
D.	bātum	scipum	hornum	scinum	glofum	oxum	ēarum	heortum

ADJECTIVES

| | STRONG DECLENSION | | | | | | WEAK DECLENSION | | |
| | Short stem | | | Long stem | | | | | |
	M	N	F	M	N	F	M	N	F
Sg. N.	til	til	tilu	wīs	wīs	wīs	wīsa	wīse	wīse
G.	tiles	tiles	tilre	wīses	wīses	wīsre	wīsan	wīsan	wīsan
D.	tilum	tilum	tilre	wīsum	wīsum	wīsre	wīsan	wīsan	wīsan
A.	tilne	til	tile	wīsne	wīs	wīse	wīsan	wīse	wīsan
I.	tile	tile	tilre	wīse	wīse	wīsre	wīsan	wīsan	wīsan
Pl. N.A.	tile	tilu	tila, -e	wīse	wīs	wīsa, -e	wīsan	wīsan	wīsan
G.	tilra	tilra	tilra	wīsra	wīsra	wīsra	wīsena	wīsena	wīsena
D.I.	tilum	tilum	tilum	wīsum	wīsum	wīsum	wīsum	wīsum	wīsum

PRONOUNS

| | | PERSONAL | | | | | | | DEMONSTRATIVE | | |
| | | Sg. | Dual | Pl. | | Third Person | | | M. | N. | F. |
						Masc.	Neut.	Fem.			
First Person	N.	ic	wit	wē	Sg. N.	hē	hit	hēo	ðēs	ðis	ðēos
	G.	mīn	uncer	ūre	G.	his	his	hiere	ðis(s)es	ðis(s)es	ðisse
	D.	mē	unc	ūs	D.	him	him	hiere	ðis(s)um	ðis(s)um	ðisse
	A.	mē	unc	ūs	A.	hine	hit	hīe	ðisne	ðis	ðās
					I.	—	—		ðȳs	ðȳs	ðisse
Second Person	N.	ðū	ġit	ġē							
	G.	ðīn	incer	ēower	Pl. N.A.	hīe	hīe	hīe	ðās	ðās	ðās
	D.	ðē	inc	ēow	G.	hiera	hiera	hiera	ðissa	ðissa	ðissa
	A.	ðē	inc	ēow	D.I.	him	him	him	ðis(s)um	ðis(s)um	ðis(s)um

MINOR DECLENSIONS

stems in -u	Root Consonant
M.F.	M.F.
sunu	fōt
suna	fōtes
suna	fēt
sunu	fōt
suna	fēt
suna	fōta
sunum	fōtum

DEFINITE ARTICLE

	N.	F.
ð…	ðæt	sēo
…s	ðæs	ðǣre
…m	ðǣm	ðǣre
…e	ðæt	ðā
ðȳ		ðǣre
…a	ðā	ðā
…	ðāra	ðāra
…m	ðǣm	ðǣm

INTER-ROGATIVE

M.F.	N.
hwā	hwæt
hwæs	hwæs
hwǣm	hwǣm
hwone	hwæt
hwȳ	hwȳ

VERBS

Present Tense

	STRONG VERBS	WEAK I (short)	WEAK I (long)	WEAK II	PRET. PRESENT	"TO BE"
Indicative Sg. 1	drīfe	fremme	hǣle	hopie	wāt	ēom bēo
2	drīf(e)st	fremest	hǣl(e)st	hopast	wāst	eart bist
3	drīf(e)ð	fremeð	hǣl(e)ð	hopað	wāt	is bið
Pl.	drīfað	fremmað	hǣlað	hopiað	witon	sindon bēoð
Subj. Sg.	drīfe	fremme	hǣle	hopie	wite	sīe bēo
Pl.	drīfen	fremmen	hǣlen	hopien	witen	sīen bēon
Imp. Sg.	drīf	freme	hǣl	hopa	wite	wes bēo
Pl.	drīfað	fremmað	hǣlað	hopiað	witað	wesað beoð
Infinitive	drīfan	fremman	hǣlan	hopian	witan	wesan bēon
Gerund	tō drīfenne	tō fremmenne	tō hǣlenne	tō hopienne	tō witenne	tō bēonne
Participle	drīfende	fremmende	hǣlende	hopiende	witende	wesende bēonde

Past Tense

	STRONG VERBS	WEAK I (short)	WEAK I (long)	WEAK II	PRET. PRESENT	"TO BE"
Indicative Sg. 1	drāf	fremede	hǣlde	hopode	wiste	wǣs
2	drife	fremedest	hǣldest	hopodest		wǣre
3	drāf	fremede	hǣlde	hopode	wiste	wǣs
Pl.	drifon	fremedon	hǣldon	hopodon	wiston	wǣron
Subj. Sg.	drife	fremede	hǣlde	hopode	wiste	wǣre
Pl.	drifen	fremeden	hǣlden	hopoden	wisten	wǣren
Participle	drifen	fremed	hǣled	hopod	witen	

CLASSES OF STRONG VERBS

	Infinitive	Present 2d Sing.	Present 3d Sing.	Past 1 Sing.	Past Plural	Past Participle
1	drīfan	drīfst	drīfð	drāf	drifon	drifen
2	crēopan	crīepst	crīepð	crēap	crupon	cropen
3	singan	singst	singð	sang	sungon	sungen
3	helpan	hilpst	hilpð	healp	hulpon	holpen
3	hweorfan	hwierfst	hwierfð	hwearf	hwurfon	hworfen
4	stelan	stilst	stilð	stæl	stǣlon	stolen
5	sprecan	spricst	spricð	spræc	sprǣcon	sprecen
6	bacan	bæcst	bæcð	bōc	bōcon	bacen
7	lācan	lǣcst	lǣcð	lēc	lēcon	lācen
7	flōwan	flēwst	flēwð	flēow	flēowon	flōwen

mildhɛortnɛsiɛ ɔvɛr hinɛ aiˈstyrɛd. θa: jɛˈnæiɔlæixtɛ hei ɑnd wraiθ his wundɑ ɑnd ɔn aiˈjæiɔt ɛlɛ ɑnd wiin ɑnd hinɛ ɔn his niiɔtɛn sɛtiɛ ɑnd jɛˈlæidiɛ ɔn his læitʃɛhuis ɔnd hinɛ laiknɔdɛ; ɑnd broixtɛ oiðrum dæjɛ tweijɛn pɛniŋgɑs ɑnd sæɔldɛ θaim læitʃɛ ɑnd θus kwæθ, "bɛˈjiiɔm his; ɑnd swai hwæt swai θu: mairɛ toi jɛˈdeist, θɔniɛ itʃ kumɛ, itʃ hit fɔrˈjiɔldɛ θei."

26. Old English Inflections. The inflectional system of Old English was quite complex. Noun declensions, of which there were several, included four or five cases: nominative, genitive, dative, accusative, and sometimes instrumental; two numbers, singular and plural; and three genders, which, like those of Modern German, were largely independent of sex. The personal pronoun, though failing to distinguish between the dative and instrumental cases, had the dual as a third number category. There was both a strong and a weak declension of the adjective, depending upon the presence or absence of an article, a demonstrative, or some other number and case distinctive form before the adjective (gode ne man; þone godan man). The verb had distinctive forms for the three persons of the singular in the present conjugation, and in many places in the conjugation the indicative and subjunctive were inflectionally distinctive. Thus, on the whole, the inflections of the language at this time were sufficiently distinct in form to permit a considerable degree of freedom in word order. The chart on pages 22 and 23 indicates most of the important Old English inflectional forms and categories.

27. Old English Dialects. The English language as it was spoken and written during the period between the Anglo-Saxon invasion in the fifth century and the Norman Conquest of the mid-eleventh varied considerably throughout the island. Four principal dialects of Old English are recognized: West-Saxon, Kentish, Mercian, and Northumbrian.

The distribution of these dialects follows the general pattern of the settlement of England. Northumbrian, as its name indicates, the dialect spoken north of the Humber River, included the territory of the kingdoms of Bernicia and Deira. At the other extremity of the island, settled originally by the Jutes, the Kentish dialect was spoken in the county which still bears that name and which occupies the southeastern corner of England. To the west of Kent, and south of the Thames and the mouth of the Severn was the territory of the West Saxons, where prevailed that dialect of Old English in which the great majority of the literary texts are written. The dialect of the region between the Thames and the Humber, settled originally by Anglian tribes, was called Mercian. Sometimes Northumbrian and Mercian together are spoken of as Anglian, but each of them does possess certain distinctive features.

The following statement presents a brief summary of the characteristic features of the four Old English dialects, with particular emphasis upon those differences which are reflected in the later development of the English language. Since the Early West-Saxon dialect is the one best known to students of Old English, the statement is put into the form of a comparison of the sounds of Early West-Saxon with those of the other dialects. Divergent developments in Late West-Saxon are also pointed out. The several developments are given in the chronological order of their occurrence, except that those numbered 9b, 9c, 10, 11, and 12 took place at approximately the same period.

For an account of the normal development of West Germanic sounds into the West-Saxon dialect of Old English, see Moore and Knott, *Elements of Old English*, Paragraphs 222–262.

1. West Germanic **ā**, which became **ǣ** in West-Saxon except before the consonants **w, p, ġ,** or **k,** when followed by a back vowel, underwent a further raising to **ē** in the Kentish, Northumbrian, and the greater part of the Mercian area: e.g., WS **dǣd, bǣron;** Kentish, Northumbrian, Mercian **dēd, bēron.** The **ǣ** region is believed to have included the counties of Norfolk, Cambridge, Hertford, Buckingham, Oxford, Gloucester, and Worcester, and the counties to the south of these, (except for Kent) as well as the West-Saxon territory. See Moore and Knott, *Elements of Old English*, Paragraph 229.

2. West Germanic **a** regularly became Prehistoric Old English **æ** except when it occurred before a nasal consonant, **w,** or any single consonant followed by a back vowel. See Moore and Knott, *Elements of Old English*, Paragraph 224. When followed by **l** plus a consonant or by double **l** (not the product of gemination), this **æ** was broken to **ea** in West-Saxon and Kentish, but developed into **a** in Mercian and Northumbrian: e.g., Prehistoric OE ***hældan, *fællan;** WS and Kentish **healdan, feallan;** Mercian and Northumbrian **haldan, fallan.** See Moore and Knott, *Elements of Old English*, Paragraph 248.

3. In early West-Saxon the vowels **e, æ,** and **ǣ** (corresponding to non-West-Saxon **ē**) were diphthongized to **ie, ea,** and **ēa** when they were preceded by **ġ, ċ,** or **sc;** e.g., EWS **ġieldan,** Kentish, Mercian, Northumbrian **ġeldan;** EWS **scield,** Kentish, Mercian, Northumbrian **sceld;** EWS **ċeaster,** Kentish, Mercian, Northumbrian **ċæster;** EWS **ġēar,**

ENGLAND

NORTH-

UMBRIAN

WALES
(CELTIC)

M E R C I A N

WEST   SAXON

KENTISH

CORNWALL
(CELTIC)

THE   OLD   ENGLISH   DIALECTS

NORTH OF THE BROKEN LINE WGmc a > e
SOUTH OF THE BROKEN LINE WGmc a > æ .
(except for Kent)

Kentish, Mercian, Northumbrian ġēr. See Moore and Knott, *Elements of Old English*, Paragraph 250.

4. Prehistoric Old English æ, which developed from West-Germanic a as described in 2 above, remained æ in West-Saxon, Northumbrian, and the greater part of the Mercian territory, but became e in Kentish and southwest Mercian: e.g. WS, Mercian, Northumbrian **fæder, wæter;** Kentish, Southwest Mercian **feder, weter.**

5. The following dialect differences resulted from the operation of the **i**-umlaut. See Moore and Knott, *Elements of Old English*, Paragraph 251.

> a. Prehistoric OE ā became ǣ in all the dialects but later developed into ē in Kentish; e.g., Prehistoric OE *dāli; WS, Mercian, Northumbrian **dǣl;** Kentish **dēl.**
>
> b. Prehistoric OE **ea** became early West-Saxon **ie** but Kentish, Mercian, and Northumbrian **e:** e.g. Prehistoric OE *wearmjan; EWS **wierman;** Kentish, Mercian, Northumbrian **werman.**
>
> c. Prehistoric OE **ēa** became early West-Saxon **īe** but Kentish, Mercian, and Northumbrian **ē:** e.g. Prehistoric OE *hēarjan; EWS **hīeran;** Kentish, Mercian, Northumbrian **hēran.**
>
> d. Prehistoric OE **io** became early West-Saxon **ie** but remained Kentish, Mercian, and Northumbrian **io** (later becoming **eo** according to 7 below): e.g., Prehistoric OE *ġiornjan; EWS **ġiernan;** Kentish, Mercian, Northumbrian **ġiornan.**[35]
>
> e. Prehistoric OE **īo** became early West-Saxon **īe** but remained Kentish, Mercian, and Northumbrian **īo** (later becoming Mercian and Northumbrian **ēo** according to 7 below): e.g., EWS **dīere;** Kentish, Mercian, Northumbrian **dīore).**
>
> f. Prehistoric OE **u** and **ū** became **y** and **ȳ** in all the dialects but developed afterwards in Kent and adjacent counties into **e** and **ē:** Prehistoric OE *guldin; WS, Mercian, Northumbrian **gylden;** Kentish **gelden;** Prehistoric OE *hūdjan; WS, Mercian, Northumbrian **hȳdan;** Kentish **hēdan.** The region in which **y** and **ȳ** developed into **e** and **ē** appears to have included

---

[35] This **io** was the result of the breaking of Prehistoric OE **i.** But the breaking of **i** did not always occur in Mercian and Northumbrian when the second syllable of the word contained **i** or **j.** When no breaking occurred, the **i** was not modified by the **i**-umlaut.

at least the counties of Sussex, Surrey, Middlesex, Essex, and Suffolk as well as Kent.

6. About 700 the vowels **æ, e,** and **i,** when they preceded a single consonant which was in turn followed by one of the back vowels (**u,o,** or **a**), were diphthongized to **ea, eo,** and **io** respectively. This process is called velar or **u-, o-, a-**umlaut. It will be observed that this umlaut is similar to breaking in that the same vowels were affected, and they developed into the same diphthongs. In this instance the influence causing the development of the glide was the following back vowel.

Velar umlaut occurred throughout England when the intervening consonant was a liquid or a labial: **herot**>**heorot**; **silufr**>**siolfor**; **sifun** >**siofun**; **clipode**>**cliopode.**

With intervening consonants other than liquids or labials, velar umlaut was generally confined to non-West-Saxon dialects, thus· West-Saxon **ġewita;** Kentish, Mercian, and Northumbrian **ġewiota;** West-Saxon **etan;** Kentish, Mercian, and Northumbrian **eotan.** The velar umlaut of **æ** appears only in Kentish and southwest Mercian: West-Saxon, Mercian, and Northumbrian **ġatu, hafoc;** Kentish and southwest Mercian **ġeatu, heafoc.** See Moore and Knott, *Elements of Old English,* Paragraph 252.

7. The earliest Old English texts generally maintain the distinction between the diphthongs **ēo** and **eo** on the one hand and **īo** and **io** on the other. During the ninth, tenth, and eleventh centuries there appear in the various dialects some tendencies on the part of these diphthongs to merge or coalesce into a single diphthongal combination:

a. In West-Saxon, Mercian, and (considerably later in) Northumbrian, **īo** became **ēo: dīofol**>**dēofol; frīond**>**frēond.** (See also 5e above.)

b. In Kentish, **ēo** became **īo: bēodan**>**bīodan; dēop**>**dīop.**

c. In West-Saxon, Mercian, and (considerably later in) Kentish, **io** became **eo: siolfor**>**seolfor;** Kentish and Mercian **iorre** >**eorre.** (See also 5d above.)

Recall however that because of the operation of **i-**umlaut, there were fewer words with **io** in West-Saxon than in the other dialects.

8. Short vowels and short diphthongs were lengthened (probably not later than the year 900) when they were followed by such voiced homorganic consonant clusters as **ld, rd, mb, nd, ng, rl, rn,** [rð], or [rz]. Earlier OE **feld, findan, grund,** later OE **fēld, findan, grūnd;** EWS and earlier Kentish **eald,** LWS and later Kentish **ēald;** Kentish, Mercian,

and Northumbrian **ġiornan,** later **ġiornan;** earlier Mercian and Northumbrian **ald,** later Mercian and Northumbrian **āld.** This lengthening did not occur when the group was followed by a third consonant; e.g., OE **ċild, ċildru,** later OE **ċīld, ċīldru,** MnE **child, children.**

9. The tendency of OE diphthongs to become simple vowels because of the influence of an adjacent palatal or velar consonant (or the combination of a liquid and a palatal or velar) is called smoothing. This process operated to some extent in all the OE dialects, but as will be seen from the statements which follow, it took place earlier in Mercian and Northumbrian than in West-Saxon and Kentish, and operated under a wider range of circumstances.

    a. Mercian and Northumbrian **ea, ēa, eo, ēo, io,** and **īo** were "smoothed" to the simple vowels **æ, ǣ, e, ē, i,** and **ī** when they were followed by **c, ġ, h, rc, rġ, rh, lc, lġ,** or **lh.** The æ which was the immediate result of the smoothing of **ea** subsequently became **e** except before **h,** and the **ǣ** which was the immediate result of the smoothing of **ēa** subsequently became **ē** under all conditions: **feaht** became **fæht; mearc** became **mærc,** later **merc; ēac** became **ēc; weorc** became **werc; flēogan** became **flēġan; tiohhian** became **tihhian; betwīoh** became **betwīh.**

    b. Early West-Saxon and Kentish **ea** and **ēa** became late West-Saxon and Kentish **e** and **ē** when they were followed by **c, ġ,** or **h:** EWS and Kentish **ēac, ēaġe, meahte, hēah;** LWS and Kentish **ēc, ēġe, mehte, hēh.**

    c. Early West-Saxon **ea** and **ēa** became LWS **e** and **ē** when they were preceded by **ċ, ġ,** or **sc:** EWS **ċeaster, ċēas, ġeaf, ġēar, sceal, scēap;** LWS **ċester, ċēs, ġef, ġēr, scel, scēp.**

10. The following developments occurred before the groups **hs, ht,** and **hþ** unless a back vowel followed the group:

    a. Early West-Saxon and Kentish **eo** became late West-Saxon and Kentish **i,** and early West-Saxon **ēo** became late West-Saxon **ī;** e.g., EWS and Kentish **cneoht** became LWS and Kentish **cniht** (but EWS and Kentish **feohtan** remained unchanged because of the back vowel that followed the consonant group); EWS **lēoht** became LWS **līht.**

    b. Kentish **īo** became **ī;** e.g. earlier Kentish **līoht,** later Kentish **līht.**

c. Kentish, Mercian, and Northumbrian **e** became **i**, and Mercian and Northumbrian **ē** became **ī**; e.g., Kentish *__hlehþ__ (from Prehistoric *__hleahiþ__ by i-umlaut according to 5, b above) became **hlihþ**; Mercian and Northumbrian **cneht** (from **cneoht** by smoothing according to 9a above) became **cniht**; Mercian and Northumbrian **lēht** (noun, from **lēoht** by smoothing) became **līht**.

11. Late West-Saxon development of early West-Saxon **ie** and **īe**.

The early West-Saxon diphthongs **ie** and **īe** became simple vowels in late West-Saxon. Even in the early West-Saxon texts they are rather frequently written as **i** and sometimes (especially after **w**) as **y**. In late West-Saxon texts they are always written as **y** or **i**. It is possible that the sounds developed differently in different parts of the West-Saxon territory, but if so we are unable to determine the geographical limits of the divergent developments. Before **ċ**, **ġ**, or **h** and groups of consonants containing these sounds (such as **nġ**, **lġ**, etc.) early West-Saxon **ie** and **īe** seem, however, to have always developed into late West-Saxon **i** and **ī** unless a labial consonant preceded.

12. Late West-Saxon development of early West-Saxon **y** and **ȳ**.

In parts of the West-Saxon territory there seems to have been a tendency for early West-Saxon **y** and **ȳ** to develop, by unrounding, into **i** and **ī**, especially before **ċ**, **ġ**, or **h** and groups of consonants containing these sounds. Certain phonetic environments, however, were favorable to the preservation of the rounded vowel, and in such environments we not only find that **y** and **ȳ** tended to remain but also that early West-Saxon **i** tended to be rounded to **y**. The conditions particularly favorable to the retention or development of a rounded vowel were a preceding labial consonant and a following **l** or **r**; e.g., EWS **hyġe, dryhten, hryċġ, drȳġe, wyrċan, byrġ, libban, ċiriċe**; LWS **hiġe** or **hyġe, drihten** or **dryhten, hriċġ** or **hryċġ, driġe** or **drȳġe, wyrċan, byrġ, lybban** or **libban, ċyriċe** or **ċiriċe**.

As a qualification, however, to this statement of the dialect differences in Old English it should be said that although we have satisfactory evidence of the existence of these differences we have no equally good evidence as to their precise geographical distribution. This is particularly true of the developments that were peculiar to early West-Saxon, that is 2, 3, and 5 b, c, d, e above. The forms showing these developments are on the whole the prevailing forms in the group of texts called "pure" West-Saxon, but forms showing the developments that occurred in the non-West-Saxon dialects appear occasionally even in these texts and with much greater frequency in texts which, though not "pure" West-Saxon, are certainly not Kentish, Mercian, or Northumbrian. And in the Southern Middle English texts also we find alongside of the forms that would have developed from the specifically West-Saxon forms others that seem to have developed from the non-West-Saxon forms. It is quite possible, or even probable, therefore, that these West-Saxon developments were current only within certain parts of the region south of the Thames and east of the Severn.

28. Specimens of non-West-Saxon Dialects. Since most students are generally more familiar with West-Saxon than with the other dialects of Old English, the following illustrative selections have been included. Each selection will be found to demonstrate some, but not all, of the characteristics peculiar to the dialect it has been chosen to represent.

I (Northumbrian)

Cædmon's Hymn

This Northumbrian version of the poem is contained in one of the Latin manuscripts of Bede's Ecclesiastical History. A much more nearly West-Saxon form occurs in the Old English translation of Bede. The present version was probably copied during the first half of the eighth century.

Nu scylun hergan   hefaenricaes uard,
metudæs maecti   end his modgidanc,
uerc uuldurfadur;   sue he uundra gihuaes,
eci dryhtin,   or astelidæ.
He aerist scop   aelda barnum
heben til hrofe,   haleg scepen;
tha middungeard,   moncynnæs uard,
eci dryctin,   æfter tiadæ
firum foldu,   frea allmectig.

II (Mercian)

Lawsuit about Wood-Pasture

Ðy gere þe wæs from Cristes geburde agæn eahta hund winter 7 xxv 7 æfterre indictio wæs in rime 7 wæs Beornwulfes rice, Mercna cyninges, þa wæs sinodlic gemot on þære meran stowe ðe mon hateþ Clofeshous on þam se siolfa Cyning Biornwulf 7 his biscopas 7 his aldormen 7 alle þa wioton þisse þiode þær gesomnade weron. Þa wæs tiolo micel sprec ymb wuduleswe to Suþtune ongægum west on Scirhylte. Waldon þa swangerefan þa leswe forður gedrifan 7 þone wudu geþiogan þonne hit ald geryhta weron. Þonne cuæð se biscop and þara hira wiotan þæt hio him neren maran ondeta þonne hit aræded wæs on Æþelbaldes dæge, þrim hunde swina mæstes. Ða geræhte Wulfred arcebiscop 7 alle þa wiotan þet se biscop 7 þa higen moston mid aþe gecythan þet hit sua aræden were on Æþelbaldes dage 7 him mare to ne sohte. And he þa sona se biscop bewæddade Eadwulfe ðæm aldormen þæs aþes biforan allum þæm wiotum, 7 him mon þone gelædde ymb xxx næhta to þæm biscop-stole æt Wigoerna-Ceastre. In þa tiid wæs Hama Suangerefa to Suðtune, 7 he rad ðæt he wæs æt Ceastre, and þone aað gesæh 7 gesceawado sua hine his aldormon heht Eadwulf, 7 he hine hweþre ne grette.

TRANSLATIONS

I

Now we must praise the guardian of the heavenly kingdom,
the power of the Lord, and his intention,
the work of the Glorious Father, as He, the Eternal Lord,
established the foundation of every marvel.
He first created for the children of men
heaven as a roof, the Holy Creator;
Then the guardian of mankind, the Eternal God,
The Lord Almighty, afterward assigned
the middle world, the earth, to men.

II

In the year which was 825 from the birth of Christ, and was in the
course of the second Indiction, and was in the reign of Beornwulf, King
of the Mercians, there was a council meeting at the famous place which is
called Clofesho, at which the same King Beornwulf and his bishops and
his earls, and all the councillors of this nation were assembled. Then there
was a very noteworthy suit about wood-pasture at Sinton, towards the
West in Scirhylte. The reeves in charge of the swineherds wanted to ex-
tend the pasture farther and encompass more of the wood than ancient
rights permitted. Then the bishop and their advisers said that they would
not permit liability for more than had been agreed upon in Aethelbald's
day, that is, mast for three hundred swine. Then Archbishop Wulfred
and all the councillors decided that the bishop and the community might
declare by oath that it had been so agreed upon in Aethelbald's day, and
that they were not likely to obtain more. And he, the bishop, then immediately pledged security by oath to Earl Eadwulf before all the councillors, and it was taken thirty days later to the bishops seat at Worcester.
And at that time Hama, the reeve in charge of the swineherds was at
Sinton, and he rode until he reached Worcester and saw and observed
the oath, as Earl Eadwulf commanded him, but he did not challenge it.

III (Kentish)

Ic Badanoð Beotting cyðo ond writan hato, hu min willa is, ðet min ærfelond fere, ðe ic et Aeðeluulfe cyninge begæt ond gebohte mid fullum friodome on æce ærfe, æfter minum dege ond minra ærfewearda, ðet is, mines wifes ond minra bearna. Ic wille ærist me siolfne Gode allmehtgum forgeofan to ðere stowe æt Cristes cirican, ond min bearn ðer liffest ge-doan, ond wiib ond cild ðæm hlaforde ond higum ond ðære stowe befestan ober minne dei, to friðe ond to mundbyrde ond to hlaforddome on ðæm ðingum ðe him ðearf sie. Ond hie brucen londes hiora dei, ond higon gefeormien to minre tide swæ hie soelest ðurhtion megen: ond higon us mid heora godcundum godum swe gemynen swæ us arlic ond him ælmeslic sie. Ond ðonne ofer hiora dei, wifes ond cilda, ic bebeode on Godes noman ðæt mon agefe ðæt lond inn higum to heora beode him to brucanne on ece ærfe, swæ him liofast sie. Ond ic biddo higon for Godes lufe ðæt se monn se higon londes unnen to brucanne ða ilcan wisan leste on swæsend-um to minre tide, ond ða godcundan lean minre saule mid gerece swe hit mine ærfenuman ær onstellan. Ðonne is min willa ðæt ðissa gewriota sien twa gelice: oðer habben higon mid boecum, oðer mine ærfeweardas hiora dei. Ðonne is ðes londes ðe ic higum selle xvi gioc ærðelondes ond medwe, all on æce ærfe to brucanne ge minne dei, ge æfter swæ to ationne swæ me mest red ond liofast sie.

III

I, Badanoth, son of Beot, make known and command to be written what my will is concerning the disposal of my heritable property, which I received and bought from King Aethelwulf in full freedom in perpetual inheritance, after my day and that of my heirs, that is my wife and my children. First, I wish to dedicate myself to God Almighty at the foundation at Christ Church, and to place my children there, and to entrust my wife and children to the lord and to the community and to the foundation after my death, for security and for protection and for guardianship in the things which may be necessary to them. And they shall enjoy the land during their life, and provide the community at my anniversary as well as they can; and the community shall remember us in their divine services as shall be honorable to us and charitable in them. And then after the death of my wife and children, I command in God's name that the land be given to the refectory of the community for them to use in perpetuity, as they wish. And I ask the community for the love of God that the man to whom the community may grant the use of the estate, carry out the same arrangements concerning a feast at my anniversary as my heirs previously shall have appointed it, that this may obtain the divine reward for my soul. Then it is my will that there would be two of these writings: the community to have one with its documents, my heirs to have the other for their lifetime. Then, the amount of the estate which I give to the community is 16 yokes of arable land and meadow, all of it in perpetual inheritance for my lifetime, and afterwards to be dealt with as it may be wisest and best for me.

CHAPTER IV

THE LANGUAGE OF CHAUCER

29. Pronunciation of Chaucer's Language. The following table shows the vowels and diphthongs of Chaucer's dialect of Middle English, expressed in the phonetic notation given above in Section **16.** Indicated also are the spellings of those sounds, characteristic of the best manuscripts of Chaucer's works.

Sound	Spelling	Examples	Transcription
[ɑː]	a, aa	*bathed*	[bɑːðəd]
[ɑ]	a	*that*	[θɑt]
[eː][36]	ee, e	*swete*	[sweːtə]
[æː]	ee, e	*heeth*	[hæːθ]
[ɛ]	e	*wende*	[wɛndə]
[iː][36]	i, y	*ryde*	[riːdə]
[ɪ]	i, y	*swich*	[swɪtʃ]
[oː][36]	oo, o	*roote*	[roːtə]
[ɔː]	oo, o	*hooly*	[hɔːlɪ]
[ɔ]	o	*folk*	[fɔlk]
[uː][36]	ou, ow	*fowles*	[fuːləs]
[ʊ]	u, o	*ful*	[fʊl]
[ə]	e	*sonne*	[sʊnːə]
[ɪ]	i, y	*holy*	[hɔːlɪ]
[ɑu]	au, aw	*faught*	[fɑuxt]
[æɪ]	ai, ay, ei, ey	*day, wey*	[dæɪ], [wæɪ]
[ɛu]	eu, ew	*fewe*	[fɛuə]
[ɪu]	u, eu, ew	*aventure, reule*	[ɑːvɛntɪurə], [rɪulə]
[ɔɪ]	oi, oy	*coy*	[kɔɪ]
[ɔːu]	ou, ow	*soules*	[sɔːuləs]
[ɔu]	ou, ow, o	*foughten*	[fɔuxtən]

---

[36] The Modern English sounds given as the equivalents of Chaucer's [eː], [iː], [oː] and [uː] are only approximate equivalents, for the Modern English sounds which are represented by these symbols tend to be diphthongs, not simple vowels. Chaucer's [eː], [iː], [oː], and [uː] were simple vowels, pronounced like the corresponding vowels of Modern German. See Section **17** above.

Unaccented **e,** as in **sonne, saide, swete,** etc., is called "final **e.**" In the selection from Chaucer which follows, when final **e** is written but not pronounced in reading, it is printed as *e*. Such unpronounced **e**'s are said to be elided when they occur before a word beginning with a vowel or "weak **h,**" and apocopated when they occur before a word beginning with a consonant. Unaccented **e** occurring between two consonants of the same word is also printed as *e* when it is not pronounced in reading. Such **e**'s are said to be syncopated. For a fuller explanation of elision, apocope, and syncope, see Section **50** below.

Most of the consonant sounds were spelled in Chaucer's work as they are in Modern English. Those consonant sounds which were indicated by spellings somewhat different from those ordinarily used today are shown below.

Sound	Spelling	Examples	Transcription
[ŋg][37]	ng	*thing*	[θɪŋg]
[ʃ]	sh, ssh, sch	*shoures*	[ʃuːrəs]
[x][38]	gh, h	*faught*	[fɑuxt]
[z]	s, z	*esed*	[æːzəd]

r in Chaucer's speech was strongly trilled with the tip of the tongue.

[37] [ŋ] never occurred by itself as in MnE *sing* [sɪŋ], but always in combination with the velar stops [k] and [g], just as in MnE *sink* [sɪŋk] and [fɪŋgɚ].

[38] For the value of this symbol and a description of the sound it indicates see Section **16** and note **21**.

30. Chaucer's Prologue in Phonetic Notation. The pronunciation of the first 117 lines of Chaucer's *Prologue* is indicated in the texts printed below. The text on the right hand pages is transcribed in the phonetic

Whan that Aprille with his shoures soote
The droghte of March hath perced to the roote,
And bathed every veyne in swich licour
Of which vertu engendred is the flour;
5   Whan Zephirus eek with his sweete breeth
Inspired hath in every holt and heeth
The tendre croppes, and the yonge sonne
Hath in the Ram his halve cours yronne,
And smale foweles maken melodye,
10   That slepen al the nyght with open ye
(So priketh hem nature in hir corages);
Thanne longen folk to goon on pilgrimages,
And palmeres for to seken straunge strondes,
To ferne halwes kowthe in sondry londes;
15   And specially from every shires ende
Of Engelond to Caunterbury they wende,
The hooly blisful martir for to seke,
That hem hath holpen whan that they were seeke.
Bifil that in that seson on a day,
20   In Southwerk at the Tabard as I lay
Redy to wenden on my pilgrymage
To Caunterbury with ful devout corage,
At nyght was come into that hostelrye
Wel nyne and twenty in a compaignye,

notation which has been explained above in Section **16.** The text on the left hand pages, printed in the spelling of the manuscripts, is that of F. N. Robinson's *Chaucer's Complete Works.*

  hwɑn θɑt ɑːprɪl wɪθ ɪs ʃuːrəs soːtə

  θə drʊxt ɔf mɑrtʃ hɑθ peːrsəd toː θə roːtə

  ɑnd baːðəd ɛvrɪ væɪn ɪn swɪtʃ lɪkuːr

  ɔf hwɪtʃ vɛrtɪu ɛndʒɛndrəd ɪs θə fluːr

5 hwɑn zɛfɪrʊs eːk wɪθ ɪs sweːtə bræːθ

  ɪnspiːrəd hɑθ ɪn ɛvrɪ hɔlt ɑnd hæːθ

  θə tɛndər krɔpːəs ɑnd θə jʊŋgə sʊnːə

  hɑθ ɪn θə rɑm ɪs hɑlvə kuːrs ɪrʊnːə

  ɑnd smɑːlə fuːləs maːkən mɛlɔdiːə

10 θɑt sleːpən ɑl θə nɪxt wɪθ ɔːpən iːə

  sɔː prɪkəθ hɛm naːtɪur ɪn hɪr kuraːdʒəs

  θɑn lɔːŋgən fɔlk toː gɔːn ɔn pɪlgrɪmaːdʒəs

  ɑnd pɑlmɛrs fɔr toː seːkən strɑʊndʒə strɔːndəs

  toː fɛrnə hɑlwəs kuːθ ɪn sʊndrɪ lɔːndəs

15 ɑnd spɛsɪɑlɪ frɔm ɛvrɪ ʃiːrəs ɛndə

  ɔf ɛŋgəlɔnd toː kɑʊntərbrɪ θæɪ wɛndə

  θə hɔːlɪ blɪsfʊl mɑrtɪr fɔr toː seːkə

  θɑt hɛm hɑθ hɔlpən hwɑn θɑt θæɪ wæːr seːkə

  bɪfɪl θɑt ɪn θɑt sæːzuːn ɔn ə dæɪ

20 ɪn suːθwɛrk ɑt θə tɑbɑrd ɑs iː læɪ

  rɛdɪ toː wɛndən ɔn miː pɪlgrɪmaːdʒə

  toː kɑʊntərbrɪ wɪθ fʊl deːvuːt kuraːdʒə

  ɑt nɪxt wɑs kʊm ɪn toː θɑt ɔstɛlriːə

25 Of sondry folk, by aventure y-falle
    In felaweshipe, and pilgrimes were they alle,
    That toward Caunterbury wolden ryde.
    The chambres and the stables weren wyde,
    And wel we weren esed atte beste.
30 And shortly, whan the sonne was to reste,
    So hadde I spoken with hem everichon
    That I was of hir felaweshipe anon,
    And made forward erly for to ryse,
    To take oure wey ther as I yow devyse.
35 But nathelees, whil I have tyme and space,
    Er that I ferther in this tale pace,
    Me thynketh it acordaunt to resoun
    To telle yow al the condicioun
    Of ech of hem, so as it semed me,
40 And whiche they weren, and of what degree,
    And eek in what array that they were inne;
    And at a knyght than wol I first bigynne.
    A Knyght ther was and that a worthy man,
    That fro the tyme that he first bigan
45 To riden out he loved chivalrie,
    Trouthe and honour, fredom and curteisie.
    Ful worthy was he in his lordes werre,
    And thereto hadde he riden, no man ferre,
    As wel in cristendom as in hethenesse,
50 And evere honoured for his worthynesse.
    At Alisaundre he was whan it was wonne.
    Ful ofte tyme he hadde the bord bigonne
    Aboven alle nacions in Pruce;
    In Lettow hadde he reysed and in Ruce,
55 No Cristen man so ofte of his degree.

weːl niːn and twɛntɪ ɪn ɑ kʊmpæɪniːə
25 ɔf sʊndrɪ fɔlk biː aːvɛntɪʊr ɪfalːə
ɪn fɛlauʃɪp and pɪlgrɪms wæːr θæɪ alːə
θat toːward kauntərbʊrɪ woːldən riːdə
θə tʃaːmbrəs and θə staːbləs wæːrən wiːdə
and weːl weː wæːrən æːzəd atːə bɛstə
30 and ʃɔrtlɪ hwan θə sʊnːə was toː rɛstə
sɔː had iː spoːkən wɪθ ɛm ɛvrɪtʃɔːn
θat iː was ɔf ɪr fɛlauʃɪp anɔːn
and maːdə fɔrward æːrlɪ fɔr toː riːzə
toː taːk uːr wæɪ θæːr as iː juː deːviːzə
35 bʊt naːðəlæːs hwiːl iː hav tiːm and spaːsə
æːr θat iː fɛrðər ɪn θɪs taːlə pasə
meː θɪŋkəθ ɪt akɔrdaunt toː ræːzuːn
toː tɛlːə juː al θə kɔndɪsɪuːn
ɔf æːtʃ ɔf hɛm sɔː as ɪt seːməd meː
40 and hwɪtʃ θæɪ wæːrən and ɔf hwat deːgreː
and eːk ɪn hwat arːæɪ θat θæɪ wæːr ɪnːə
and at ə knɪxt θan wʊl iː fɪrst bɪgɪnːə
ə knɪxt θæːr was and θat ə wʊrðɪ man
θat frɔː θə tiːmə θat eː fɪrst bɪgan
45 toː riːdən uːt eː lʊvəd tʃɪvalriːə
troːuθ and ɔnuːr freːdoːm and kʊrtæɪziːə
fʊl wʊrðɪ was eː ɪn ɪs lɔːrdəs wɛrːə
and θæːrtoː had eː rɪdən nɔː man fɛrːə
as weːl ɪn krɪstəndoːm as ɪn hæːðənɛsːə
50 and ɛvr ɔnuːrəd fɔr ɪs wʊrðɪnɛsːə
at alɪsaundr eː was hwan ɪt was wʊnːə
fʊl ɔftə tiːm eː had θə boːrd bɪgʊnːə
abʊvən alːə naːsɪuːns ɪn prɪusə
ɪn lɛtɔːu had eː ræɪzəd and ɪn rɪusə
55 nɔː krɪstən man sɔː ɔft ɔf hɪs deːgreː

In Gernade at the seege eek hadde he be
Of Algezir, and riden in Belmarye.
At Lyeys was he and at Satalye
Whan they were wonne; and in the Grete See
60   At many a noble armee hadde he be.
At mortal batailles hadde he been fiftene,
And foughten for oure feith at Tramyssene
In lystes thries, and ay slayn his foo.
This ilke worthy knyght hadde been also
65   Somtyme with the lord of Palatye
Agayn another hethen in Turkye.
And everemoore he hadde a sovereyn prys;
And though that he were worthy, he was wys,
And of his port as meeke as is a mayde.
70   He nevere yet no vileynye ne sayde
In al his lyf unto no maner wight.
He was a verray, parfit gentil knyght.
But, for to tellen yow of his array,
His hors were goode, but he was nat gay.
75   Of fustian he wered a gypon
Al bismotered with his habergeon,
For he was late ycome from his viage,
And wente for to doon his pilgrymage.
      With hym ther was his sone, a yong Squier,
80   A lovyere and a lusty bacheler,
With lokkes crulle as they were leyd in presse.
Of twenty yeer of age he was, I gesse.
Of his stature he was of evene lengthe,
And wonderly delyvere, and of greet strengthe.
85   And he hadde been somtyme in chyvachie
In Flaundres, in Artoys, and Pycardie,

ın gɛrnaːd at θə seːdʒ eːk had eː beː

ɔf aldʒɛzır and rıdən ın bɛlmariːə

at liːæıs was eː and at sataliːə

hwan θæı wæːr wʊn and at θə græːtə sæː

60 at manɪ ə nɔːbəl armeː had eː beː

at mɔrtal batæıls had eː beːn fıfteːnə

and fɔʊxtən fɔr uːr fæıθ at tramıseːnə

ın lıstəs θriːəs and æı slæın ıs fɔː

θıs ılkə wʊrðɪ knıxt had beːn alsɔː

65 sʊmtiːmə wıθ θə lɔːrd ɔf palatiːə

agæın anoːðər hæːðən ın tʊrkiːə

and ɛvərmɔːr eː had a sʊvræın priːs

and θɔʊx θat heː wæːr wʊrðı heː was wiːs

and ɔf ıs pɔrt as meːk as ıs ə mæıdə

70 heː nɛvər jɛt nɔː vılæıniː nə sæıdə

ın al ıs liːf ʊntoː nɔː manər wıxt

heː was a vɛriːæı parfıt dʒɛntıl knıxt

but fɔr toː tɛlıən juː ɔf hıs arːæı

hıs hɔrs wæːr gɔːdə bʊt eː was nat gæı

75 ɔf fʊstıan eː wæːrəd ə dʒıpuːn

al bısmʊtərd wıθ ıs abərdʒuːn

fɔr heː was laːt ɪkʊm frɔm hıs viaːdʒə

and wɛntə fɔr toː doːn ıs pılgrımaːdʒə

wıθ ım θæːr was ıs sʊn a jʊŋg skwiːeːr

80 a lʊvjɛr and ə lʊstɪ batʃəleːr

wıθ lɔkːəs krʊl as θæı wæːr læıd ın prɛsːə

ɔf twɛntɪ jæːr ɔf aːdʒ eː was iː gɛsːə

ɔf hıs statıʊr eː was ɔf ɛvnə lɛŋgθə

and wʊndərlɪ deːlıvr and ɔf græːt strɛŋgθə

85 and heː had beːn sʊmtiːm ın tʃıvatʃiːə

ın flaʊndrəs ın artɔıs and pıkardiːə

And born hym weel, as of so litel space,
In hope to stonden in his lady grace.
Embrouded was he, as it were a meede
90   Al ful of fresshe floures, whyte and reede.
Syngynge he was or floytynge, al the day;
He was as fressh as is the month of May.
Short was his gowne with sleves longe and wyde.
Wel koude he sitte on hors and faire ryde.
95   He koude songes make and wel endite,
Juste and eek daunce and weel purtreye and write.
So hoote he loved that by nyghtertale
He sleep namoore than dooth a nyghtyngale.
Curteis he was, lowely and servysable,
100   And carf biforn his fader at the table.
        A Yeman hadde he and servantz namo
At that tyme, for hym liste ride so;
And he was clad in cote and hood of grene.
A sheef of pecok arwes, bright and kene,
105   Under his belt he bar ful thriftily,
(Wel koude he dresse his takel yemanly:
His arwes drouped noght with fetheres lowe)
And in his hand he baar a myghty bowe.
A not heed hadde he, with a broun visage.
110   Of wodecraft wel koude he al the usage.
Upon his arm he baar a gay bracer,
And by his syde a swerd and a bokeler,
And on that oother syde a gay daggere
Harneised wel and sharp as point of spere;
115   A Cristopher on his brest of silver sheene,
An horn he bar, the bawdryk was of grene;
A forster was he soothly, as I gesse.

and bɔːrn ɪm weːl as ɔf sɔː liːtəl spaːsə
ɪn hɔːp toː stɔːndən ɪn ɪs laːdɪ graːsə
ɛmbruːdəd was eː as ɪt wæːr ə mæːdə

90 al fʊl ɔf frɛʃə fluːrəs hwiːt and ræːdə
sɪŋgɪŋg eː was ɔr flɔɪtɪŋg al θə dæɪ
heː was as frɛʃ as ɪs θə moːnθ ɔf mæɪ
ʃɔrt was ɪs guːn wɪθ sleːvəs lɔːŋg and wiːdə
weːl kuːd eː sɪt ɔn hɔrs and fæɪrə riːdə

95 heː kuːdə sɔːŋgəs maːk and weːl ɛndiːtə
dʒʊst and eːk daʊns and weːl pʊrtræɪ and wriːtə
sɔː hɔːt eː lʊvəd θat biː nɪxtərtaːlə
heː sleːp namɔːr θan doːθ ə nɪxtɪŋgaːlə
kʊrtæɪs eː was lɔːʊ̇lɪ and sɛrvɪzaːbəl

100 and karf bɪfɔːrn ɪs fadər at θə taːbəl
a jeːman had eː and sɛrvants namɔː
at θat tiːm fɔr ɪm lɪstə riːdə sɔː
and heː was klad ɪn kɔːt and hoːd ɔf greːnə
a ʃæːf ɔf pæːkɔk arwəs brɪxt and keːnə

105 ʊndər ɪs bɛlt eː baːr fʊl θrɪftɪlɪ
weːl kuːd eː drɛs ɪs takəl jeːmanlɪ
hɪs arwəs druːpəd nɔʊxt wɪθ fɛðrəs lɔːʊə
and ɪn ɪs hand eː baːr ə mɪxtɪ bɔːʊə
a nɔt hæːd had eː wɪθ a bruːn vɪzaːdʒə

110 ɔf woːdəkraft weːl kuːd eː al θɪuzaːdʒə
ʊpɔn ɪs arm eː baːr ə gæɪ braːseːr
and biː ɪs siːd ə sweːrd and ə bʊkleːr
and ɔn θat oːðər siːd a gæɪ dageːrə
harnæɪzəd weːl and ʃarp as pɔɪnt ɔf spæːrə

115 a krɪstɔfr ɔn ɪs breːst ɔf sɪlvər ʃeːnə
an hɔrn eː baːr θə baʊdrɪk was ɔf greːnə
a fɔrstər was eː soːθlɪ as iː gesːə

31. Chaucer's Spelling. The spelling of the vowels and diphthongs in the manuscripts of Chaucer's works is by no means consistently phonetic. In a phonetic system of spelling each character represents one sound and only one. As will appear from the tabulation which follows, most letters or letter combinations represent two and sometimes three distinctive vowel sounds or phonemes in the works of Chaucer as they have come down to us.

a	represents	[ɑː] or [ɑ]
aa	"	[ɑː]
e	"	[eː], [æː], or [ɛ]
ee	"	[eː] or [æː]
i	"	[iː] or [ɪ]
o	"	[oː], [ɔː], [ɔ], [ʊ], or [ɔʊ]
oo	"	[oː] or [ɔː]
ou	"	[uː], [ɔːʊ], or [ɔʊ]
u	"	[ʊ] or [ɪu]
y	"	[iː] or [ɪ]

32. Chaucer's Sounds in Relation to Modern English. Despite the ambiguities of spelling indicated in the foregoing section, the pronunciation of a word in Chaucer's dialect can usually be inferred from the pronunciation of that word in Modern English. This is possible because the pronunciations of the English vowel sounds since Chaucer's time, though they have changed considerably, have changed in a consistent and systematic manner. Middle English [ɔː] has regularly developed into Modern English [o]; [hɔːlɪ] has become [holɪ], [bɔːt] has become [bot], [ɔːpən] has become [oːpən], [sɔː] has become [so]. That is, under the same conditions, a given Middle English sound has always developed into a certain corresponding Modern English sound. Therefore, the Chaucerian spellings listed below may be interpreted as follows:

aa or a represents [ɑː] if in MnE the vowel is [e]; ME *name* [nɑːmə], MnE [nem].

a   "   [ɑ] if in MnE the vowel is [æ]; ME *that* [θɑt], MnE [ðæt].

ee or e   "   [eː] or [æː] if in MnE the vowel is [i]; ME *swete* [sweːtə], MnE [swit]; ME *heeth* [hæːθ], MnE [hiθ].

e   "   [ɛ] if in MnE the vowel is [ɛ]; ME *sende* [sɛndə], MnE [sɛnd].

i or y represents [iː] if in MnE the vowel is [ɑɪ]; ME *ryde* [riːdə],
MnE [rɑɪd].

i or y   "   [ɪ] if in MnE the vowel is [ɪ]; ME *riden* [rɪdən], MnE
[rɪdn].

oo or o   "   [oː] if in MnE the vowel is [u]; ME *rote* [roːtə],
MnE [rut].

oo or o   "   [ɔː] if in MnE the vowel is [o]; ME *hooly* [hɔːlɪ],
MnE [holɪ].

o   "   [ɔ] if in MnE the vowel is [ɑ]; ME *oxe* [ɔksə], MnE
[ɑks].[39]

o   "   [ʊ] if in MnE the vowel is [ʌ]; ME *sone* [sʊnə], MnE
[sʌn].

o   "   [ɔʊ] if in MnE the vowel is [ɔ]; ME *thoght* [θɔʊxt];
MnE [θɔt].

ou or ow   "   [uː] if in MnE the vowel is [ɑʊ]; ME *hous* [huːs],
MnE [hɑʊs].

ou or ow   "   [ɔːu] if in MnE the vowel is [o]; ME *bowe* [bɔːuə],
MnE [bo].

ou   "   [ɔʊ] if in MnE the vowel is [ɔ]; ME *foughte* [fɔʊxtə],
MnE [fɔt].

u   "   [ʊ] if in MnE the vowel is [ʌ]; ME *under* [ʊndər],
MnE [ʌndɚ].

u   "   [ɪu] if in MnE the vowel is [ju] [ɪu] or [u]; ME
humour [hɪumuːr], MnE [hjumɚ] or [hɪumɚ]; ME *rude*
[rɪudə], MnE [rud].

But the characters **ai, ay, ei,** and **ey** always represent the diphthong
[æɪ] and the characters **au** and **aw** always represent the diphthong [ɑʊ].
The characters **eu** and **ew** nearly always represent the diphthong [ɪu];
they represent the diphthong [ɛu] only in **dew,** *dew*; **dronkelewe,** *ad-
dicted to drink*; **fewe,** *few*; **hewen,** *hew*; **lewed,** *ignorant*; **rewe,** *row*;
shewen, *show*; **shrewe,** *shrew*; **thewes,** *habits*, and possibly one or two
other words. The characters **oi** and **oy** always represent the diphthong
[ɔɪ].

[39] In the dialect of most parts of the United States, ME [ɔ] has become [ɑ], but
the ME vowel (or a vowel much like it) has been retained in the speech of England
and New England.

The character o represents the diphthong [ɔu] only when [x], spelled gh or h, follows.

33. The interpretations made in the foregoing section are based upon what is known of the systematic development of English sounds between 1400 and the present time when such sounds remained free of the influence of neighboring sounds. But the development of a sound is often affected by the influence of other sounds which precede or follow it. Thus, Middle English [ʊ] regularly developed into Modern English [ʌ]; [sʊnːə] has become [sʌn], [ʊndər] has become [ʌndɚ], [lʊvə] has become [lʌv]. But when Middle English [ʊ] was preceded by a lip consonant (b, p, f, or w) and was followed by l, it has been preserved in Modern English; e.g., Middle English [bʊlə], [pʊlːə], [fʊl], and [wʊlf] are Modern English [bʊl], [pʊl], [fʊl], and [wʊlf]. Moreover, vowels change not only in quality, but also in quantity. Long vowels may become short, and short vowels may become long. For example, in a number of words Middle English [oː], which has regularly become [u] in Modern English, is represented by Modern English [ʊ]. This is not because Middle English [oː] has in these words changed to [ʊ] instead of [u], but because, after [oː] had become [uː], the [uː] was shortened to [ʊ]. Thus we have Modern English [gʊd], [hʊd], and [stʊd] from Middle English [goːd], [hoːd], [stoːd]. So also with Modern English [brɛθ] from Middle English [bræːθ]; Middle English [æː] regularly changed to early Modern English [eː], which later became [i], but in this case the vowel was shortened to [ɛ] before the change to [i] occurred.

34. **Chaucer's Sounds in Relation to Old English.** The statements, therefore, that have been made with regard to the relation between Middle English sounds and Modern English sounds are not sufficient to enable us to determine the pronunciation of *all* Middle English words. But where the evidence of the Modern English pronunciation is not clear, it is generally possible to determine the Middle English pronunciation of a *native* English word from a knowledge of its pronunciation in Old English.[40]

---

[40] Likewise, the pronunciation of ME words that were borrowed from French can be determined from a knowledge of their pronunciation in **Old** French; the **Modern** French pronunciation of such words is often different.

aa or a represents [ɑ:] if in OE the vowel was a or æ in an open syllable;[41]
OE **nama, fæder**; ME **name, fader**

a   "   [ɑ] if in OE the vowel was a, æ or ea in a closed syllable;[42] OE **þanc, þæt, hearm**; ME **thank, that, harm**

ee or e   "   [e:] if in OE the vowel was ē or ēo; OE **swēte, bēon**; ME **swete, been**

ee or e   "   [æ:] if in OE the vowel was ēa, or e in an open syllable; OE **strēam, mete**; ME **streem, mete**

e   "   [ɛ] if in OE the vowel was e or eo in a closed syllable; OE **helpan, eorðe**; ME **helpen, erthe**

i or y   "   [i:] if in OE the vowel was ī or ȳ; OE **rīdan, fȳr**; ME **riden, fyr**

i or y   "   [ɪ] if in OE the vowel was i or y; OE **drincan, fyllan**; ME **drinken, fillen**

oo or o   "   [o:] if in OE the vowel was ō; OE **dōn**; ME **don**

oo or o   "   [ɔ:] if in OE the vowel was ā, or o in an open syllable; OE **hāliġ, stolen**; ME **hooly, stolen**

o   "   [ɔ] if in OE the vowel was o in a closed syllable; OE **oxa**; ME **oxe**

o   "   [ʊ] if in OE the vowel was u; OE **sunu**; ME **sone**

ou   "   [u:] if in OE the vowel was ū; OE **hūs**; ME **hous**

u   "   [ʊ] if in OE the vowel was u; OE **under**; ME **under**

By following the rules that have been given in these sections, the student will be able to ascertain the pronunciation of the great majority of the words that occur in Chaucer's works. These rules, however, are merely a practical application of our knowledge of the history of English pronunciation, which is treated systematically in Chapters III, V, and VIII of this book. The student is therefore urged to go on, after learning the use of the rules, to a study of these chapters in order that he may better understand the principles on which the rules are based.

[41] An open syllable is one that ends in a vowel. In words of two or more syllables a **single** consonant following a vowel belongs to the following syllable; in OE **nama, fæder, mete,** and **stolen, a, æ, e,** and o were in open syllables.

[42] A closed syllable is one that ends in a consonant; examples of vowels in closed syllables are **a, æ, e,** and o in OE **þanc, þæt, helpan,** and **oxa.**

35. Consonant Sounds. The consonant sounds present much less difficulty to the student of Chaucer than the vowel sounds because the changes in pronunciation that have occurred since Chaucer's time have affected the consonants much less extensively than the vowels. The principal points of difference are the following:

1. Initial **g**, **k**, and **w** were pronounced in the combinations **gn**, **kn**, and **wr**: ME **gnawe** [gnɑυə], *knight* [knɪxt], *write* [wriːtə]; MnE [nɔ], [nɑɪt], [rɑɪt].

2. **ng** was always pronounced [ŋg]: ME **yong** [juŋg], **singe** [sɪŋgə]; MnE [jʌŋ], [sɪŋ].

3. **l** was pronounced before **f**, **k**, and **m**: ME *half* [half], *folk* [fɔlk], *palmer* [palmɛr]; MnE [hæf] or [haf], [fok], [pɑːmə˞].

4. Final **s** was always pronounced [s] and initial **th** was always pronounced [θ]: ME *was* [was], *his* [hɪs], *houses* [huːzəs]; MnE [waz], [hɪz], [haυzəz]; ME *that* [θat], *than* [θan]; MnE [ðæt], [ðæn].

5. The suffix corresponding to MnE *-tion* was pronounced [sɪuːn] (two syllables) in ME: ME *nacioun* [naːsɪuːn], *condicioun* [kɔndɪsɪuːn]; MnE *nation* [neʃən], *condition* [kəndɪʃən].

6. Double consonants were lengthened (as in MnE **pen-knife, book-case, gull-like**): ME *sonne* [sυnːə], *alle* [alːə].

INFLECTIONS OF CHAUCER'S LANGUAGE

36. Declension of Nouns. The regular inflection of nouns in Chaucer, as exemplified by **dom**, *judgment*, and **ende**, *end*, is as follows:

SING. NOM., DAT., ACC.	dom	ende
GEN.	domes	endes
PLUR. NOM., GEN., DAT., ACC.	domes	endes

The following exceptions occur:

1. The genitive singular of proper nouns ending in **s** is frequently without ending; e.g., *Epicurus owne sone*, A 336.

2. The genitive singular of nouns of relationship ending in **r** is sometimes without ending; e.g., *my fader soule*, A 781; *brother sone*, A 3084.[43]

---

[43] These nouns had no ending in the genitive singular in Old English.

3. The genitive singular of nouns which belonged to the Old English weak declension is sometimes without ending; e.g., *his lady grace,* A 88; *the sonne up-riste,* A 1051.[44]

4. The plural frequently ends in **s** instead of **es**; e.g., *naciouns,* A 53; *hunters,* A 178; *fees,* A 317; this is particularly common in words of one syllable ending in a vowel and in words of two syllables ending in a consonant. The ending **-es** is often written when only **s** is sounded; e.g., *yeddinges,* A 237.

5. The plural of some nouns ends in **en** instead of **es**; e.g., *eyen,* A 152; *children,* A 1193.[45]

6. The plural of monosyllabic nouns ending in **s** is usually without ending; e.g., *caas,* A 323.

7. Some nouns which had no ending in the nominative and accusative plural in Old English have no plural ending in Chaucer; e.g., *hors,* A 74; *swyn,* A 598; *yeer,* A 82.[46]

8. The dative singular has the same form as the nominative-accusative singular, but in a few phrases consisting of a preposition immediately followed by a noun the noun has the old dative ending **-e**; e.g., *of towne,* A 566.[47]

37. Declension of Adjectives. Middle English, like Old English, has two declensions of the adjective, the strong and the weak although by Chaucer's time there was a minimum of difference between the two. The weak declension of the adjective is used when it is preceded by the definite article **the,** by a demonstrative (**this** or **that**), by a possessive pronoun, or by a noun in the genitive case; e.g., *the yonge sonne,* A 7; *this ilke monk,* A 175; *his halve cours,* A 8; *Epicurus owne sone,* A 336;

---

[44] The Old English genitive singulars of Chaucer's **lady** and **sonne** were **hlǽfdigan** and **sunnan,** which in early Middle English became **ladie(n)** and **sunne(n),** the n in parenthesis being a sound which was very often lost. The genitive singulars **lady** and **sonne** in Chaucer are the early Middle English forms without **n,** the three syllables of early Middle English **ladie** having been reduced to two.

[45] Some of these nouns, such as **eyen,** belonged in Old English to the weak declension, which had the ending **-an** in the nominative and accusative plural. Others, such as **children,** from Old English **čild,** plural **čildru,** did not belong in Old English to the weak declension but assumed the weak ending **-en** in Middle English from the analogy of nouns which had been weak in Old English.

[46] These were neuter nouns in Old English with a long root syllable. See the declension of *horn* on p. 22.

[47] See note 58 below.

the weak declension is also used when the adjective precedes a noun used in direct address; e.g., *faire fresshe May*, A 1511; it may also be used when the adjective precedes a proper name not used in direct address; e.g., *faire Venus*, A 2663. The strong declension is used chiefly when the adjective, unaccompanied by article or demonstrative precedes the noun or when it is used as a predicate adjective.

The forms of the strong and weak declensions of the adjectives **good** and **swete** are as follows:

Strong Declension

Singular	**good**	swete
Plural	**goode**	swete

Weak Declension

Singular	**goode**	swete
Plural	**goode**	swete

It will be observed that:

(1) Adjectives like **swete** are invariable in form.

(2) Adjectives like **good** have in the strong declension the ending **-e** in the plural.

(3) Adjectives like good have in the weak declension the ending **-e** in both singular and plural.

The following exceptions occur:

1. Plural adjectives used predicatively or post-substantively are often not inflected, though such adjectives are frequently written with a final e even when the e is not sounded; e.g., *whiche they weren*, A 40; *And of another thing they were as fayn*, A 2707; *His limes grete, his brawnes harde*, A 2135.

2. Adjectives of two or more syllables ending in a consonant are usually not inflected, either in the plural or in the circumstances which call for the use of the weak inflection; e.g., *mortal batailles*, A 61; *He which that hath the shortest shal biginne*, A 836.

3. A trace of the old genitive plural of the adjective **all** appears occasionally in the form **aller, alder** (from Old English **ealra**, genitive plural of **eal**); e. g., *hir aller cappe*, "the cap of them all," A 586; *alderbest*, "best of all," A 710.

38. Personal Pronouns. The personal pronouns are inflected as follows in Chaucer; forms that are rare are placed in parentheses. Though not indicated in the diagram all forms of the second person plural were used with singular meaning in certain social situations.

	First person	Second person
SING. NOM.	**I, (ich)**	**thou**
GEN.	**my, myn**	**thy, thyn**
DAT., ACC.	**me**	**the**
PLUR. NOM.	**we**	**ye**
GEN.	**our, (oure), oures**	**your [juːr], (youre), youres**
DAT., ACC.	**us**	**you [juː]**

Third person

	Masc.	Fem.	Neut.
SING. NOM.	**he**	**she**	**hit, it**
GEN.	**his**	**hir, (hire) her(e)s; her, (here)**	**his**
DAT., ACC.	**hym**	**hir, (hire); her, (here)**	**hit, it**

All genders

PLUR. NOM.	**they**
GEN.	**hir, (hire); her, (here)**
DAT., ACC.	**hem**

39. Demonstratives. The demonstratives **this** and **that** are inflected as follows in Chaucer; forms that are rare are placed in parentheses.

SING.	**this**	**that**
PLUR.	**this, thise; thes, these**	**tho [θɔː]**

A trace of the old dative singular of **that** appears in the phrase *for the nones*, A 379, from Old English *for þæm ānes* (literally "for that once"); the early Middle English form of this phrase was *for then ones*, which by incorrect word division, came to be written in Chaucer's time *for the nones*. A survival of the old instrumental case of **that** appears in the adverbial **the** (Old English þē); e.g., *the more mery*, A 802, literally "more merry by that."

The demonstrative **that** is historically the same word as the definite article **the,** for both are derived from Old English **sē, sēo, þæt,** which was used both as demonstrative and article. Survivals of the Old English and early Middle English use of **that** in the function of article appear in such expressions as *that other syde,* A 113.

40. Strong and Weak Verbs. In Middle English, as in Old English and all other Germanic languages, there are two conjugations of verbs, the strong and the weak. Weak verbs form their preterit by means of a suffix containing **d** or **t.** Strong verbs do not form their preterit by means of a suffix containing **d** or **t** but by a change in the vowel of the stem of the verb. For example, the preterits of the weak verb **loven** and the strong verb **riden** are as follows:

Pret. Ind. Sing.	1	lovede, loved	rood
	2	lovedest	ride
	3	lovede, loved	rood
Plur.		lovede(n),[48] loved	ride(n)

Weak verbs may be recognized from the fact that their preterit indicative first and third persons singular end in **-ede, -ed, -de,** or **-te** and from the fact that their past participles end in **-ed, d,** or **t.** Strong verbs may be recognized from the fact that their preterit indicative first and third persons singular are **without ending,** and from the fact that their past participles end in **-en** or **e.**

41. Weak Verb Conjugations. There are two types of weak verbs in Middle English. Weak verbs of Type I have preterits ending in **-ede** or **-ed** and past participles ending in **-ed.** Weak verbs of Type II have preterits ending in **-de** or **-te** and past participles ending in **-ed, d,** or **t.** The principal parts of representative verbs are as follows:

Type I	love(n)	lovede, loved	loved
	stire(n)	stirede, stired	stired

---

[48] **e(n)** indicates that the ending **-en** interchanges with the ending **-e.** This interchange of **-en** and **-e** was the result of a general tendency to the loss of final **n** in unstressed syllables which began in very early Middle English but which was never fully carried out in Chaucer's dialect. Survivals of the Middle English double forms still exist in the Modern English past participles **(for)gotten, (for)got; broken, broke; frozen, froze,** etc.

Type II	here(n)	herde	herd
	fele(n)	felte	feled, felt
	fede(n)	fedde	fed
	seke(n)	soughte	sought[49]

The complete conjugations of the two types of weak verbs, exemplified by **love(n)** and **here(n)** respectively, are as follows:

	TYPE I	TYPE II
PRES. IND. SING.	1 lov-e	her-e
	2 lov-est	her-est
	3 lov-eth	her-eth
PLUR.	lov-e(n)	her-e(n)
PRES. SUBJ. SING.	lov-e	her-e
PLUR.	lov-e(n)	her-e(n)
PRET. IND. SING. 1	lov-ede, lov-ed	her-de
2	lov-edest	her-dest
3	lov-ede, lov-ed	her-de
PLUR.	lov-ede(n), lov-ed	her-de(n)
PRET. SUBJ. SING.	lov-ede, lov-ed	her-de
PLUR.	lov-ede(n), lov-ed	her-de(n)
IMPERATIVE SING.	lov-e	her
PLUR.	lov-eth, lov-e	her-eth, her-e
INFINITIVE	lov-e(n)	her-e(n)
GERUND	to lov-e(n)	to her-e(n)
PRES. PARTICIPLE	lov-inge, lov-ing	her-inge, her-ing
PAST PARTICIPLE	lov-ed	her-d

42. Strong Verb Conjugations. Strong verbs form their preterit by means of a change in the vowel of the stem of the verb. The vowel of the preterit plural is often different from that of the preterit singular, so that there are four principal parts, the infinitive, the preterit indicative first person singular, the preterit indicative plural, and the past partici-

---

[49] The past participles of both strong and weak verbs often have the prefix -y (from the OE prefix -ǧe); e.g. **yronne** A 8, **yfalle** A 25, **ytaught** A 127 **ywroght** A 196.

ple.[50] For further information concerning the types of vowel alternation occurring in the various strong verb conjugations see the inflectional chart of Old English, Chapter III, p. 23, and the table in connection with Section 97, Chapter VI.

The principal parts of representative strong verbs are as follows:

ride(n)	[riːdən]	rood	[rɔːd]	ride(n)	[rɪdən]	ride(n)	[rɪdən]
crepe(n)	[kreːpən]	creep	[kræːp]	crope(n)	[krɔːpən]	crope(n)	[krɔːpən]
binde(n)	[biːndən]	bond	[bɔːnd]	bounde(n)	[buːndən]	bounde(n)	[buːndən]
helpe(n)	[hɛlpən]	halp	[halp]	holpe(n)	[hɔlpən]	holpe(n)	[hɔlpən]
sterve(n)	[stɛrvən]	starf	[starf]	storve(n)	[stɔrvən]	storve(n)	[stɔrvən]
bere(n)	[bæːrən]	bar	[bar]	bere(n)	[beːrən]	bore(n)	[bɔːrən]
		baar	[baːr]	bare(n)	[baːrən]		
		beer	[beːr]				
speke(n)	[spæːkən]	spak	[spak]	speke(n)	[speːkən]	spoke(n)	[spɔːkən]
				spake(n)	[spaːkən]		
shake(n)	[ʃaːkən]	shook	[ʃoːk]	shoke(n)	[ʃoːkən]	shake(n)	[ʃaːkən]
slepe(n)	[slæːpən]	sleep	[sleːp]	slepe(n)	[sleːpən]	slepe(n)	[sleːpən]
holde(n)	[hɔːldən]	heeld	[heːld]	helde(n)	[heːldən]	holde(n)	[hɔːldən]

The endings of the strong verbs, exemplified by ride(n) and bere(n), are as follows:

PRES. IND. SING.
1 rid-e   ber-e
2 rid-est   ber-est
3 rid-eth, rit [rɪt][51]   ber-eth
PLUR. rid-e(n)   ber-e(n)

PRES. SUBJ. SING. rid-e   ber-e
PLUR. rid-e(n)   ber-e(n)

PRET. IND. SING.
1 rood   bar
2 rid-e, rood   ber-e, bar
3 rood   bar
PLUR. rid-e(n)   ber-e(n)

[50] The vowel of the infinitive occurs also in the present indicative, present subjunctive, imperative, gerund, and present participle; the vowel of the preterit indicative first person singular occurs also in the preterit indicative third person singular; the vowel of the preterit indicative plural occurs also in the preterit indicative second person singular and in the preterit subjunctive; the vowel of the past participle occurs in that form only.

[51] Contracted forms like rit are frequent in verbs whose stems end in d or t; the contraction originated in Old English. See Moore and Knott, *Elements of Old English*, Sections 124, 125.

Pret. Subj. Sing.	rid-e	ber-e
Plur.	rid-e(n)	ber-e(n)
Imperative Sing.	rid	ber
Plur.	rid-eth, rid-e	ber-eth, ber-e
Infinitive	rid-e(n)	ber-e(n)
Gerund	to rid-e(n)	to ber-e(n)
Pres. Participle	rid-inge, rid-ing	ber-inge, ber-ing
Past Participle	rid-e(n)	bor-e(n)

43. Preteritive-Present Verbs. The preteritive-present (or strong-weak) verbs have **present** indicatives which are like the **preterit** indicatives of strong verbs in that they have no ending in the first and third persons singular.[52] The **preterits** of these verbs are **weak.** For the most part these verbs are employed as modal auxiliaries, but on occasions they assume independent meaning. The principal forms of the more important preteritive-present verbs that occur in Chaucer are as follows:

Pres. Ind. Sing. 1	**can,** *know how, be able*	dar, *dare*
2	**canst**	darst
3	**can**	dar
Plur.	**conne(n)** [kʊnɪən], can	dorre(n) [dʊɪrən], dar
Pret. Ind. Sing. 1	couthe[kuɪðə], coude[kuɪdə]	dorste [dʊrstə]

Pres. Ind. Sing. 1	**may,** *be able*	moot, *be permitted,* *be under obligation*
2	**mayst**	most
3	**may**	moot
Plur.	**mowe(n)** [muɪən], may	mote(n), moot
Pret. Ind. Sing. 1	**mighte** [mɪxtə]	moste

Pres. Ind. Sing. 1	**shal,** *be under obligation,* *be about to*	wot [wɔɪt], *know*
2	**shalt**	wost [wɔɪst]
3	**shal**	wot
Plur.	**shulle(n), shul, shal**	wite(n), wot
Pret. Ind. Sing. 1	**sholde** [ʃʊldə], [ʃoɪldə]; **shulde**	wiste

[52] See Moore and Knott, *Elements of Old English*, Chapter XXIII; also Sections 100, 101 in this book.

44. Anomalous Verbs. The forms of **bee(n)**, *be*, are as follows:

PRES. IND. SING. 1 **am**
2 **art**
3 **is**
PLUR. **bee(n)** [beːn], **be** (beː]

PRES. SUBJ. SING. **be**
PLUR. **bee(n), be**

PRET. IND. SING. 1 **was**
2 **were** [wæːrə]
3 **was**
PLUR. **were(n)** [wæːrən]

PRET. SUBJ. SING. **were**
PLUR. **were(n)**

IMPERATIVE SING. **be**
PLUR. **beeth, be**

INFINITIVE **bee(n), be**
GERUND **to bee(n), to be**
PRES. PARTICIPLE **being**
PAST PARTICIPLE **bee(n), be**

The forms of **wille(n)**, *will*, are as follows:[53]

PRES. IND. SING. 1 **wil, wol** [wul]
2 **wilt, wolt**
3 **wil, wol**
PLUR. **wille(n), wolle(n), wil, wol**

PRET. IND. SING. 1 **wolde** [woːldə]
2 **woldest**
3 **wolde**
PLUR. **wolde(n)**

---

[53] Although some forms of the subjunctive of this verb do occur in the works of Chaucer, they are not found in all persons and numbers, and moreover, subjunctive forms cannot always be distinguished with certainty from the indicative. Therefore the subjunctive has been omitted from the conjugation.

FINAL e IN CHAUCER'S LANGUAGE

45. Inflectional and Etymological Final e. Final e's in Chaucer's language are, with a few exceptions, either **inflectional** or **etymological.** Inflectional final e's are those which occur in some forms of a word but not in others, their occurrence or non-occurrence depending on grammatical considerations. For example, the adjective **good** has no final e in such an expression as *A good man was ther of religioun* (A 477), but it has a final e in the expressions *His hors were gode* (A 74) and *his gode name* (A 3049). In A 74 **gode** has a final e because the noun it modifies is plural. In A 3049 it has a final e because, being preceded by a possessive pronoun, it is a weak adjective (see **37** above). But in A 477 **good** is without final e because it is neither plural nor weak, modifying a noun in the singular and not being preceded by an article, demonstrative, or possessive pronoun. Since **good,** derived from Old English **gōd** may appear either with or without final e, those final e's which are added to it in keeping with certain grammatical considerations are considered inflectional.

On the other hand, the adjective **lene** in A 287, *As lene was his hors as is a rake,* a construction virtually parallel to that of **good** in A 477, does have a final e, though like **good** it is neither plural nor weak. Here the explanation of the final e is not grammatical but etymological; the word has a final e because it ended in e in Old English, being derived from OE **hlǣne.** Thus, if a final e cannot be explained upon grammatical or inflectional grounds, it is very probably there because the root or stem of the word in question originally ended in a vowel, which had become e by Chaucer's time. Such e's are called etymological.

46. Inflectional Final e. Inflectional final e occurs in adjectives and verbs.

1. Adjectives (see **37** above)

Final e occurs:

    a. In the weak form of the adjective

    b. In the plural form of the adjective[54]

---

[54] When it modifies a plural noun the pronoun **his** is very commonly written **hise** in good manuscripts, and the final e is sometimes pronounced. This final e is from the analogy of the final e of plural adjectives. So also is the final e of **these, thise** plural of **thes, this** (see **39** above).

2. Verbs (see **41-43** above)

Final **e** occurs:

a. In the present indicative first person singular of **strong** and **weak** verbs.

b. In the present subjunctive singular of **strong** and **weak** verbs

c. In the preterit indicative first and third persons singular of **weak** verbs

d. In the preterit indicative second person singular of **strong** verbs

e. In the preterit subjunctive singular of **strong** and **weak** verbs

f. In the imperative singular of many **weak** verbs

g. Sometimes in the gerund of **monosyllabic** verbs, e.g., **to done,** F 334[55]

h. In the present participle of **strong** and **weak** verbs e.g. **singinge,** A 91[56]

Final **e** interchanging with **en** occurs:

i. In the present indicative plural of **strong** and **weak** verbs

j. In the present subjunctive plural of **strong** and **weak** verbs

k. In the preterit indicative plural of **strong** and **weak** verbs

l. In the preterit subjunctive plural of **strong** and **weak** verbs

m. In the infinitive and gerund of **strong** and **weak** verbs

n. In the past participle of **strong** verbs[57]

---

[55] The gerund in OE was made up of the proposition **tō** and an inflected form of the infinitive having the ending **-e**, e.g. **tō rīdenne**. Even in OE, however, gerunds with an uninflected infinitive, e.g. **tō rīdan**, appear occasionally. In ME the inflected infinitive became less and less common in the gerund, so that for most verbs the usual form of the gerund was **to riden** or **to ride**. The inflected infinitive still occurs sometimes in Chaucer in the gerunds of verbs like **doon** and **seen** which have monosyllabic infinitives.

[56] The present participle should be distinguished from the verbal noun in **-inge** or **-ing** (e.g. **winning,** A 275, **lerninge,** A 300, **turneyinge,** A 2557) which corresponds historically to the OE verbal nouns in **-ing** or **-ung**. But OE had only a limited number of these verbal nouns, whereas in ME they were formed with the greatest freedom, even from verbs of French derivation. The OE verbal nouns in **-ing** or **-ung** were feminines, and like other feminines ending in a consonant acquired a final **-e**, in ME (see **47.1b** below). But they occur more frequently in Chaucer without final **-e**.

[57] For simplicity the preteritive-present verbs are ignored in this paragraph. Their preterits are like those of weak verbs, and their present indicative plural either has the ending **-e(n)** or is without ending. (See **43** above.)

47. Etymological Final e. Etymological final **e** occurs in nouns, adjectives, pronouns, adverbs, prepositions, and conjunctions.

1. Nouns

   Final **e** occurs:

   a. In nouns derived from Old English nouns which ended in a vowel (**a, e** or **u**); e.g., **tyme,** from OE **tīma** (A 44); **sonne,** from OE **sunne** (A 7); **tale,** from OE **talu** (A 36)

   b. In nouns derived from Old English **feminine** nouns which ended in a consonant; e.g., **reste,** from OE **rest,** fem. (A 30)

   c. In some nouns derived from Old English nouns ending in **-en;** e.g., **mayde,** from OE **mæġden** (A 69)

   d. In nouns derived from Old French nouns ending in **e;** e.g., **corage,** from OFr **corage** (A 22)

   e. In the "petrified" dative which occurs in certain phrases consisting of a preposition immediately followed by a noun; e.g., **out of towne** (A 566)[58]

2. Adjectives

   Final **e** occurs:

   a. In adjectives derived from Old English adjectives ending in **e;** e.g., **lene,** from OE **hlǽne** (A 287)

   b. In the comparative form of a few adjectives; e.g., **more,** from OE **māra, māre**[59]

   c. In the "petrified" dative which occurs in certain phrases consisting of a preposition immediately followed by an adjective used as a noun; e.g., **with-alle** (A 127)

   d. In adjectives derived from Old French adjectives ending in **e;** e.g., **straunge,** from OFr **estrange** (A 13)

3. Pronouns

   Final **e** is usually written and occasionally pronounced in **oure**

---

[58] The final **e** in **of towne** is not a genuine inflection in the English of Chaucer's time. In early Middle English the dative singular always ended in **e,** but in the course of time the accusative was substituted for the dative wherever the two cases differed in form. A few phrases, however, like **of towne, on live, to bedde,** etc., were in such constant use that they were preserved at times long after the dative form had become obsolete in the language as a whole. We find therefore that Chaucer says **of towne** in A 566, but **of the toun** in A 217.

[59] The usual comparative ending is **-er.**

from OE ūre; in **hire, here** (*her*), from OE **hire;** and in
hire, here (*their*) from OE **hira, heora**

4. Adverbs, Prepositions, and Conjunctions

Final **e** occurs:

a. In adverbs derived from adjectives; e.g., **faire** (A 94), from the
adjective **fair** (A 154)

b. In adverbs, prepositions, and conjunctions whose originals
had a final vowel in Old English; e.g., **sone,** from OE **sōna**
(B 1702); **thanne,** from OE **þonne** (D 2004); **inne,** from OE
inne (A 41); **ẅhanne,** from OE **hwonne** (F 1406)

c. In adverbs, prepositions, and conjunctions whose originals in
Old English ended in -**an;** e.g., **bifore,** from OE **beforan**
(A 377); **with-oute,** from OE **wiþūtan** (A 343); **sithe,** from
OE **siþþan**

48. Inorganic Final e. A few nouns and adjectives in Middle English
had final **e**'s (not inflectional) which cannot be explained upon any of the
etymological grounds stated in Section **47;** e.g., **hewe** (F 587), from OE
hīw, neut.; **weye** (B 385), from OE **weġ,** masc.; **pere** (F 678), from OFr
per; bare (A 683), from OE **bær; harde** (G 665), from OE **heard.** Such final **e**'s we call **inorganic** final **e**'s. These words acquired final **e** in early
Middle English as the result of some analogy which in most cases we are
not able to trace with certainty.[60]

49. Scribal e. Occasionally even in the best and earliest manuscripts of Chaucer, and frequently in the later manuscripts, final **e**'s are
written which were never pronounced in Middle English. For example,
in the Lansdowne MS of the *Canterbury Tales,* written early in the
fifteenth century, the rime words of A 43f. are written **manne** and **be-
ganne.** Such **e**'s we call **scribal e**'s.

50. Elision, Apocope, and Syncope. If one pronounces in reading
Chaucer's verse all the final **e**'s that are grammatically or etymologically
justifiable, the metrical structure of the verse is often seriously impaired
or entirely destroyed. It is clear that Chaucer did not intend that every
possible final **e** should be sounded. Final **e** is usually **elided** when the

---

[60] On this point see Ruth B. McJimsey, *Chaucer's Irregular -E,* New York, 1942,
pp. 57–61.

following word begins with a vowel or "weak h";[61] e.g., in **couthe** (A 14) and **dresse** (A 106). Moreover, final **e** is often lost before words beginning with a consonant; e.g., **wiste** (A 224), **tyme** (A 102), **mete** (A 136). The loss of final **e** before consonants is called **apocope** or **apocopation.** This is to be distinguished from **syncope** or **syncopation,** which is the loss of a vowel **between** two consonants of the same word; e.g., *"Com(e)th neer," quod he, "my lady prioresse"* (A 839).

In using apocopated forms in his verse, however, Chaucer was not doing violence to the language of his time, as a modern writer would be doing if he omitted the final vowel of *navy* or *china.* In Chaucer's time the final **e** was beginning to be lost, and by the end of the fifteenth century it had entirely disappeared from the language. In Chaucer's time the final **e** was still pronounced, but not universally, so that double forms with and without final **e** were in use. Chaucer used the apocopated forms freely within the line, but neither apocope nor elision occur at the end of the line in his verse.[62]

---

[61] "Weak h" is the **h** in words like **he, him, hem, her, hath, hadde,** etc., in which the **h** was pronounced only when the word was strongly stressed, and the silent **h** in French words like **honour,** etc.

[62] The pronunciation of final **e** at the end of the line in Chaucer's poetry has been the topic of recent controversy. See J. G. Southworth, "Chaucer's Final *-e* in Rhyme," *PMLA* 62 (1947) 910–935. E. Talbot Donaldson, "Chaucer's Final *-e*," *PMLA* 63 (1948), 1101–24. J. G. Southworth, "Chaucer's Final *-E* (continued)," *PMLA* 64 (1949) 601–610.

CHAPTER V

The Development of Middle English Sounds

51. Sound Change and Linguistic Science. The regularity and consistency of behavior of the sounds of a language in their development from one period or point in time to another has already been briefly discussed (Section 32). This concept, however, is so basic to the scientific study of language that it merits repetition. The phonologist or historian of the sounds of a language assumes that a sound change generally affects all members of a phonetic category in the same way. Such changes as that of Chaucer's pronunciation [stɔːn] to Modern English [ston] and of [sʊn] to Modern English [sʌn], affecting the majority of words which were pronounced [ɔː] and [ʌ] respectively at that time, constitute what may be called normal or regular developments.

It is by no means unusual for certain words to remain unaffected or to be affected in a manner somewhat different from the so-called normal or regular development. It will be recalled that Middle English [pʊt] and [fʊl], among others, did not lower and unround to [ʌ], but retained their older pronunciation. The phonologist assumes also that such exceptions to the general rule or deviations from the norm can be accounted for. In the case of **put** and **full** he proceeds to do so by pointing out that the rounding of the lips demanded by the initial consonants in these particular words would constitute enough resistance to a general unrounding tendency to prevent their participation in the "regular" or "normal" change.

Some seventy-five years ago linguistic scientists were so insistent upon these postulates that they regularly spoke of sound changes as phonetic laws. The term *law* suggested for these language processes the same kind of inviolability that is characteristic of the operation of the physical universe. Today, students of language are somewhat less doctrinaire about such hypotheses than were their predecessors. The linguist of the mid-twentieth century is more likely to speak of a sound change as a historical event than as a law, but still basic to his science is the concept of regularity of change with the corollary assumption that departures from the norm may be accounted for.

The ground is now cleared for our initial step in tracing the development of English sounds. This first step will consist of a comparison of the sounds of Old English with those into which they developed during the next stage of the history of the language, namely the Middle English period.

In this connection, however, we must remember that these sound changes took place very gradually and that not all changes took place at precisely the same time. Thus, when it is said that Old English [ɑː] became Middle English [ɔː], we must realize that there was no precise point in time at which everyone ceased using the older sound and adopted the new. Quite possibly for a generation or more, some speakers in a given locality used the older sound whereas others employed the newer one, or at least something more like it than [ɑː]. Moreover, this change may have taken place at one time in one locality or part of England and not until considerably later in other portions of the country.

Thus it should be understood that a table of equivalents between the sounds of the language at two different periods, such as is drawn up in the section which follows, is unquestionably an over-simplification of a highly complex situation, but is justifiable on the ground that it is able to present in broad outline a synthesis of a highly complex series of interrelated developments. The only danger lies in the misuse, not in the proper use, of such a tabulation by the student.

52. Normal Development of Old English Stressed Vowels. The normal development of the Old English stressed vowel sounds into Middle English of the East Midland dialect is shown in the following table:

Old English[63]			Middle English		
[ɑː]	stān	[stɑːn]	[ɔː]	ston	[stɔːn]
[ɑ]	crabba	[krɑbːɑ]	[ɑ]	crabbe	[krɑbːə]
[æ]	þæt	[θæt]	[ɑ]	that	[θɑt]
[æː]	clǣne	[klæːnɛ]	[æː]	cleene	[klæːnə]
[eː][64]	swēte	[sweːtɛ]	[eː]	swete	[sweːtə]

[63] The Old English sounds which are taken as the basis of this table are those of the east **Mercian** dialect, which was that from which the East Midland dialect of Middle English was derived. The sounds of the **Mercian** dialect differed in certain respects from those of **West-Saxon** (WS), which is the dialect in which most of the Old English literature is preserved and upon which the Old English dictionaries are based. For example, the Mercian dialect did not contain the early West-Saxon (EWS) diphthongs **ie** and **ie**, and it had the vowel **ē** in many words which in West-Saxon have the vowel **ǣ**; e.g., WS **dǣd** was Mercian **dēd**. In the Mercian dialect the vowel **ǣ** was always the result of the i-umlaut of WGmc **ā**. See also Section **27**.

[64] The Modern English sounds given as the equivalents of Old and Middle English [eː], [iː], [oː] and [uː] are only approximate equivalents, for (as explained above in Sec-

Old English			Middle English		
[ɛ]	helpan	[hɛlpɑn]	[ɛ]	helpe(n)	[hɛlpən]
[iː]⁶⁴	rīdan	[riːdɑn]	[iː]	ride(n)	[riːdən]
[ɪ]	drincan	[drɪŋkɑn]	[ɪ]	drinke(n)	[drɪŋkən]
[oː]⁶⁴	fōda	[foːdɑ]	[oː]	fode	[foːdə]
[ɔ]	oxa	[ɔksɑ]	[ɔ]	oxe	[ɔksə]
[uː]⁶⁴	hūs	[huːs]	[uː]	hous	[huːs]
[ʊ]	sunu	[sʊnʊ]	[ʊ]	sone	[sʊnə]
[yː]	mȳs	[myːs]	[iː]	mis	[miːs]
[ʏ]	fyllan	[fʏlːɑn]	[ɪ]	fille(n)	[fɪlːən]
[æːə]	strēam	[stræːəm]	[æː]	streem	[stræːm]
[æə]	earm	[æərm]	[ɑ]	arm	[ɑrm]
[eːo]	dēop	[deːop]	[eː]⁶⁵	deep	[deːp]
[ɛo]	heorte	[hɛortɛ]	[ɛ]⁶⁵	herte	[hɛrtə]

These developments may be conveniently summarized as follows: of the eighteen distinctive vowel sounds and diphthong combinations in Old English, ten remained unchanged. Of the eight which did change, the two high front rounded vowels [yː] and [ʏ] were unrounded to the two corresponding high front vowels [iː] and [ɪ]. The low front unround [æ] was retracted to [ɑ]; the low back unround [ɑː] was rounded to [ɔː]. This accounts for four of the eight changes. The remaining four consist of the simplification of the Old English diphthongs to simple vowels, consisting in three cases of the unmodified first element, and in the final instance, [æə], of this first element then participating in the general retraction of all the Old English æ sounds to [ɑ].

These changes did not all take place at the same time. The unrounding of [yː] and [ʏ] had already begun in Late Old English (see Section 27.12). The simplification of the diphthongs was possibly next in point of time; one may even be justified in wondering whether the Old English phenomenon called smoothing was not an initial step in this direction (see Section 27.9-11). At all events it is assumed to have been virtually completed during the course of the eleventh century except for the unrounding of [œː] and [œ] to [eː] and [ɛ],⁶⁴ which is supposed to have taken place

---

tion 17) the Modern English sounds represented by [eː], [iː], [oː], and [uː] tend to be diphthongs, not simple vowels. Old and Middle English [eː], [iː], [oː] and [uː] were simple vowels, like the corresponding vowels in Modern German.

⁶⁵ OE ēo and eo first changed to early ME [œː] and [œ], which developed later into [eː] and [ɛ].

during the twelfth. The retraction of [æ] to [ɑ] was next in point of time. This was followed by the rounding of [ɑː], which occurred in the south of England during the twelfth century and progressed northward very slowly, not reaching the North Midlands until the fourteenth.

53. Special Developments in Middle English. Special phonological developments in Middle English are in general of two kinds. On the one hand there occurred certain changes in the quantity of vowels, dependent generally upon syllabic structure. In addition, certain specific combinations or types of combinations of vowels and consonants gave rise to a series of new diphthongs.

CHANGES IN THE QUANTITY OF VOWELS

54. Shortening of Long Vowels.

1. Old English long vowels were shortened in early Middle English when they were followed by a double consonant or by a group of two or more consonants; excepting, however those combinations which caused lengthening in late Old English (see Section **27.8** and **54.3** below): OE sōfte, ME softe [sɔftə]; OE fifta, ME fifte [fɪftə]; OE cēpte, ME kepte [kɛptə]; OE wīsdom, ME wisdom [wɪzdoːm]. The shortening of Old English ǣ and ēa appears in Middle English as both a and e; e.g. OE lǣssa, ME lasse, lesse; OE lǣdde, ME ladde, ledde; OE hēafdes, g.s., ME hafdes, hefdes.

That this change occurred before the rounding of [ɑː] to [ɔː] is evidenced by such words as Modern English ask [æsk], ME aske(n), from OE āscian, and Modern English Lammas [læməs] from OE hlāfmæsse. Had OE [ɑː] become [ɔː] before the shortening took place, we would now have an [ɔ] sound in these words.

2. Old English long vowels followed by a single consonant or by a consonant group that caused lengthening in late Old English (see Section **54.3** below) were shortened in early Middle English when they occurred in the first syllable of trisyllabic words; e.g. OE sūðerne, ME sutherne [suðərnə]; OE hāliġdōm, ME halidom [halɪdoːm]; late Mercian OE ālderman (EWS ealderman), ME alderman [aldərmɑn]. The shortening of long vowels in trisyllabic words occurred before the change of [ɑː] to [ɔː] (cf. **alderman** above), and affected all the words in which the conditions for its occurrence existed at that time. Short vowels that developed in the inflected forms of disyllables were frequently extended by analogy to the uninflected forms. OE līnenes, ME linenes [lɪnənəs],

hence **linen** [lɪnən]; Mercian OE **hēringas** (WS **hǣringas**), ME **heringes** [hɛrɪŋgəs], hence **hering** [hɛrɪŋg].

3. It will be recalled that in late Old English all short vowels were lengthened when they were foliowed by **ld, mb, nd, ng, rd, rl, rn,** [rz], or [rð]. Lengthening did not occur, however, before the consonant group if a third consonant followed, so that we have MnE [tʃaild] from late OE **ċild,** ME [tʃiːld], but MnE [tʃɪldrən] from OE **ċildru,** ME [tʃɪldrən]; MnE [hɑʊnd] from late OE **hūnd,** but MnE [hʌndrəd] from OE **hundred.** Many long vowels which originated in this way remained long throughout the Middle English period and have developed in Modern English like the other Middle English long vowels; e.g., late OE **fēld,** ME **feeld** [feːld], MnE [fiːld]; late OE **findan,** ME **finde(n)** [fiːndən], MnE [fɑɪnd]; late OE **grūnd,** ME **ground** [gruːnd], MnE [grɑʊnd]. Modern English [old] is from Midland Middle English [ɔːld], which developed regularly from late Old English **āld,** earlier **ald** (West-Saxon **eald**). But in a great many words these lengthened vowels were again shortened in Middle English, or else forms with short vowels continued to exist alongside the lengthened forms.

55. Lengthening of Short Vowels. In the thirteenth century the short vowels **a, e,** and **o** were lengthened in open syllables of dissyllabic words,[66] so that **a** became [ɑː], **e** became [ɛː], and **o** became [ɔː]; e. g., OE **nama,** ME **name** [nɑːmə]; OE **fæder,** ME **fader** [fɑːdər]; OE **mete,** ME **mete** [mɛːtə]; OE **stolen,** ME **stole(n)** [stɔːlən]. That this change took place after the rounding of Old English [ɑː] to Middle English [ɔː] is indicated by the fact that the [ɑː] in words like ME [nɑːmə] from OE **nama** never became [ɔː].

Shortening or lengthening of vowels often occurred in some forms of a word but not in others because the phonetic environment of the vowel in different forms of the same word was different. For example, the shortening of long vowels before consonant groups did not occur in dissyllables if the consonant group was of such a nature that the syllable division came between the vowel and the consonant group. The shortening therefore occurred in ME **gast** [gɑst] from OE **gāst** but not in the inflected forms of the word, e.g. ME **gostes** [gɔːstəs], genitive singular, from OE **gāstes.** No shortening occurred in ME **sori** [sɔːrɪ] from OE **sāriġ,** but shortening did occur (after loss of

---

[66] An open syllable is one that ends in a vowel; in words of two or more syllables a single consonant following the vowel belongs to the following syllable.

secondary stress on the second syllable) in the trisyllabic plural form sorie [sɔrɪə]. Similarly, in ME fader from OE fæder the vowel [ɑ] was in an open syllable and was lengthened, but no lengthening occurred in the plural form fadres or faderes because here the vowel either was not in an open syllable or the word was trisyllabic. After these divergent developments had taken place, both the long and the short vowel were likely to be generalised in *all* the forms of the word, so that double forms arose: [gɑst] and [gɔːst], [sɔrɪ] and [sɔːrɪ], [fɑdər] and [fɑːdər]. Eventually one of the alternative forms came into general use and the other became obsolete. Modern English *ghost* is based on the Middle English form that had a long vowel, but Modern English *sorry* and *father* are based on the Middle English forms that had a short vowel; some of the modern dialects, however, still preserve the form [feːðr], which is based on the Middle English form that had a lengthened vowel.

DEVELOPMENT OF NEW DIPHTHONGS

As may be seen from the table of sound changes given above in Section 52, the Old English diphthongs ēa, ea, ēo, and eo became simple vowels in Middle English. In Middle English, however, there developed a new series of diphthongs, arising largely from new juxtapositions of vowels and consonants which had been brought together in the main through the operation of the normal or regular phonetic developments. These may most conveniently be considered in terms of the phonetic situations which gave rise to them.

56. Combinations of Front Vowels and Palatal Consonants. The diphthong [æɪ],[67] composed of two front vowel elements, developed from:

1. OE æ followed by [j], spelled ġ: OE dæġ [dæj], ME [dæɪ]; OE sæġde [sæjdɛ], ME [sæɪdə].

2. OE ǣ or ē followed by [j], spelled ġ: OE twēġen [tweːjɛn], ME [twæɪən]; OE ǣġ [æːj], ME [æɪ].

3. OE e followed by the [j] sound which was already [j] in Old English or by the [j] sound that developed in Middle English out of Old English [ɣ]: OE weġ [wɛj], ME [wæɪ]; OE pleġa [plɛɣɑ], ME [plæɪə].

[67] In early Middle English the diphthong which developed as a result of the combination described in 56.1 had the sound of [ɑɪ]. The diphthong which developed as the result of the combinations described in 56.2, 3, and 4 had the sound of [ɛɪ]. In late Middle English the two diphthongs became identical. Although it is possible that they were levelled under [ɑɪ] or [ɛɪ], it seems more likely that both developed into a diphthong that approximated [æɪ].

4. Middle English [ɛ] followed by [x]:[68] early ME **nehhebur** [nɛxːə-buːr] (from Mercian OE **nēhhebūr**, EWS **nēahġebūr**), later ME [næɪxə-buːr].

57. Combinations of Front Vowels and Velar Consonants. The diphthong [ɪu],[69] composed of a front vowel followed by a back vowel, developed from:

1. Old English **ēa** or **ǣ** followed by **w**: OE **fēawe** [fæːəwɛ], ME **fewe** [fɪuə]; OE **lǣwede** [læːwɛdɛ], ME **lewed(e)** [lɪuədə].

2. Old English **ī** followed by **w**: OE **stīweard, ME steward** [stɪuɑrd].

3. Old English **ēo** followed by **w** when it remained a falling diphthong (see Section 15 above): OE **cnēow, ME knew** [knɪu].

But the commonest source of [ɪu] in Middle English was the French vowel [yː], which was written **u**. The sound [yː] did not occur in the East Midland dialect of Middle English, and therefore French loanwords which contained this sound were pronounced in this dialect with the diphthong [ɪu], which was the nearest English equivalent; e. g. ME **cure** [kɪurə], from Old French **cure** [kyːrə].

58. Combinations of Back Rounded Vowels and Velar Consonants. The diphthong [ɔːu], composed of two back rounded vowel elements developed from:

1. Old English **ā** or **ō** followed by **w**: OE **cnāwan** [knaːwɑn], Middle English **knowe(n)** [knɔːuən]; OE **ġrōwan** [groːwɑn], ME **ġrowe(n)** [grɔːuən].

2. Old English **ā** followed by [ɣ],[70] spelled **ġ**; OE **āġen** [aːɣɛn], ME **owe:n;** [ɔːuən].

3. Old English **o** when it was in an open syllable followed by [ɣ]) e.g , OE **boġa** [bɔɣɑ], ME **bowe** [bɔːuə].

4. Old English **ā** or **ō** followed by **h**: OE **āh** [aːx], ME **ough** [ɔːux]; OE **bōh** [boːx], ME **bough** [bɔːux].

[68] See note 21 above.

[69] In early Middle English the diphthong which resulted from the combinations described in Section 57.1 had the sound of [ɛu]. The diphthong which developed from the combinations described in Section 57.2 and 3 had the sound of [ɪu]. In late Middle English both sounds were levelled under [ɪu], and for that reason they are so described here. Chaucer's rhymes, however, appear to indicate that he maintained the distinction between the two sounds; accordingly they are so described in the preceding chapter, Section 32.

[70] This sound, the **ġ** of North German **saġen**, is not a stop consonant (like **g** in **go**) but a voiced velar fricative. It resembles the spirant [w] in English **woo** but is made without any rounding of the lips.

5. Old English ēo followed by w when it became a rising diphthong (see Section 15 above); e.g. OE trēowian, ME trowe(n) [trɔːʊən].

6. [ɔʊ], the shortened form of the diphthong, developed out of Old English o or ō, followed by ht: OE bohte, ME boughte [bɔʊxtə]; OE sōhte, ME soghte [sɔʊxtə].[71]

59. Combinations of Back Unrounded Vowels and Velar Consonants.

The diphthong [ɑʊ], composed of two back rounded vowel elements developed from:

1. Old English a followed by w: OE clawu [klɑwʊ], ME clawe [klɑʊə].

2. Old English a followed by [ɣ], spelled g: OE dragan [drɑɣɑn], ME drawe(n) [drɑʊən].

3. Old English æ followed by h: Mercian OE fæht (EWS feaht) ME faught [fɑʊxt].

4. Old English ā followed by ht: OE tāhte, ME taughte [tɑʊxtə].

60. The Diphthong [ɔɪ] occurs almost exclusively in French loan words; e.g., ME joie from Old French joie.

61. Special Developments Resulting in [iː] and [uː].

1. Old English i followed by ġ became [iː]; e.g. OE liġeþ [lɪjɛθ], ME lieth [liːəθ].

2. Old English ē followed by the [j] sound that developed in Middle English out of Old English [ɣ] became Middle English [eɪ], which developed later into Middle English [iː]; e. g. Mercian OE lēgan (WS lēogan), ME leie(n) [leɪən], later lie(n) [liːən]; Mercian OE ēge (EWS ēage), ME eye [eɪə], later eye or ye [iːə].

3. Old English ē followed by h became [eɪ], which developed later into [iː]; e.g. Mercian OE hēh (EWS hēah), ME heigh [heɪx] later high [hiːx]; Mercian OE þēh (WS þēoh), ME þeigh [θeɪx], later thigh [θiːx].

4. Old English u followed by g became [uː]; e.g. OE sugu [sʊɣʊ], ME sowe [suːə].

5. Old English ō followed by g became [uː]; e.g. OE wōgian [woːɣɪɑn], ME wowe(n) [wuːən]; OE bōgas [boːɣɑs], ME bowes [buːəs].

From the quantitative and combinative developments described in Sections 54-61, there resulted the following additional sounds·not listed in the table in Section 52.

---

[71] The ō of OE sōhte was shortened before ht (see Section 54.1, above).

[ɑː]⁷²	name	[nɑːmə]
[ɑu]	faught	[fɑuxt]
[æɪ]	seil	[sæɪl]
[ɪu]	humour	[hɪumuːr], rude [rɪudə], fewe [fɪuə]
[ɔɪ]	boy	[bɔɪ]
[ɔːu]	soule	[sɔːulə]
[ɔu]	thought	[θɔuxt]

The special developments resulting in new diphthongs and in [iː] and [uː] did not all occur at the same period. The earliest to occur were those that resulted from the combination of vowels with Old English w and with the [j] sound that was already [j] in Old English; the next those that resulted from the combination of vowels with sounds that developed out of Old English [ɣ]; the latest those that resulted from the combination of vowels with h.

62. Vowels in Unaccented Syllables. The sound changes which have been explained in the preceding sections are those which were undergone by vowels in accented syllables. A detailed account of the changes undergone by vowels in unaccented syllables would involve complexities of treatment which would be inconsistent with the scope and character of this book. The following account aims only at giving the barest essentials.

1. Unaccented Old English **a, e, o,** and **u** became a vowel which was usually written **e** and which probably (cf. Section **69** below) approximated in sound to [ə]; e.g., OE **oxa** [ɔksɑ], ME **oxe** [ɔksə]; OE **belle** [bɛlːɛ], ME **belle** [bɛlːə]; OE **nacod** [nɑkɔd], ME **naked** [nɑːkəd]; OE **sunu** [sunu], ME **sune** [sunə]. This development was completed by the year 1100 in the Southern dialect, at least as early or earlier in the Midland dialect, and perhaps as early as the year 1000 in the Northern dialect.

But unaccented Old English **i** remained Middle English [ɪ]; e.g., OE **englisc** [ɛŋglɪʃ], ME **english** [ɛŋglɪʃ]; OE **scilling** [ʃɪlːɪŋg], ME **shilling** [ʃɪlːɪŋg].

In unaccented prefixes, however, Old English **o** (except in the prefix **on-**) and **u** remained unchanged, but Old English **æ** and **ā** became [ɑ], **e** usually became [ɪ], **on** became [ɑ], and **ym** became [um]. OE **forberan,** ME **forbere(n)**; OE **fulfyllan,** ME **fulfille(n)**; OE **ætstandan,** ME

---

⁷² The [ɑː] which was present in the language during the Old English period had become [ɔː] in Middle English. This new [ɑː] sound resulted from the lengthening of OE **a** in an open syllable.

atstande(n); OE ārīsan, ME arise(n); OE becuman, ME bicume(n); Mercian OE ondrēdan (WS ondrǣdan), ME adrede(n); OE ymbstōdon (preterit plural of ymbstandan), ME umbistode(n).

2. There was a tendency in certain phonetic situations, especially before r, l, h, and w, to the development of glide vowels. The vowel that developed before r and l was usually e [ə] but before h and w it was usually [ʊ] or [ɔ]; e.g., OE glædra, ME gladre, gladere; OE æfre, ME evre, evere; OE burh, ME burh, buruh; OE folgian [fɔlɣɪan], ME folwie(n), folwe(n), folowe(n).

3. Final e disappeared at a fairly early period in Middle English in words of three syllables which contained no secondary stress; e.g., OE ælmesse, ME almesse, later almes; OE lufode, ME luvede, later luved; OE frēondscipe, ME frendshipe, later frendship (but frendshipe when the secondary stress on the second syllable was retained); OE æfre, ME evere (according to 62.2 above), later ever; OE glædra, ME gladere (according to 62.2 above), later gladder.

4. Middle English medial e was frequently syncopated in words of three syllables; e.g., OE munecas, ME munekes, later munkes; OE stedefæst, ME stedefast, later stedfast; Mercian OE nēhhebūr (EWS nēahġebūr), ME neighebur, later neighbour [næɪxbuːr]. In four syllable words which ended in e and which had secondary stress on the third syllable, there first occurred syncopation of an e in the second syllable and later, after loss of the secondary stress on the third syllable, loss of final e according to 62.3 above; e.g., OE mynecene, ME minechene, later minchene, later minchen; OE gaderode, ME gaderede, later gadrede, later gadred.

63. Consonant Sounds. The most important changes that took place in the consonant sounds between the Old and Middle English periods are these:

1. Old English initial hn, wl, hl, and hr became Middle English n, l, l, and r: OE hnecca, ME necke; OE wlispian, ME lispe(n); OE hlāf, ME lof; OE hring, ME ring.

2. Final ċ [tʃ] was lost in unstressed syllables: OE ānliċ, ME onli [ɔːnlɪ]; OE dēadliċ, ME dedly [dɛdlɪ].

3. Old English final m in unstressed syllables became late Old English or very early Middle English n: OE endum, ME ende(n).

4. Final n was very frequently lost in unstressed syllables, so that the common inflectional ending -en was very often reduced to -e: OE singan, ME singen or singe.

5. Old English [ɣ] always underwent change in Middle English:
a. Initial Old English [ɣ] became Middle English [g]; e.g., OE gōd [ɣoːd], ME good [goːd].
b. When preceded by a vowel Old English [ɣ] became Middle English [j] or [w]. If in Old English it was preceded by a front vowel and followed by a back vowel, it became [j] in Middle English after the following back vowel had become [ə]; e.g., Mercian OE lēgan (WS lēogan), ME leie(n), later lie(n) [liːən]; Mercian OE ēgan, nom. plur. (EWS ēagan, LWS ēgan), ME eien, later yen [iːən]. In the other situations in which it occurred Old English [ɣ] preceded by a vowel developed into Middle English [w]. Subsequently the Middle English [j] or [w] which had developed out of Old English [ɣ] united with the preceding vowel and underwent the developments treated above in Sections **56-61.**
c. When preceded by a consonant Old English [ɣ] became Middle English [w]; e.g., OE folgian, ME folwie(n), folwe(n).

64. Middle English Spelling. Just as the sounds of the language do not remain static but show distinct lines of development from one period, and even from one century, to another, so spelling has its own series of changes and its own history. Even though spelling has as its function the indication of pronunciation, and at certain stages of the language it constitutes some of our best evidence for pronunciation, the history of spelling and the history of pronunciation are by no means identical.

We know, for example that early in the Middle English period Old English æ became [ɑ], Old English ā became [ɔː], the Old English diphthongs ēa and ea became the simple vowels [æː] and [ɑ], Old English ēo and eo became [œː] and [œ], which later developed into [eː] and [ɛ], and a number of new diphthongs—[æɪ], [ɑʊ], etc.—developed out of Old English simple vowels followed by ġ, w, and h. While these changes were going on and for some time after they had been carried out, people continued to spell words in the way they had been spelled in Old English. For example, Old English þæt was spelled with æ, Old English bēon[73] was spelled with eo, Old English strēam was spelled with ea, and Old English stān was spelled with a; the words retained these spellings long after their respective pronunciations had become [θɑt], [bœːn] or [beːn], [stræːm], and [stɔːn].

[73] The Old English manuscripts as a rule make no distinction between long and short vowels and diphthongs; bēon, for example, with a long diphthong, and weorc, with a short diphthong, are both spelled with eo. The marks of length are added by modern editors. Nor do the manuscripts distinguish ċ [tʃ], from c [k], or ġ [j] from g, [ɣ]. The dot is added by modern editors.

But the changes that had taken place in pronunciation were so numerous that it proved to be impossible to maintain the old system of spelling. Confusion in spelling soon arose. After words that were spelled with **eo** and with **e** came to have the same sound in Middle English, people regarded the two signs as interchangeable; they would therefore spell Old English **bēon** and **weorc** with **e,** and Old English **swēte** and **helpan** with **eo.** Moreover, **ea** and **eo** were enough alike in appearance to be confused in use, so that [beːn], from Old English **bēon** was sometimes spelled with **ea** and [stræːm], from Old English **strēam** was sometimes spelled with **eo.** As a result, the spelling of the vowel sounds in the earliest Middle English texts exhibits great confusion, which gradually diminished, however, as the digraphs **ea** and **eo** fell more and more into disuse and as the character **æ** gave place to **a** as a means of representing the vowel [ɑ].

65. Influence of Old French Spelling. There is no doubt that in the course of time the confusion of early Middle English spelling would have been done away with and that a good system of spelling Middle English might have been evolved on the basis of the Old English system, had English people been left to themselves. But they were not left to themselves. French was the language of the superior class from 1066 to the middle of the fourteenth century. Educated people read French books and were expected to be able to write as well as speak the French language; French words were adopted into the language and kept their French spellings when used in writing. As a result, people began to spell certain English sounds according to the French system of spelling. The most important changes that came about were these:

1. [æː], spelled in OE with **æ** and in early ME with **æ** or **ea,** came to be spelled with **e,** as in French: early ME **hæþ,** later ME **heþ** or **heeth.**

2. [u], spelled in OE and early ME with **u,** was often spelled with **o** in later ME, particularly in proximity to letters like **n, m, v,** and **w:** early ME **sune,** later ME **sone.**

3. [uː], spelled in OE and early ME with **u,** was usually spelled in late ME with **ou:** early ME **hus,** late ME **hous.**

4. [y] and [yː], which were spelled in OE with **y** and had the sound of French **u,** were spelled in Southern ME and in the other ME dialects which contained this sound, with **u,** as in French; [yː] was also sometimes spelled **ui.** OE **fyllan,** Southern ME **vulle(n);** OE **fȳr,** Southern ME, **vur, vuir.**

5. [eː], spelled in early ME with **e** or **eo** is often spelled in late ME

with **ie**: OE **spēdan**, early ME **spede(n)**, late ME **spede(n)** or **spiede(n)**.

6. [v], spelled in OE and in the earliest ME with **f**, came to be spelled with **v**, as in French: OE **life**, ME **live**.

7. [tʃ], spelled in OE with **c**, came to be spelled in ME with **ch**, as in French: OE **ċīdan**,[74] ME **chide(n)**.

8. [kw], spelled in OE with **cw**, came to be spelled in ME with **qu**, as in French: OE **cwēn**, ME **quen** or **queen**.

The influence of French spelling on English spelling **began** soon after the Norman conquest, but the changes which it brought about were not completed until after the middle of the thirteenth century.

66. Spelling of Middle English Vowels and Diphthongs. The table given below shows the spellings which are most commonly used in Middle English manuscripts to represent the various vowels and diphthongs. The first column contains the sounds as represented in phonetic notation; the second column contains the spellings by which these sounds are represented in the earlier Middle English manuscripts (roughly, before 1250); the third column contains the spellings by which these same sounds are represented in the later Middle English manuscripts (roughly, after 1250). Spellings which are decidedly less frequent than the others are placed in parentheses.[75]

ME Sound	Early ME Spelling	Late ME Spelling
[ɑː]	a	a, aa
[ɑ]	a, æ, ea	a
[eː]	e, eo, (ea)	e, ee, (ie)
[æː]	æ, ea, e, (eo)	e, ee
[ɛ]	e, eo, (æ)	e
[iː]	i, (y)	i, ii, y, (ei), (ey)
[ɪ]	i(y)	i, y
[oː]	o	o, oo
[ɔː]	a, o, (oa)	o, oo
[ɔ]	o	o

---

[74] As to **ċ**, see the preceding note.

[75] The tables given in **32** and **34** were not intended to include **all** of the spellings that occur in Middle English manuscripts, but only those that are fairly common in Chaucer.

ME Sound	Early ME Spelling	Late ME Spelling
[uː]	u, v[76]	ou, ow, (o)
[u]	u, v	u, v, o
[yː]	y, u, v, ui	u, v, ui
[y]	y, u, v	u, v
[œː]	eo	eo, o, u, oe, ue
[œ]	eo	eo, o, u, oe, ue
[aɪ]	ai, æi, aʒ, æʒ	ai, ay
[æɪ]		ai, ay, ei, ey
[ɑu]	au, aw, aʒ, ag, agh[77]	au, aw
[ɛɪ]	ei, æi, eʒ, æʒ	ei, ey
[ɛu]	eu, ew	eu, ew
[ɪu]	iu, iw, eu, ew, eou, eow[77]	iu, iw, eu, ew, u, ui
[ɔːu]	au, aw, aʒ, ag, agh, ou, ow, oʒ, ɒg, ogh[77]	ou, ow
[ɔu]	ou, ow, o	ou, ow, o
[ɔɪ]	oi	oi, oy

The student should remember that all diacritical marks which he finds in Middle English texts are supplied by modern editors.

67. Spelling of Middle English Consonants. The table given below shows the spellings which are most commonly used in Middle English manuscripts to represent consonant sounds, so far as the spelling of these sounds differs from that of Modern English.

ME Sound	EME Spelling	LME Spelling
[hw]	hw, wh	wh, qu
[j]	ʒ,[78] g	y, ʒ
[ʃ]	sc, ss, s	sch, ssch, sh, ssh, s

[76] The letters **u** and **v** were used interchangeably by the Middle English scribes, the choice of character often depending on its position in the word.

[77] The Middle English diphthongs are variously spelled in early Middle English for two reasons. First, the sounds of which they were composed were variously spelled, [ɔː], for example, being spelled either **a** or **o**. Second, the diphthongs themselves were of various origin (see **56-60** above); [ɑu] sometimes developing out of OE **a** followed by **w** or **g**, or out of OE **æ** followed by **h**. Many of the early Middle English spellings of these diphthongs are traditional spellings which do not represent adequately the true nature of the sounds. See also note 78 below.

[78] The character ʒ was called **ʒoʒ** [jɔx], and was a slight modification of the Old English form of the letter **g**. The Old English **g** represented two sounds, that of [j],

ME Sound	EME Spelling	LME Spelling
[θ]	þ, ð	þ, th
[ð]	þ, ð	þ, th
[v]	f, v, u	v, u
[w]	w (initially)	w
[w]	w, ȝ, g, gh, h (medially)[79]	w
[x]	h, ȝ,[78] g	gh, h, ȝ, ch

in dæȝ, and that of [ɣ] in āgen. This latter sound is a fricative like the g of North German sagen. In Middle English the sound of [j] was preserved if it occurred at the beginning of a word, as in ȝe, from OE ȝē. But when it .was preceded by a vowel it united with the vowel to form a diphthong, as in ME dai from OE dæȝ. The Old English sound [ɣ] became [w] in early ME when preceded by a back vowel, and then it united with the preceding vowel to form a diphthong, as in ME owen [ɔːuən] from OE āgen. In the few words in which it was followed by a vowel and preceded by a consonant, OE [ɣ] became [w] in ME, e.g., in halwien, from OE hālgian. OE initial [ɣ] however, became in ME a stop consonant like the g in Modern English good. This stop g was then spelled with a new variety of the letter g which was very much like the modern g. The Old English form of the letter g, slightly modified, as shown above, was then used to spell the sounds other than stop g which had developed out of the two Old English sounds of g. That is, it was used to represent:

1. The sound of [j], e.g., in ȝe, from OE ȝē;
2. The sound of [w], e.g., in halȝien, from OE hālgian;
3. The second element of the diphthong [æɪ], e.g., in daȝ from OE dæȝ and weȝ from OE weg;
4. The second element of the diphthongs [au] and [ɔːu], e.g., in draȝen from OE dragan, and aȝen or oȝen from OE āgen.

It was also used to represent:

5. The sound of [x], e.g., in niȝt from OE niht.

[79] [w] is spelled ȝ, g, h, or gh when it developed out of OE [ɣ], e.g., in halȝien, alghien from OE hālgian. See note 78 above.

CHAPTER VI

The Development of Middle English Inflections

68. The Old English Inflectional System has already been briefly outlined in Section **26** and set forth in detail in the accompanying table (pp. 22, 23). The combination of case, number, and gender forms for the nouns, the somewhat greater differentiation in the adjectives, and the formal distinctions for person, tense, and mood in the various verb conjugations, although not approaching ancient Greek or even Latin in general complexity, nevertheless is a far cry from a flexionless system. The inflectional system of the late Middle English of Chaucer, on the other hand, was extremely simple. All distinctions of case were lost in Middle English except the genitive singular in nouns. The distinctions of grammatical gender were lost altogether. And even the grammatical categories that remained were more simply expressed, for in late Middle English the single ending **-es** had replaced the variety of endings which had indicated the genitive singular and the plural of nouns in Old English. The simplification that took place in the inflectional system was the result of two causes, **sound-change** and **analogy**.

69. Sound-Change. The sound-changes that take place in accented syllables usually have little or no effect on the inflectional system of the words in which they occur. The changes that take place in the pronunciation of unaccented syllables, however, very frequently (though not necessarily) do result in a modification of the inflectional system. The inflectional pattern of the language was very little modified by the sound-changes that took place in accented syllables during the Middle English period (shown above in Sections **52-61**) but was profoundly affected by certain of the changes that took place in the vowels of unaccented syllables as set forth in Section **62**.

Those changes in unaccented syllables which had considerable influence upon the inflectional structure of Middle English may be briefly restated as follows:

Old English **a, e, o,** and **u** became in unaccented syllables the vowel which was commonly written **e** and which probably was pronounced [ə];[80] e.g.

[80] This unstressed vowel (when followed by a consonant, as in the endings **-es** and **-ed**) was also frequently written **i,** particularly in the North of England. It is probable that this variation of spelling represents a variation of pronunciation between [ə]

OE belle [bɛlːɛ]   ME belle [bɛlːə]
OE oxa [ɔksɑ]   ME oxe [ɔksə]
OE nacod [nɑkɔd]   ME naked [nɑːkəd]
OE sunu [sʊnʊ]   ME sune [sʊnə]

This change in the pronunciation of vowels of unaccented syllables is the most important difference between Old English and Middle English.

The effect on the inflectional system of these changes in the quality of unaccented vowels can be appreciated only after a thorough study of the forms tabulated below in Sections **72-100,** but it may be illustrated by considering the more obvious effects that are shown in the inflection of the Old English feminine noun **lufu** (Section **75**). In this noun the Old English distinction between nominative singular **lufu** [lʊvʊ], genitive-dative-accusative singular **lufe** [lʊvɛ], and nominative-genitive-accusative plural **lufa** [lʊvɑ] were obliterated in Middle English, for all three forms became **luve** [lʊvə], a form distinctive as to neither number or case.

The Middle English fate of the dative plural **lufum** [lʊvʊm] of this same noun shows the far-reaching effects on the inflectional system that resulted from another sound-change that took place in unaccented syllables. In very late Old English final **m** changed in unaccented syllables to **n.** At the very beginning of the Middle English period final **n,** including the **n** that had developed from original **m,** tended to disappear in unaccented syllables (see Section **63.**3, 4 above). As the result of this change of **m** to **n,** the loss of **n,** and the change in the quality of the unaccented vowel, the Old English dative plural form **lufum** became Middle English **luven** or **luve.** From this it can be seen that the process of sound change alone could result in extensive modification of the inflectional system. The inflectional pattern even of the earliest Middle English is radically different from that of Old English.

70. Analogy. The inflectional forms that appear in the earliest documents that we can call Middle English (e.g., the homilies in MSS Bodley 343 and Cotton Vespasian Dxɪv) can for the most part be accounted for on the basis of the sound-changes that took place in unaccented syllables. In later texts, however, we find occurring with increasing frequency forms that cannot be accounted for in this way. In the inflection of feminine nouns like **luve,** for example, we find the

---

and [ɪ]. Much less frequently it is written u when followed by a consonant (as in the endings -es and -ed); this spelling is interpreted by some as indicating a rounded variety of the [ə] sound.

form **luves** appearing as genitive singular and as plural. In the inflection of masculine nouns like **doom** we find the uninflected form appearing in phrases which in the earliest Middle English had the specifically dative form **doome**. These changes were not the result of sound-change, for there was no general tendency in Middle English to add **s** to words that did not originally have it nor does Middle English of this period and dialect show any general tendency to loss of final **e**. Changes of this kind are the result not of sound-change but of those processes that we designate by the term analogy.

Analogy is easier to illustrate than to define. It is a process that is constantly operating in speech. When we use in the plural a noun (*assonance*, for example) that we happen never to have used or to have heard others use before in the plural, or when a child uses the plural form *mans* or the preterit *hurted*, it is analogy that supplies the form that is used. By this we mean that there has occurred the extension of an already existing and operative formal (in this case an inflectional) pattern to an individual lexical unit of the language. The speaker has presumably never made this particular combination of unit and pattern, that is word and suffix, before. In his linguistic experience it is a new creation.

The results of the process that operates in these cases can be shown schematically by such proportions as:

ASSONANCES : *assonance* : : *alliances* : *alliance* (*chances* : *chance, dunces* : *dunce,* etc.)

MANS : *man* : : *cans* : *can* (*pins* : *pin, lambs* : *lamb,* etc.)

HURTED : *hurt* : : *wanted* : *want* (*waited* : *wait, needed* : *need,* etc.)

But although such proportions may constitute a convenient schematic representation of analogical formations, these are not to be interpreted as explanations of the psychological processes involved.[81] When we make such formations in our speech we are not conscious of the fact that we are making them and we are not conscious of any process of comparison. The psychology of analogical formations has never been adequately set forth, even by the Gestalt psychologists in whose field such phenomena would appropriately seem to fall.[82] It seems correct to say in general terms

---

[81] The proportional representation of analogy was employed several decades ago by such linguistic scientists as Hermann Paul principally as a safeguard against a previous tendency on the part of historians of the language to apply the term analogy too widely to phenomena which did not seem to admit of any other explanation.

[82] This statement implies that the whole mechanism for the formation of regular plurals, the addition of [s] to stems ending in voiceless consonants other than the three

that when we make an analogical formation, an established speech habit or pattern functions unconsciously in a situation which is similar to but not identical with situations in which it has functioned before.[83] For example, it is a firmly established habit, when we speak of two or more things whose name ends in the sound [s] to employ the plural form [-səz]. This habit is so thoroughly established by years of exercise that it functions as readily when we have occasion to say *assonances* for the first time as it does when we say *chances* or *pieces* for the thousandth time.

An analogical formation such as *assonances* is "correct," that is, it is the form that anyone would use who had occasion to use that word in the plural, for it conforms to the traditional usage of our speech. Analogical formations like *mans* and *hurted* are "incorrect," that is, they are very rarely used except by young children whose speech habits are not yet perfectly conformed to those of the older persons from whom they receive the tradition of speech. But the psychological process that operates in the two kinds of analogical formations is identical. Such forms as *mans* and *hurted* occur in the speech of adults only as "slips of the tongue." But if for any reason the same "slip" is made frequently by many persons the analogical form becomes a part of the speech tradition and is "learned" by other persons, especially younger persons whose speech habits are still in process of formation or relatively susceptible of change. Such analogical formations are likely in time to displace entirely the older traditional forms. Language, however, does not undergo numerous and extensive changes through the operation of analogy unless the traditional patterns of speech have been radically modified by some other cause, usually sound-change. This condition did result from the sound-changes that took place in unaccented syllables at the very beginning of the Middle English period.

---

sibilants, the addition of [z] to voiced sounds other than the three sibilants, and the addition of [əz] to the six sibilants, taken in its entirety constitutes a Gestalt or configuration. In all honesty I must assume responsibility for this interpretation of analogy. A.H.M.

[83] It is not intended to suggest that this statement is true of all the phenomena that psychologists and students of language include under the general term analogy. In fact it is likely that many of these phenomena, including such "contaminations" as *evoid* for *evade* (cf. *avoid*) and most of the phenomena referred to by Thumb and Marbe in their *Experimentelle untersuchungen über die psychologischen grundlagen der sprachlichen analogiebildungen*, are the result of psychological processes essentially different from those which operate in the "proportional" analogy formations, which are dealt with here.

NOUNS

71. Development of the Middle English Noun Declensions. The historical development of the Middle English noun declensions is shown in the tables printed below. In the first column are given the Old English (Late West-Saxon) forms. In the second column are given the forms that occur in the earliest Middle English. These forms are, with one exception, historical forms, that is forms developed from those of Old English by the process of sound-change alone; they are the Old English forms pronounced in the new way. The exception is the nominative singular of nouns of the feminine ō-declension which ended in a consonant in Old English (Section 76); in this type of inflection a new nominative singular **hwile** developed by analogy at the very beginning of the Middle English period.[84] This analogical form is distinguished from the historical forms that developed through sound-change by being printed in italic type instead of Roman. In the third column are given the late Middle English forms such as occur in the language of Chaucer and his contemporaries. In this column the forms that are identical with those of early Middle English (except the nominative singular **while,** which is the early Middle English analogical form **hwile**) are printed in Roman type and the numerous analogical forms that developed in later Middle English are printed in italic type. The words in the first column exemplify the eleven principal types of noun declension in Old English: the masculine a-declension nouns (strong masculines) **dōm** (*judgment*) and **ende** (end); the u-declension noun **sunu** (*son*); the feminine ō-declension nouns (strong feminines) **lufu** (*love*) and **hwīl** (*time*); the neuter a-declension nouns (strong neuters) **lim** (*limb*), **hors** (*horse*), and **wīte** (*punishment*); the weak masculine noun **hunta** (*hunter*); the weak feminine noun **sunne** (*sun*); and the weak neuter noun **ēare** (*ear*).

In these tables the Old English forms in the first column are given in their Old English spelling, the early Middle English forms in the second column are given in their early Middle English spelling, and the late Middle English forms in the third column are given in their late Middle English spelling. These spellings must always be interpreted, however, in terms of the sounds which they represent. We frequently find changes of spelling which do not represent any corresponding change of pronunciation (e.g., Old English **dōm**, Middle English **doom**, Early Middle

[84] For a more comprehensive treatment of this particular analogical development see S. Moore, "Earliest Morphological Changes in Middle English," *Language* 4: (1928), 238–266.

English **sune,** Late Middle English **sone**), and changes of pronunciation which are not represented by any corresponding change of spelling (e.g., Old English **ende** [ɛndɛ], Middle English **ende** [ɛndə]).

In connection with these tables and those that will occur later it is to be understood that the forms given as early Middle English are those that occur in the earliest Southern Middle English manuscripts that we have (written during the twelfth century), and that the forms given as late Middle English are those that occur in the best Southern and Midland manuscripts of the period of Chaucer. The forms that occur in the Southern manuscripts written between about 1200 and 1350 and in the very earliest Midland manuscripts are partly the early Middle English and partly the late Middle English forms. In each dialect the proportion of early Middle English forms is greater in the earlier manuscripts than in the later ones.

	OLD ENGLISH	MIDDLE ENGLISH	
		Early ME	Late ME
72. dōm, masculine:			
SING. Nom.	**dōm**	**doom**	**doom**
Gen.	**dōmes**	**doomes**	**doomes**
Dat.	**dōme**	**doome**	*doom*
Acc.	**dōm**	**doom**	**doom**
PLUR. Nom., Acc.	**dōmas**	**doomes**	**doomes**
Gen.	**dōma**	**doome**	*doomes*
Dat.	**dōmum**	**doome(n)**[85]	*doomes*
73. ende, masculine:			
SING. Nom.	**ende**	**ende**	**ende**
Gen.	**endes**	**endes**	**endes**
Dat.	**ende**	**ende**	**ende**
Acc.	**ende**	**ende**	**ende**
PLUR. Nom., Acc.	**endas**	**endes**	**endes**
Gen.	**enda**	**ende**	*endes*
Dat.	**endum**	**ende(n)**	*endes*

[85] As stated above in Section **63.4** the ending **-en** was very frequently reduced to **-e** through the loss of the final **n;** in these tables, therefore, the ending is printed **-e(n).**

OLD ENGLISH		MIDDLE ENGLISH	
		Early ME	Late ME
74. sunu, masculine:			
SING. Nom.	**sunu**	**sune**	**sone**
Gen.	**suna**	**sune**	*sones*
Dat.	**suna**	**sune**	**sone**
Acc.	**sunu**	**sune**	**sone**
PLUR. Nom., Acc.	**suna**	**sune**	*sones*
Gen.	**suna**	**sune**	*sones*
Dat.	**sunum**	**sune(n)**	*sones*
75. lufu, feminine:			
SING. Nom.	**lufu**	**luve**	**love**
Gen.	**lufe**	**luve**	*loves*
Dat.	**lufe**	**luve**	**love**
Acc.	**lufe**	**luve**	**love**
PLUR. Nom., Acc.	**lufa**	**luve**	*loves*
Gen.	**lufa**	**luve**	*loves*
Dat.	**lufum**	**luve(n)**	*loves*
76. hwil, feminine:			
SING. Nom.	**hwil**	*hwile*	*while*
Gen.	**hwile**	**hwile**	*whiles*
Dat.	**hwile**	**hwile**	**while**
Acc.	**hwile**	**hwile**	**while**
PLUR. Nom., Acc.	**hwila**	**hwile**	*whiles*
Gen.	**hwila**	**hwile**	*whiles*
Dat.	**hwilum**	**hwile(n)**	*whiles*
77. lim, neuter:			
SING. Nom.	**lim**	**lim**	**lim**
Gen.	**limes**	**limes**	**limes**
Dat.	**lime**	**lime**	*lim*
Acc.	**lim**	**lim**	**lim**
PLUR. Nom., Acc.	**limu**	**lime**	*limes*
Gen.	**lima**	**lime**	*limes*
Dat.	**limum**	**lime(n)**	*limes*

	OLD ENGLISH	MIDDLE ENGLISH	
		Early ME	Late ME

78. hors, neuter:

SING. Nom.	hors	hors	hors
Gen.	horses	horses	horses
Dat.	horse	horse	*hors*
Acc.	hors	hors	hors
PLUR. Nom., Acc.	hors	hors	*horses*
Gen.	horsa	horse	*horses*
Dat.	horsum	horse(n)	*horses*

79. flicce, neuter:

SING. Nom.	flicce	flicche	flitche
Gen.	flicces	flicches	flitches
Dat.	flicce	flicche	flitche
Acc.	flicce	flicche	flitche
PLUR. Nom., Acc.	fliccu	flicche	*flitches*
Gen.	flicca	flicche	*flitches*
Dat.	fliccum	flicche(n)	*flitches*

80. hunta, weak masculine:

SING. Nom.	hunta	hunte	hunte
Gen.	huntan	hunte(n)	*huntes*
Dat.	huntan	hunte(n)	hunte
Acc.	huntan	hunte(n)	hunte
PLUR. Nom., Acc.	huntan	hunte(n)	*huntes*
Gen.	huntena, huntan	huntene, hunte(n)	*huntes*
Dat.	huntum	hunte(n)	*huntes*

81. sunne, weak feminine:

SING. Nom.	sunne	sunne	sonne
Gen.	sunnan	sunne(n)	*sonnes*
Dat.	sunnan	sunne(n)	sonne
Acc.	sunnan	sunne(n)	sonne
PLUR. Nom., Acc.	sunnan	sunne(n)	*sonnes*
Gen.	sunnena, sunnan	sunnene, sunne(n)	*sonnes*
Dat.	sunnum	sunne(n)	*sonnes*

| | | OLD ENGLISH | MIDDLE ENGLISH | |
| | | | Early ME | Late ME |

82. ēare, weak neuter:

		OLD ENGLISH	Early ME	Late ME
SING.	Nom.	ēare	ere	ere
	Gen.	ēaran	ere(n)	*eres*
	Dat.	ēaran	ere(n)	ere
	Acc.	ēare	ere	ere
PLUR.	Nom., Acc.	ēaran	ere(n)	*eres*
	Gen.	ēarena, ēaran	erene, ere(n)	*eres*
	Dat.	ēarum	ere(n)	*eres*

83. An analysis of the tables given above shows that the analogical changes that took place in the inflection of nouns were these:

1. The nominative singular became identical with the accusative singular in the strong feminine nouns ending in a consonant, which in Old English had different forms for the two cases.

2. The ending **-es** became the endings of the genitive singular of nouns which in Old English had other endings.

3. The dative singular became identical with the accusative singular in those nouns which in Old English had different forms for the two cases.

4. The ending **-es** became the ending of the nominative-accusative plural of those nouns which in Old English had other endings.

5. The genitive and dative plural became identical with the nominative-accusative plural.

84. Retention and Extension of the Weak Noun Inflection. One other statement is needed, however, to complete this account of the Middle English noun inflections. A few nouns that belonged to the Old English weak declension retained their weak inflection, at least in part, even in Late Middle English. The development of this type of inflection, as exemplified by Old English **oxa** (*ox*), is shown in the following table:

| | | OLD ENGLISH | MIDDLE ENGLISH | |
| | | | Early ME | Late ME |

		OLD ENGLISH	Early ME	Late ME
SING.	Nom.	oxa	oxe	oxe
	Gen.	oxan	oxe(n)	*oxes*
	Dat.	oxan	oxe(n)	oxe
	Acc.	oxan	oxe(n)	oxe

	OLD ENGLISH		MIDDLE ENGLISH	
			Early ME	Late ME
PLUR. Nom., Acc.	oxan		oxe(n)	oxen
Gen.	oxena, oxan		oxene, oxe(n)	oxen
Dat.	oxum		oxe(n)	oxen

The weak plural inflection was frequently extended in early Middle English to nouns that were not weak nouns in Old English; e.g., OE nom. plur. **dēda**, f. (WS **dǣda**), **suna**, m., **limu**, n., **word**, n., **čildru**, n., ME **deden, sunen, limen, worden, children.** Likewise the weak genitive plural ending **-ene** was sometimes extended to nouns that were not weak in Old English; e.g., **kingene king** *king of kings.*

ADJECTIVES

85. Declension of Adjectives. In Old English, as in Modern German, every adjective was inflected according to either one of two declensions, the strong or the weak. In general the strong (i.e. the more highly differentiated) declension was employed in the absence of some other accompanying gender, case, and number distinctive form such as the definite article or demonstrative pronoun. The weak or less distinctive declension was used if the adjective was preceded by a definite article, a demonstrative, or a possessive, or if the adjective modified a noun used in direct address. In the Middle English both declensions of the adjective were retained, but with much simplification of forms.

There were two types of strong adjectives in Old English, those ending in a consonant, like **gōd**, *good,* and those ending in **-e**, like **swēte**, *sweet.* The historical development of the strong inflection in these two types of adjective is shown in the tables printed below. In the first column are given the Old English (Late West-Saxon) forms, in the second the historical forms that developed in the earliest Middle English by the process of sound-change, and in the third those that occur in late Middle English. In the third column the forms that are identical with the historical forms of early Middle English are printed in Roman type and the analogical forms that developed later are printed in italic type.

86. Strong Declension. Type 1, Ending in a Consonant.

	OLD ENGLISH	MIDDLE ENGLISH	
		Early ME	Late ME
	Masculine		
SING. Nom.	gōd	good	good
Gen.	gōdes	goodes	*good*
Dat.	gōdum	goode(n)	*good*
Acc.	gōdne	goodne	*good*
	Feminine		
SING. Nom.	gōd[85]	good	good
Gen.	gōdre	goodre, gooder	*good*
Dat.	gōdre	goodre, gooder	*good*
Acc.	gōde	goode	*good*
	Neuter		
SING. Nom.	gōd	good	good
Gen.	gōdes	goodes	*good*
Dat.	gōdum	goode(n)	*good*
Acc.	gōd	good	good
	All Genders		
PLUR. Nom., Acc.	gōde[86]	goode	goode
Gen.	gōdra	goodre, gooder	*goode*
Dat.	gōdum	goode(n)	goode

87. Strong Declension. Type 2, Ending in -e.

	Masculine		
SING. Nom.	swēte	swete	swete
Gen.	swētes	swetes	*swete*
Dat.	swētum	swete(n)	swete
Acc.	swētne	swetne	*swete*

[86] Actually the neuter nominative-accusative plural originally had no inflection when the adjective was a long monosyllabic stem (**gōd**) and a -u inflection when the stem was short (**sumu**) or a disyllable ending in -e (**swētu**). Even in Old English the long stemmed adjectives like **gōd** already had an alternative form **gōde,** owing to analogy with the other genders. Such forms as **sumu** and **swētu** became **sume** and **swete** in early Middle English by the regular process of levelling of unstressed vowels. This was also true of the feminine accusative singular, except that **gōd** did not here acquire the -e inflection.

| | OLD ENGLISH | MIDDLE ENGLISH | |
| | | Early ME | Late ME |

Feminine

SING. Nom.	swētu	swete	swete
Gen.	swētre	swetre, sweter	*swete*
Dat.	swētre	swetre, sweter	*swete*
Acc.	swēte	swete	swete

Neuter

SING. Nom.	swēte	swete	swete
Gen.	swētes	swetes	*swete*
Dat.	swētum	swete(n)	swete
Acc.	swēte	swete	swete

All Genders

PLUR. Nom., Acc.	swēte	swete	swete
Gen.	swētra	swetre, sweter	*swete*
Dat.	swētum	swete(n)	swete

88. Weak Declension.

Masculine

SING. Nom.	gōda	goode	goode
Gen.	gōdan	goode(n)	goode
Dat.	gōdan	goode(n)	goode
Acc.	gōdan	goode(n)	goode

Feminine

SING. Nom.	gōde	goode	goode
Gen.	gōdan	goode(n)	goode
Dat.	gōdan	goode(n)	goode
Acc.	gōdan	goode(n)	goode

Neuter

SING. Nom.	gōde	goode	goode
Gen.	gōdan	goode(n)	goode
Dat.	gōdan	goode(n)	goode
Acc.	gōde	goode	goode

All Genders

PLUR. Nom., Acc.	gōdan	goode(n)	goode
Gen.	gōdena, gōdan	goodene, gode(n)	goode
Dat.	gōdum	goode(n)	goode

Pronouns

89. Declension of Personal Pronouns. The development that took place in nouns and adjectives in Middle English resulted in a very great simplification of inflections, chiefly as the result of numerous analogical formations. No such simplification of inflection took place, however, in the Middle English development of the personal pronouns. In the first and second personal pronouns there is a one-for-one correspondence between the Old English and the Middle English forms, and in the third personal pronoun there is a one-for-one correspondence except that in late Middle English there are no distinctive forms for the dative and accusative.[87] Analogical processes played a very much smaller part in the development of the personal pronouns than in the development of nouns and adjectives.

But although the development of the personal pronouns is simple from this point of view, it is more complex in some other respects.

One reason is that the Old English pronouns often had variant forms, any one of which might become the basis of a corresponding Middle English form. Another reason is that variant forms might develop in Middle English from the same Old English form. All of the Old English forms containing the diphthong ēo were subject to divergent development in Middle English because of the fact that this sound developed variously, according to circumstances, into [œː] which later became [eː]; [ɪu]; [ɔːu]; [oː]; or [uː].

There is a more fundamental reason, however, that made for complexity in the development of the personal pronouns in Middle English. Pronominal words are in all languages particularly liable to divergent development because of the fact that they have "strong" forms, which are used when the word is strongly stressed, and "weak" forms, which are used when the word is weakly stressed (cf. Modern English [hɪm] and [ɪm]. These strong and weak forms are never phonetically identical. If the strong form has a long vowel, the corresponding weak form will have a half-long or short vowel, which may be of the same quality as that of the stressed form or of slightly different quality. If the strong form has a short vowel, the vowel of the weak form will be shorter and possibly obscured (cf. MnE [ʌs] and [əs]).

---

[87] Note that in the first and second persons, the dative forms **mē, þē, ūs,** and **ēow** had in Old English almost completely replaced the older, distinctively accusative **mec, þec, ūsic, ēowic.** The same process in the third personal pronoun did not occur until several centuries later.

Now when we consider (1) that the strong forms of pronouns are stressed syllables and that the weak forms are unstressed syllables, (2) that the sound-changes that take place in stressed syllables are seldom identical with those that take place in unstressed syllables, and (3) that the sound-changes undergone by long vowels are frequently different from those undergone by short vowels, we can understand that when pronouns are affected by sound-change the resulting strong and weak forms are apt to be less similar than they were before the sound-change took place. But if the dissimilarity is too great, either the strong or the weak form is likely to be modified by becoming assimilated to the other, so that similarity between the two is restored. In Old English, for example, the nominative singular of the first personal pronoun was [ɪtʃ], which was also the early Middle English stressed form. In Middle English, however, final [tʃ] was lost in unstressed syllables, so that the unstressed form of the pronoun became [ɪ]. From this weak form a new strong form [iː] was then developed, and from this strong form there probably developed in late Middle English a new weak form with half-long [i]. Through such processes as these strong and weak forms are continually multiplying each other, and the results of sound-changes are repeatedly modified by assimilation of strong forms to weak or vice-versa. (Cf. **129** below.)

The tables in the following sections show the historical development of the stressed forms of the personal pronouns in Middle English.[88]

90. First Personal Pronoun.

	OLD ENGLISH		MIDDLE ENGLISH	
SING. Nom.	iċ		ich	[ɪtʃ], I [iː]
Gen.	mīn		mi(n)	[miːn]
Dat.	mē		me	[meː]
Acc.	mē		me	[meː]
PLUR. Nom.	wē		we	[weː]
Gen.	ūre		ure, ures	[uːrə], [uːrəs]
Dat., Acc.	ūs		us	[uːs], [ʊs]

91. Second Personal Pronoun. The variety of forms that occurs in the second personal pronoun is the result of the various developments

[88] These tables do not attempt to give *all* the Middle English pronominal forms, but only the commoner and more characteristic ones. No account is taken of mere variations of spelling.

that occurred in Middle English of the Old English sound combination ēow. When it remained a "falling" diphthong (Section 15 above),
the Middle English development was [œːʊ], which later became [eːʊ]
and then [ɪu]. If it became a "rising" diphthong, it lost its first element
and then developed into [ɔːu]. The explanation to be given of the [uː]
in ʒur and ʒu depends on the explanation we accept as to the origin of
the initial [j]. One explanation regards the ʒ-forms as analogical formations developed from the [ɔːʊ] forms under the influence of the nominative
ʒe, with later change of [ɔːʊ] into [uː]. A simpler explanation is that
they developed from the Middle English [ɪu] forms as the result of the
falling diphthong becoming a rising diphthong.

It was during the Middle English period also that the plural forms of
the second person pronoun began to be used with singular meaning. The
table which follows should be interpreted with this syntactical feature in
mind. For a further discussion of this subject see Section 131.2.

OLD ENGLISH		MIDDLE ENGLISH	
SING. Nom.	þū	þu	[θuː]
Gen.	þīn	þi(n)	[θiːn]
Dat.	þē	þe	[θeː]
Acc.	þē	þe	[θeː]
PLUR. Nom.	ġē	ʒe	[jeː]
Gen.	ēower	eower [œːʊər]; euer [eːʊər], [ɪuər]; ower	
		[ɔːʊər]; ʒur [juːr], ʒures	
Dat., Acc.	ēow	eow [œːʊ]; eu [eːʊ], [ɪu]; ow [ɔːʊ]; ʒu [juː]	

92. Third Personal Pronoun. The variety of forms that occurs in
the feminine nominative and accusative singular and in the nominative
and accusative plural of the third personal pronoun is the result of the
various Middle English developments of the Old English diphthongs
ēo and ie. When these remained falling diphthongs, they developed
respectively into [œː], which later became [eː], and [iː]. If they became
rising diphthongs, they developed respectively into [hjoː] and [hjeː]
if their first elements were retained, and into [hoː] and [heː] if their first
elements were lost.

OLD ENGLISH   MIDDLE ENGLISH

Analogical
forms

MASCULINE SINGULAR

Nom.	hē	he	[he]	
Gen.	his	his	[hɪs]	
Dat.	him	him	[hɪm]	
Acc.	hine	hine	[hɪnə]	*him*

FEMININE SINGULAR

Nom.	hēo	heo [hœː]; he [heː];		
		hʒo [hjoː]; ho [hoː]		
	hīe	hi [hiː]; hʒe [hjeː]; he [heː]		
Gen.	hire	hire, hires	[hɪrə]	*here*
Dat.	hire	hire	[hɪrə]	*here*
Acc.	hēo	heo [hœː]; he [heː];		*hire, here*
		hʒo [hjoː]; ho [hoː]		
	hīe	hi [hiː]; hʒe [hjeː]; he [heː]		

NEUTER SINGULAR

Nom.	hit	hit	[hɪt]	
Gen.	his	his	[hɪs]	
Dat.	him	him	[hɪm]	*hit*
Acc.	hit	hit	[hɪt]	

PLURAL (ALL GENDERS)

Nom.	hēo	heo [hœː]; he [heː];	
		hʒo [hjoː]; ho [hoː]	
	hīe	hi [hiː]; hʒe [hjeː]; he [heː]	
Gen.	hira, heora	hire [hɪrə]; heore, here	
Dat.	him, heom	him [hɪm]; heom, hem	
Acc.	hēo	heo [hœː]; he [heː]	*him, hem*
		hʒo [hjoː]; ho [hoː]	
	hīe	hi [hiː]; hʒe [hjeː]; he [heː]	

The feminine nominative singular and the plural pronouns given above are those which occur in the Southern and the South-Midland dialects of Middle English, but in the Northern and the North-Midland dialects these forms began to be displaced before the end of the twelfth century by the feminine pronoun **she, sho** and the plural pronouns **þei, þeir, þeim** (later **þem**). The origin of **she, sho** is uncertain, some scholars deriving it from Old English **sēo**, the feminine nominative singular of the demonstrative, and some from the Old Norse feminine (and masculine) nominative singular pronoun **sjā.** The new plural pronouns were certainly derived from or developed under the influence of the Old Norse plural pronouns **þeir, þeira, þeim,** for the diphthong that occurs in the Middle English forms cannot be accounted for on the basis of **þā, þāra, þām** (the plural forms of the demonstrative) which are the nearest corresponding Old English forms, though Old English **þām** would be a perfectly possible original for the later Middle English **þem.**

93. Demonstrative Pronouns and Definite Article. The forms **sē, sēo, þæt** were used in Old English both as demonstrative and as definite article and were inflected for gender, case, and number. In late Middle English we find that the definite article has lost all inflection and has been reduced to the invariable form **þe,** and that the demonstrative has lost all inflection for gender and case and has been reduced to the two forms **þat** (singular) and **þo** (plural). The details of the development that took place within the Middle English period and the causes that cooperated in this process of simplification and differentiation of forms are too complex and too uncertain to deal with here. It seems best merely to give the early Middle English and late Middle English forms as they appear in the manuscripts, without attempting a phonetic interpretation of the forms and without attempting to show how much of the late ME development can be accounted for as the result of sound-change and how much is to be regarded as the result of analogy. Among the early Middle English forms, however, the nominative *þe* and *þeo,* which had begun to replace **se** and **seo,** are unquestionably analogical formations and are therefore printed in italics.

OLD ENGLISH		MIDDLE ENGLISH	
		Early ME	Late ME
			Def. Art. Dem.

MASCULINE SINGULAR

			Def. Art.	Dem.
Nom.	sē	se, þe	þe	þat
Gen.	þæs	þes, þas	þe	þat
Dat.	þæm, þām	þam, þen, þan	þe	þat
Acc.	þone, þœne	þon(e),[89] þen(e), þan(e)	þe	þat
Inst.	þȳ, þon, þē	þi, þon, þe		

FEMININE SINGULAR

			Def. Art.	Dem.
Nom.	sēo	seo, þeo	þe	þat
Gen.	þǣre	þer(e), þar(e)	þe	þat
Dat.	þēre	þer(e), þar(e)	þe	þat
Acc.	þā	þo, þa	þe	þat

NEUTER SINGULAR

			Def. Art.	Dem.
Nom.	þæt	þet, þat	þe	þat
Gen.	þæs	þes, þas	þe	þat
Dat.	þǣm, þām	þam, þen, þan	þe	þat
Acc.	þæt	þet, þat	þe	þat
Inst.	þȳ, þon, þē	þi, þon, þe	þe	

PLURAL (ALL GENDERS)

			Def. Art.	Dem.
Nom.	þā	þo, þa	þe	þo
Gen.	þāra, þǣra	þar(e), þer(e)	þe	þo
Dat.	þǣm, þām	þam, þen, þan	þe	þo
Acc.	þā	þo, þa	þe	þo

The Old English demonstrative þēs, þēos, þis underwent a similar development in Middle English, for it lost all inflection for gender and

---

[89] When preceded by a stressed syllable final e was retained in Middle English until the fourteenth century or later, but it was very generally lost even in Early Middle English when preceded by an unstressed syllable (see 62.3 above). This condition occurred (1) in words of three or more syllables, none of which had secondary stress, and (2) in the weak forms of words which were frequently used without stress, such as the personal pronouns and article.

case and was reduced to the invariable form þes or þis. This form was commonly used both as singular and plural, though in later ME the specifically plural forms þese and þise, which were formed from the analogy of the plural adjective, were also used. Not much attention has been given by scholars to the Middle English development of this demonstrative and no attempt will be made here to indicate how much of it can be accounted for as the result of sound-change and how much is to be attributed to analogy. The more frequent forms that appear in early Middle English and late Middle English are given below as they appear in the manuscripts, without phonetic interpretation.

OLD ENGLISH	MIDDLE ENGLISH	
	Early ME	Late ME

MASCULINE SINGULAR

	OLD ENGLISH	Early ME	Late ME
Nom.	þēs	þes	þes, þis
Gen.	þis(s)es	þis(s)es, þes(s)es	þes, þis
Dat.	þis(s)um	þis(s)e(n), þes(s)e(n)	þes, þis
Acc.	þisne	þisne	þes, þis

FEMININE SINGULAR

	OLD ENGLISH	Early ME	Late ME
Nom.	þēos	þeos, þes	þes, þis
Gen.	þisse, þissere	þisse, þesse, þissere, þessere	þes, þis
Dat.	þisse, þissere	þisse, þesse, þissere, þessere	þes, þis
Acc.	þās	þas, þos, þise, þese	þes, þis

NEUTER SINGULAR

	OLD ENGLISH	Early ME	Late ME
Nom.	þis	þis	þes, þis
Gen.	þis(s)es	þis(s)es, þes(s)es	þes, þis
Dat.	þis(s)um	þis(s)e(n), þes(s)e(n)	þes, þis
Acc.	þis	þis	þes, þis

PLURAL (ALL GENDERS)

	OLD ENGLISH	Early ME	Late ME
Nom.	þās	þas, þos	þes, þis, þese, þise
Gen.	þissa, þissera	þisse, þissere	þes, þis, þese, þise
Dat.	þis(s)um	þis(s)e(n), þes(s)e(n)	þes, þis, þese, þise
Acc.	þās	þas, þos	þes, þis, þese, þise

VERBS

94. Weak Verbs, Type I. In Middle English, as in Old English and all other Germanic languages, there are two conjugations of verbs, the strong and the weak. Weak verbs form their preterit by means of a suffix containing **d** or **t** followed by endings indicative of person and number. From the point of view of their development in Middle English, we may say that there were two types of weak verbs in Old English. Verbs of the first type had preterits ending in **-ede** or **-ode** and past participles ending in **-ed** or **-od**:

fremman (*make*)	fremede	fremed
erian (*plow*)	erede	ered
lufian (*love*)	lufode	lufod

In Middle English the distinction between **lufian**, with preterit in **-ode**, and **fremman** and **erian**, with preterits in **-ede**, was done away with by the process of sound change, so that the earliest Middle English forms of these verbs were

fremme(n)	fremede	fremed
erie(n)	erede	ered
luvie(n)	luvede	luved

These verbs, which we shall call weak verbs of Type I, therefore had in Middle English preterits ending in **-ede** and past participles ending in **-ed**. In early Middle English the infinitive of these verbs ended in **-e(n)** or **-ie(n)**, but in late Middle English, by the process of analogy, the ending **-ie(n)** was displaced by the commoner ending **-e(n)**.

95. Weak Verbs, Type II. Old English verbs of the second type had preterits ending in **-de** or **-te** and past participles ending in **-ed, -d,** or **-t**:

dēman (*judge*)	dēmde	dēmed
fēlan (*feel*)	fēlde	fēled
fēdan (*feed*)	fēdde	fēded, fēdd
wendan (*turn*)	wende	wended, wend
cēpan (*keep*)	cēpte	cēped
mētan (*meet*)	mētte	mēted, mētt
settan (*set*)	sette	seted, sett
sēċan (*seek*)	sōhte	sōht
þenċan (*think*)	þōhte	þōht

In Middle English these verbs developed, according to the regular laws of sound change, as follows:

deme(n) [deːmən]	demde [deːmdə]	demed [deːməd]
fele(n) [feːlən]	felte [fɛltə]	feled [feːləd]
fede(n) [feːdən]	fedde [fɛddə]	fed [fɛd]
wende(n) [wɛndən]	wente [wɛntə]	went [wɛnt]
kepe(n) [keːpən]	kepte [kɛptə]	keped [keːpəd]
mete(n) [meːtən]	mette [mɛtːə]	met [mɛt]
sette(n) [sɛtːən]	sette [sɛtːə]	set [sɛt]
seche(n) [seːtʃən]	soughte [sɔuxtə]	sought [sɔuxt]
þenche(n) [θɛntʃən]	þoughte [θɔuxtə]	þought [θɔuxt]

These Type II weak verbs, therefore had in Middle English preterits ending in **-de** or **-te** and past participles ending in **-ed, d,** or **t.** It will be observed (cf. **54.**1 above) that the long vowels of **felen, feden, kepen,** and **meten** are shortened in the preterit, where they were followed by a double consonant or a combination of consonants. For **felte** see Section **140.**3 below.

96. Weak Verb Inflections. The historical development of the Middle English forms of the weak verb is shown in the tables printed below. Weak verbs of Type I are exemplified by Old English **erian** (*plow*) and **lufian** (*love*); weak verbs of Type II are exemplified by Old English **dēman** (*judge*). In the first column are given the Old English forms, in the second the historical forms that developed in early Middle English by sound-change, and in the third the analogical forms that developed in later Middle English.

OLD ENGLISH	MIDDLE ENGLISH	
	Historical forms	Analogical forms
TYPE I		
PRES. IND. SING. 1 erie	erie	*ere*
2 erest	erest	
3 ereþ	ereþ	
PLUR. eriaþ	erieþ	*ereþ, ere(n)*[90]
PRES. SUBJ. SING. erie	erie	*ere*
PLUR. erien	erie(n)	*ere(n)*

[90] The ending **-e(n)** in the present indicative plural is a characteristic of the Midland dialect; the ending **-eþ** is a characteristic of the Southern dialect.

OLD ENGLISH	MIDDLE ENGLISH	
	Historical forms	Analogical forms
PRET. IND. SING. 1 erede	erede, ered[91]	
2 eredest	eredest	
3 erede	erede, ered[91]	
PLUR. eredon	erede(n)	
PRET. SUBJ. SING. erede	erede, ered[92]	
PLUR. ereden	erede(n)	
PRES. IMP. SING. 2 ere	ere	
PLUR. 2 eriaþ	erieþ	*ereþ*
INFINITIVE erian	erie(n)	*ere(n)*
GERUND tō erienne	to eriene	*to erene*
tō erian	to erie(n)	*to ere(n)*
PRES. PARTICIPLE eriende	eriende, eriinde[93]	*erende, erinde,[93] eringe, ering[93]*
PAST PARTICIPLE ered	ered	
PRES. IND. SING. 1 lufie	luvie, luvi[92]	*luve*
2 lufast	luvest	
3 lufaþ	luveþ	
PLUR. lufiaþ	luvieþ	*luveþ, luve(n)[94]*
PRES. SUBJ. SING. lufie	luvie, luvi[92]	*luve*
PLUR. lufien	luvie(n), luvi(n)	*luve(n)*
PRET. IND. SING. 1 lufode	luvede, luved[92]	
2 lufodest	luvedest	
3 lufode	luvede, luved[92]	
PLUR. lufodon	luvede(n)	
PRET. SUBJ. SING. lufode	luvede, luved[92]	
PLUR. lufoden	luvede(n)	
PRES. IMP. SING. 2 lufa	luve	
PLUR. 2 lufiaþ	luvieþ	*luveþ*

[91] For the loss of final e see note 89 above.

[92] For the loss of final e see note 89 above.

[93] The ending -inde is a characteristic of the Southern dialect, the ending -ende of the Midland dialect.

[94] The ending -e(n) in the present indicative plural is a characteristic of the Midland dialect; the ending -eþ is a characteristic of the Southern dialect.

	OLD ENGLISH	MIDDLE ENGLISH	
		Historical forms	Analogical forms
INFINITIVE	lufian	luvie(n), luvi(n)	*luve(n)*
GERUND	tō lufienne	to luviene	*to luvene,*
	tō lufian	to luvie(n), to luvi(n)	*to luve(n)*
PRES. PARTICIPLE	lufiende	luviende, luviinde[95]	*luvende, luvinde, luvinge, luving*[96]
PAST PARTICIPLE	lufod	luved	

TYPE II

		OLD ENGLISH	MIDDLE ENGLISH	
PRES. IND. SING.	1	dēme	deme	
	2	dēmest, dēmst	demest, demst	
	3	dēmeþ, dēmþ	demeþ, demþ	
PLUR.		dēmaþ	demeþ	*deme(n)* [97]
PRES. SUBJ. SING.		dēme	deme	
PLUR.		dēmen	deme(n)	
PRET. IND. SING.	1	dēmde	demde	
	2	dēmdest	demdest	
	3	dēmde	demde	
PLUR.		dēmdon	demde(n)	
PRET. SUBJ. SING.		dēmde	demde	
PLUR.		dēmden	demde(n)	
PRES. IMP. SING.	2	dēm	dem	*deme*
PLUR.	2	dēmaþ	demeþ	
INFINITIVE		dēman	deme(n)	
GERUND		tō dēmenne	to demene	
		tō dēman	to deme(n)	
PRES. PARTICIPLE		dēmende	demende, deminde[95]	*deminge, deming*[96]
PAST PARTICIPLE		dēmed	demed	

[95] The ending **-inde** is a characteristic of the Southern dialect, the ending **-ende** of the Midland dialect.

[96] For the loss of final **e** see note 89 above.

[97] The ending **-e(n)** in the present indicative plural is a characteristic of the Midland dialect; the ending **-eþ** is a characteristic of the Southern dialect.

97. Strong Verbs. Strong verbs are those that do not form their preterit by the addition of a suffix containing **d** or **t** but by a particular kind of vowel change called "ablaut"; the strong verbs are therefore frequently called "ablaut verbs." The preterit plural of these verbs usually has a different vowel from the preterit singular; the principal parts therefore are the infinitive, the preterit indicative first person singular, the preterit indicative plural, and the past participle.

In Old English there were seven classes of strong verbs; the principal parts of verbs representative of these seven classes are given in the first of the two tables shown below.[98] The Old English forms given are those that were common to the West-Saxon and the Mercian dialects. Where the West-Saxon and the Mercian forms were not the same both forms are given.

By the operation of the sound changes which have been explained in Sections **52-55**, these Old English forms developed in Middle English as shown in the second of the two tables opposite the following page, the West-Saxon forms corresponding to those of the Southern dialect and the Mercian forms to those of the East Midland dialect.

98. Analogical Developments in the Principal Parts of Strong Verbs. The forms that developed from the Old English forms by sound change are those that occur in early Middle English, but in later Middle English

[98] See also the table of Old English inflections, p. 23, and Moore and Knott, *Elements of Old English*, pp. 170–180.

OLD ENGLISH

I.	rīdan (*ride*)	rād	ridon	riden
II.	crēopan (*creep*)	crēap	crupon	cropen
III.	bindan (*bind*)	band	bundon	bunden
	helpan (*help*)	WS healp Merc. halp	hulpon	holpen
	steorfan (*die*)	stearf	sturfon	storfen
IV.	beran (*bear*)	bær	WS. bǣron Merc. bēron	boren
V	specan (*speak*)	spæc	WS. spǣcon Merc. spēcon	specen
VI.	scacan (*shake*)	scōc	scōcon	scacen
VII.	WS. slǣpan (*sleep*) Merc. slēpan	slēp	slēpon	WS. slǣpen Merc. slēpen
	WS. healdan (*hold*) Merc. haldan	hēold	hēoldon	WS. healden Merc. halden

we meet with a good many analogical forms. The most important results of analogy were these:

1. Strong verbs often acquired weak preterits; e.g., **crepte** [krɛptə], **slepte** [slɛptə], in place of **creep, sleep.**
2. The vowel of the preterit plural was often substituted for the vowel of the preterit singular; e.g., **beer,** with the vowel of the preterit plural, displaced **bar.**
3. The vowel of the preterit singular was often substituted for the vowel of the preterit plural; e.g., **bare(n)** [baːrən], with the vowel of the preterit singular (lengthened when it came to stand in an open syllable),[99] displaced **bere(n)**.
4. The vowel of the past participle was often substituted for the vowel of the preterit plural; e.g., **crope(n)** [krɔːpən], with the vowel of the past participle, displaced **crupe(n)**.
5. In the past participles of verbs of Class V the vowel **o** [ɔː] was substituted for the original vowel **e,** from the analogy of the past participle of verbs of Class IV; e.g., **spoke(n)** [spɔːkən], with the vowel of **bore(n)** [bɔːrən], displaced **speke(n)** [spæːkən].

99. Strong Verb Inflections. The historical development of the Middle English forms of the strong verb, exemplified by Old English **ridan** (*ride*) and **bindan** (*bind*), is shown in the tables printed below.

[99] See Section **55** above.

MIDDLE ENGLISH

ride(n) [riːdən]	rod [rɔːd]	ride(n) [rɪdən]	ride(n) [rɪdən]
crepe(n) [kreːpən]	creep [kræːp]	crupe(n) [krupən]	crope(n) [krɔːpən]
binde(n) biːndən]	bond [bɔːnd]	bunde(n) [buːndən]	bunde(n) [buːndən]
helpe(n) [hɛlpən]	halp [halp]	hulpe(n) [hulpən]	holpe(n) [hɔlpən]
sterve(n) [stɛrvən]	starf [starf]	sturve(n) [sturvən]	storve(n) [stɔrvən]
bere(n) [bæːrən]	bar [bar]	Sth. bere(n) [bæːrən] Mdl. bere(n) [beɪrən]	bore(n) [bɔːrən]
speke(n) [spæːkən]	spak [spak]	Sth. speke(n) [spæːkən] Mdl. speke(n) [speɪkən]	speke(n) [spæːkən]
shake(n) [ʃaːkən]	shook [ʃoːk]	shooke(n) [ʃoːkən]	shake(n) [ʃaːkən]
Sth. slepe(n) [slæːpən] Mdl. slepe(n) [sleipən	sleep [sleːp]	sleepe(n) [sleːpən]	slepe(n) [slæːpən] Mdl. slepe(n) [sleipən
Sth. helde(n) [hæːldən] Mdl. holde(e)[hɔːldən]	heeld [heːld]	heelde(n) [heːldən]	Sth. helde(n) [hæːldən] Mdl. holde(n) [hɔːldən]

VERBS

OLD ENGLISH			MIDDLE ENGLISH	
			Historical forms	Analogical forms
PRES. IND.	SING.	1 rīde	ride	
		2 rīdest, rītst	ridest, ritst [rɪtst]	
		3 rīdeþ, rītt	rideþ, rit [rɪt]	
	PLUR.	rīdaþ	rideþ	ride(n)[100]
PRES. SUBJ.	SING.	rīde	ride	
	PLUR.	rīden	ride(n)	
PRET. IND.	SING.	1 rād	rood	
		2 ride[101]	ride	rood
		3 rād	rood	
	PLUR.	ridon	ride(n)	
PRET. SUBJ.	SING.	ride	ride	
	PLUR.	riden	ride(n)	
PRES. IMP.	SING.	2 rid	rid	
	PLUR.	2 rīdaþ	rideþ	
INFINITIVE		rīdan	ride(n)	
GERUND		tō rīdenne	to ridene	
		tō rīdan	to ride(n)	
PRES. PARTICIPLE		rīdende	ridende, ridinde[102]	ridinge, riding[103]
PAST PARTICIPLE		riden	ride(n)	
PRES. IND.	SING.	1 binde	binde	
		2 bindest, bintst	bindest, bintst	
		3 bindeþ, bint	bindeþ, bint	
	PLUR.	bindaþ	bindeþ	binde(n)[100]
PRET. SUBJ.	SING.	binde	binde	
	PLUR.	binden	binde(n)	

[100] The ending -e(n) in the present indicative plural is a characteristic of the Midland dialect; the ending -eþ is a characteristic of the Southern dialect.

[101] It should be observed that the preterit indicative 2 singular of the strong verbs has the vowel of the preterit plural.

[102] The ending -inde is a characteristic of the Southern dialect, the ending -ende of the Midland dialect.

[103] For the loss of final e see note 89 above.

	OLD ENGLISH	MIDDLE ENGLISH	
		Historical forms	Analogical forms
PRES. IND. SING. 1	band	bond	
2	bunde[101]	bunde	*bond*
3	band	bond	
PLUR.	bundon	bunde(n)	
PRET. SUBJ. SING.	bunde	bunde	
PLUR.	bunden	bunde(n)	
PRES. IMP. SING. 2	bind	bind	
PLUR. 2	bindaþ	bindeþ	
INFINITIVE	bindan	binde(n)	
GERUND	tō bindenne	to bindene	
	tō bindan	to binde(n)	
PRES. PARTICIPLE	bindende	bindende	*bindinge, binding*[104]
		bindinde[105]	
PAST PARTICIPLE	bunden	bunde(n)	

100. Preteritive-Present Verbs. The preteritive-present (or strong-weak) verbs have **present** indicatives which are like the **preterit** indicatives of strong verbs in that they have no ending in the first and third persons singular and have the ending **-e(n)** (from Old English **-on**) in the plural.[106] The **preterits** of these verbs are **weak.** The indicative forms of Middle English **shal,** for example, are as follows:

PRES. IND. SING. 1 **shal**
2 **shalt**
3 **shal**
PLUR.   **shule(n)**

PRET. IND. SING. 1 **sholde**
2 **sholdest**
3 **sholde**
PLUR.   **sholde(n)**

[104] For the loss of final **e** see note 89 above.
[105] See note 102 above.
[103] The present indicative forms of these verbs are also like the preterit indicative forms of strong verbs in showing differences of ablaut (see Section **97**) between singular and plural. Compare **wāt-witon** and **rād-ridon; cann-cunnon** and **band-bundon; mōt-mōton** and **scōc-scōcon.** See Moore and Knott, *Elements of Old English,* Chapter XXIII.

The most important of the preteritive-present verbs remaining in Middle English are:

owen, *own, be under obligation*
cunnen, *know, be able*
muwen, *be able*
moten, *be permitted, be under obligation*
shulen, *be under obligation, be about to*
witen, *know*

101. The historical development of the preteritive-present verbs is shown in the following tables:

	OLD ENGLISH	MIDDLE ENGLISH	
		Historical forms	Analogical forms
PRES. IND. SING. 1	**āh, āg**	**ouh** [ɔːʊx], **ow** [ɔːʊ]	*owe* [ɔːuə]
2	**āhst**	**auhst** [ɑuxst]	*ouhst* [ɔuxst],[107] *owest* [ɔːʊəst]
3	**āh, āg**	**ouh** [ɔːʊx], **ow** [ɔːʊ]	*oweþ* [ɔːʊəθ]
PLUR.	**āgon**	**owe(n)** [ɔːʊən]	*oweþ* [ɔːʊəθ][108]
PRET. IND. SING. 1	**āhte**	**auhte** [ɑuxtə]	*ouhte* [ɔuxtə][107]
INFINITIVE	**āgan**	**owe(n)** [ɔːʊən]	
PRES. IND. SING. 1	**cann, conn**	**can**	
2	**canst, const**	**canst**	
3	**cann, conn**	**can**	
PLUR.	**cunnon**	**cunne(n)**	
PRET. IND. SING. 1	**cūþe**	**cuþe** [kuːðə]	*cude* [kuːdə]
INFINITIVE	**cunnan**	**cunne(n)**	

[107] The shortening of long vowels before two or more consonants (see Section 54) occurred previous to the change of [ɑː] to [ɔː], so that the historical form had the diphthong **au.**

[108] This plural form occurs only in the Southern dialect.

OLD ENGLISH		MIDDLE ENGLISH	
		Historical forms	Analogical forms
PRES. IND. SING. 1	mæᵹ	mai,	
2	meaht,[109]	meight, maught,	maist
	miht	might	
3	mæᵹ	mai,	
PLUR.	magon, mugon[110]	mawe(n), muwe(n)	
PRET. IND. SING. 1	meahte[109]	meighte, maughte,	mughte,
	mihte	mighte	moughte[111]
INFINITIVE	magan, mugan[110]	mawe(n), muwe(n)	
PRES. IND. SING. 1	mōt	mot	
2	mōst	most	
3	mōt	mot	
PLUR.	mōton	mote(n)	
PRET. IND. SING. 1	mōste	moste	
INFINITIVE	mōtan	mote(n)	
PRES. IND. SING. 1	sceal, scel, scæl[112]	shal, shel	
2	scealt, scelt, scælt[112]	shalt, shelt	
3	sceal, scel, scæl[112]	shal, shel	
PLUR.	sculon	shule(n)	
PRET. IND. SING. 1	scolde	sholde	shulde
INFINITIVE	sculan	shule(n)	
PRES. IND. SING. 1	wāt	wot	
2	wāst	wast	wost
3	wāt	wot	

[109] The forms **meaht** and **meahte**, which at one period were common to all the Old English dialects, developed later in the Kentish and West-Saxon dialects into **meht** and **mehte**, which were the basis of Middle English **meight** and **meighte**, and in the Mercian dialect into **mæht** and **mæht**, which were the basis of Middle English **maught** and **maughte**.

[110] The forms **mugon** and **mugan** are not recorded in Old English, but are inferred from the Middle English forms.

[111] Old English **mugan** and **mugon** became, according to 61. 4 above, Middle English [muːən], which was the basis of the analogical form [muːxtə], later [mʊxtə].

[112] The forms **sceal** and **scealt** were early West-Saxon; **scel** and **scelt** occurred in the Kentish dialect and in late West-Saxon; **scæl** occurred in the Mercian dialect.

OLD ENGLISH		MIDDLE ENGLISH	
		Historical forms	Analogical forms
PLUR.	witon	wite(n)	
PRET. IND. SING. 1	wiste	wiste, wuste	
INFINITIVE	witan	wite(n)	

102. Anomalous Verbs. As the term suggests, the anomalous verbs are those so irregular, confused, or strangely blended in conjugation that they defy classification with any of the recognized conjugational patterns. In both Old and Middle English the verbs **be, do, will,** and **go** are considered anomalous.

1. The historical development of the Middle English verb **bee(n)**, *be*, was as follows:

OLD ENGLISH			MIDDLE ENGLISH		
			Historical forms		Analogical forms
PRES. IND. SING. 1	eom	bēo	em	be	
	eam[113]		am		
2	eart	bist	art	bist	*beest*
3	is	biþ	is	biþ	*beeþ*
PLUR.	sindon	bēoþ	sinde(n)	beeþ	*biþ, bee(n)*[116]
	earon[114]		are(n)[115]		
PRES. SUBJ. SING.	sīe	bēo	si	be	
PLUR.	sīen	bēon	si(n)	bee(n)	
PRET. IND. SING. 1	wæs		wes, was		
2	WS. wǣre		Sth. were [wæːrə]		
	Merc. wēre		Mdl. were [weːrə]		
3	wæs		wes, was		
PLUR.	WS. wǣron		Sth. were(n) [wæːrən]		
	Merc. wēron		Mdl. were(n) [weːrən]		
PRET. SUBJ. SING.	WS. wǣre		Sth. were [wæːrə]		
	Merc. wēre		Mdl. were [weːrə]		
PLUR.	WS. wǣren		Sth. were(n) [wæːrən]		
	Merc. wēren		Mdl. were(n) [weːrən]		
PRES. IMP. SING. 2		bēo	be		
PLUR. 2		bēoþ	beeþ		
INFINITIVE		bēon	bee(n)		

[113] **eam** is the Mercian form, **eom** the West-Saxon.
[114] **earon** is the Mercian form; **sindon** was used in all the Old English dialects.
[115] **are(n)** was not used in the Southern dialect, but only in the Midland and North.
[116] **bee(n)** and **do(n)** are Midland forms; they were not used in the South.

2. The historical development of the Middle English verbs **do(n)**, *do*, **ga(n)**, *go*, and **wille(n)**, *will*, in the indicative was as follows:

		OLD ENGLISH	MIDDLE ENGLISH	
			Historical forms	Analogical forms
PRES. IND. SING.	1	**dō**	**do**	
	2	**dēst**	**dest**	*dost*
	3	**dēþ**	**deþ**	*doþ*
PLUR.		**dōþ**	**doþ**	*do(n)*[116]
PRET. IND. SING.	1	**dyde**	**dide, dude [dydə]**	
	2	**dydest**	**didest, dudest**	
	3	**dyde**	**dide, dude**	
PLUR.		**dydon**	**dide(n), dude(n)**	
PAST PARTICIPLE		**dōn**	**don**	

		OLD ENGLISH	MIDDLE ENGLISH	
			Historical forms	Analogical forms
PRES. IND. SING.	1	**ǥā**	**ǥo**	
	2	**ǥǣst**	**ǥest**	*ǥost*
	3	**ǥǣþ**	**ǥeþ**	*ǥoþ*
PLUR.		**ǥāþ**	**ǥoþ**	*ǥo(n)*
PRET. IND. SING.	1	**ēode**	**ʒede, ʒode**	*wente*[117]
	2	**ēodest**	**ʒedest, ʒodest**	*wentest*
	3	**ēode**	**ʒede, ʒode**	*wente*
PLUR.		**ēodon**	**ʒede(n), ʒode(n)**	*wente(n)*
PAST PARTICIPLE		**ǥān**	**ǥon, yǥon**	
PRES. IND. SING.	1	**wille**	**wille, wulle**	*wile, wule*
	2	**wilt**	**wilt, wult**	
	3	**wile**	**wile, wule**	*wille, wulle*
PLUR.		**willaþ**	**willeþ, wulleþ**	*wille(n), wulle(n)*[118]
PRET. IND. SING.	1	**wolde**	**wolde**	*wulde*
	2	**woldest**	**woldest**	*wuldest*
	3	**wolde**	**wolde**	*wulde*
PLUR.		**woldon**	**wolde(n)**	*wulde(n)*

[117] Strictly speaking **wente, wentest** are not analogical forms but rather outright borrowings from the Old English weak verb **wendan** which also meant 'to go.'

[118] **wille(n)** and **wulle(n)** are Midland forms.

CHAPTER VII

MIDDLE ENGLISH DIALECTS

103. The Nature of the Materials. Two major difficulties are encountered in any attempt to define the features of the Middle English dialects. The first lies in the nature of the materials. There are very few Middle English literary texts which have been preserved in definitely localized and dated manuscripts. Often the manuscripts which have been preserved are copies made by scribes who wrote and spoke a dialect different from that of the original author. Naturally such manuscripts are likely to represent a mixture in which the regional features of the language of composition cannot easily be isolated from those of the final—and in some cases, intermediate—transmission.

As a consequence investigators of the dialects of Middle English have come more and more to depend upon such materials as wills, inventories, court records, etc. (*i.e.* documents rather than literature), for evidence of dialect characteristics. Unfortunately such documentary evidence exists in quantity only after the middle of the fourteenth century; it is later than much of the literature. Therefore, if it is assumed that the areas of concentration of regional features of language may shift over a period of time, the boundaries of certain features of speech as they occur in the late fourteenth and early fifteenth century documents may not always be applicable to earlier Middle English, where dependable dialect information might be extremely useful in furnishing clues to the history of certain literary texts.

Second, the student of Middle English dialects must always reckon with the encroachment of features of the south-east Midland dialect, and of the London area in particular, which was already beginning to assert itself as the accepted standard of the English language throughout the island. Because of this, much writing of the period shows a tendency to display forms characteristic of the London standard, even when such forms do not represent the actual speech of the author. He may have pronounced a word in the Gloucestershire manner even though he spelled it according to the London fashion. Moreover, many speakers in the north, southeast, and west of England often *partially* adopted certain features of London speech. That is to say, they may at times have consciously employed a London pronunciation or a London inflectional form in a word, but a moment later, when using the same or a similar word, they would often lapse unconsciously into the regional form which was habitual to them. In other words, London was a focal area from which there was cultural spreading of many language features.

104. The Middle English Dictionary Study of Dialect. Because of these considerations the necessity of a fresh examination of the whole question of Middle English dialects impressed itself upon Samuel Moore almost immediately after he took over the editorship of the Middle English Dictionary in 1930. This was the first task that he set for himself and his two associates, Sanford B. Meech and Harold Whitehall. The result of their examination of 266 documents and 43 literary texts, all furnishing some nonlinguistic evidence of the time and place of composition[119] appeared under the title, "Middle English Dialect Characteristics and Dialect Boundaries," in Volume XIII of the University of Michigan series *Essays and Studies in English and Comparative Literature.*[120]

Since the conclusions which Professor Moore reached in this study represent a considerable advance both in content and in method over his treatment of the Middle English dialects even in his latest edition of the *Historical Outlines*, the reviser has undertaken to alter this section of the book quite radically and to present the Middle English dialects in the light of Professor Moore's last important investigation in this field. He died before the article cited above had appeared in published form.

105. Middle English Dialect Areas. The major dialect areas which emerged as a result of this investigation are shown in the accompanying map. It is apparent that these principal Middle English dialects correspond in a general way to the four chief dialects of Old English. The area which is called Southern, although Southwestern might be a more appropriate term for it, occupies much the same territory as the West Saxon dialect of Old English and developed out of it. (Compare the map of Old English dialects on p. 26.) The Kentish dialect of Old English became Kentish Middle English, with but little change in territorial boundaries. This, too, might be more appropriately termed Southeastern, were it not for the force of tradition. Northern Middle English, a development of the Northumbrian dialect of Old English, is the region north of the Humber, the Ribble, and the Lune. Mercian Old English, the dialect of central

---

[119] Evidence of time and place of composition must be non-linguistic to avoid circularity of reasoning.

[120] University of Michigan Press, Ann Arbor, 1935, pp. 1–60.

MIDDLE ENGLISH DIALECT AREAS

England, is generally designated as Midland for the Middle English period. Here it is convenient to recognize a number of sub-areas. West and East Midland differ from each other in several important respects, and the East Midland area may again be divided into a northern and a southern part.

106. Criteria of Middle English Dialects. The dialect boundaries shown on the accompanying map are labelled with letters ranging from **A** to **J.** These letters represent the principal features of Middle English which Professors Moore, Meech, and Whitehall, upon the basis of their examination of definitely localized texts, came to accept as satisfactory dialect criteria. The dialect characteristics established by means of this investigation are as follows:

1. Line **A** represents the southern limit of Old English **ā** retained as an unround vowel, spelled **a, ai, ay,** as in **mar** 'more,' **baith** 'both,' **hayl** 'whole.'[121] The characterization of this line as the southern limit means that unrounded forms are not found to occur south of this line, although rounded forms, spelled **o** or **oo** might be found north of it. Such rounded forms were, of course, a feature of the emerging standard form of English and had spread from London and central England as a focal point well beyond the southern limit of the **a** forms. This illustrates a cardinal point in the procedure of determining these dialect boundaries: the lines (isoglosses or isophones, as they are sometimes called) represent always the farthest extension of the regressive or non-standard characteristic. In the dialect map, Line **A** constitutes the boundary of the Northern dialect of Middle English.

2. Line **B** represents the southern limit of -(**e**)**s** as the present indicative plural inflection. In general the Midland inflection for this form of the verb, which ultimately became that of Standard English also, was -(**e**)**n** or -**e.** The extension of the -**s** type of inflection to the present plural was a feature of the North and extreme northern Midland. Lines **A** and **B** coincide for a short distance in northwestern England; then line **B** swings slightly to the south, cutting the Northeast Midland area just about in half.

3. Line **C** represents the southern limit of **sal** and **sulde** or **solde** for

[121] In determining this line, words in which **ā** developed in late Old English from earlier **a** through lengthening before a homorganic consonant group (e.g. **lāmb, lāng, lānd, āld;** see also Section 27.8) and those in which OE **ā** was followed by **w,** with which it coalesced in Middle English to form a diphthong (e.g. **cnāwan;** see also Section 58.1) were disregarded.

standard English *shall* and *should*. Like **B,** this line coincides with **A** for a short distance. Then it proceeds southward down the center of England until it is approximately opposite The Wash, at which point it turns to the east. While proceeding southward this line is part of a composite boundary separating West from East Midland; in its final eastward course it is the boundary of one of several features distinguishing Northeast from Southeast Midland.

4. Line **D** represents the eastern and southern limits of the rounding of Old English **a** before nasals, indicated in Middle as in Old English by **o** spellings, as in **mon, nome, ronk.** Excluded as valid evidence in this category, however, would be such words as OE **lang, land,** or **camb,** where the homorganic consonant group following the vowel would have produced Late OE **ā** (see Section **27.**8), which would have become ME [ɔː], spelled **o, oo,** even in areas where unrounding before nasals was prevalent. However, words like OE **nama** (**noma**) are admissible as evidence because in them the lengthening in open syllables (see Section **55**) took place after the development of OE [ɑː] to ME [ɔː]. In determining this line the words *thank* and *many* were also disregarded because of irregularities of behavior. This boundary, identical with **C** and **E** in the north and with **F** in central England, sets off the West Midland from the other dialect areas.

5. Line **E** represents the northern limit of the **h** forms of the object pronouns in the plural—**hem, ham, hom** for **them.** Although **hem** was still the more frequent form in the written English of London in the fifteenth century, **them,** moving down from the north, was already a powerful intruder, foretelling its ultimate establishment as the standard form. Lines **C** and **E** are virtually identical, first dividing East and West Midland, and after their shift to the east, serving to distinguish Northeast from Southeast Midland.

6. Line **F** indicates the eastern and northern limit of ME [ʏ] and [y], spelled **u, ui,** as in **hull** 'hill,' **fuir** 'fire,' and [œ], [œː], spelled **u, ue, eo,** or **o,** as in **huerte** 'heart,' **preost, prust** 'priest.' The sources of ME [ʏ], [yː] were Old English **y, ȳ** respectively, which had developed as the **i**-umlaut of WGmc **u, ū,** but which had generally unrounded in the eastern dialects (see Sections **27.**12, **52**). In determining this line, words in which original Old English [ɪ], [iː] became [ʏ], [yː] in late Old English were ignored. The sources for Middle English [œ], [œː] within the area encompassed by line **F** were OE **eo, ēo,** which generally developed into [ɛ] and [eː] in the eastern part of England (see Section **52** and footnote 64). Line **F** begins in the Northwest Midland area, runs slantwise toward the center of England,

joins **D** for a short distance in separating the East and West Midland areas, then continues southward to the English Channel, separating East Midland and Kentish from Southern.

7. Line **G** constitutes the southern limit for the -(e)s inflection in the third person singular, present indicative of verbs. Although this inflection was destined to become established as the regular inflectional form in Standard English, it had not yet attained such status in the Southeast Midland dialect as employed by Chaucer and his contemporaries, but as Moore suggests, it may often have been pronounced when -eth was written. Line **G** moves from west to east, bisecting the West Midland area, and then with lines **C** and **E** serving to separate Northeast from Southeast Midland.

8. Line **H** represents the northern limit of the -eth inflection in the present indicative plural. As already stated with reference to Line **B,** the Midland -e(n), -e was strongly intrusive, crowding the -(e)s inflections northward, and pushing downward into the territory of the -eth inflections, which were derived from the form which was standard during the Old English period. So powerful had this drive become, that in eastern England the Thames constituted the northern boundary of the -eth inflection, although in the west the line projects a considerable distance into West Midland territory. In the east, however, line **H** serves to divide the Kentish from the Southeast Midland dialect.

9. Line **I** indicates the northern limit of initial v for Old English initial **f.** Presumably all three of the Old English voiceless fricatives became voiced, when initial, in the southern part of England quite early in the Middle English period. The reluctance of many scribes to use the letter **z,** and the impossibility of determining vocal quality in the various spellings of the interdentals [θ] and [ð] at this period, leave the alternation between **f** and **v** as the only feasible criterion of this change. In the east of England, lines **I** and **H** are virtually identical, but in the west, line **I** does not reach quite as far to the north as **H.**

10. Line **J** marks the northern limit of the reflexes of the West Saxon umlauts of Old English **ea** and **ēa** and of the diphthongization of **e** after initial palatals. The i-umlauts of **ea** and **ēa** were **ie** and **īe** in early West Saxon, which in late West Saxon developed into **i** or **y** and **ī** and **ȳ**; in the other dialects of Old English the umlauts of these sounds were **e** and **ē.** Likewise early OE **e** preceded by **ġ, c,** or **sc** became **ie** in early West Saxon, which in late West Saxon developed into **i** or **y**; in the other dialects of OE, however, original **e** was not changed by a preceding **c, ġ,** or **sc.**

Middle English forms that developed out of the late West Saxon forms of these words would have [ɪ] or [ʏ] spelled **i** or **u** from late West Saxon **y**, and [iː] or [ʏː] spelled **i, u,** or **ue,** from late West Saxon **ȳ**; whereas Middle English forms that developed out of the non-West Saxon forms would have [ɛ] or [eː], spelled **e** in such words. Early West Saxon **dierne** 'dern' and **hīeran** 'hear,' which became late West Saxon **dyrne** or **dirne** and **hȳran** or **hīran,** would become Middle English **durne** or **dirne** and **huren** or **hiren,** whereas non-West Saxon **derne** and **hēran** would become ME **derne** and **heren.** Likewise early West Saxon **ȝielpan** 'yelp,' which became late West Saxon **ȝylpan** or **ȝilpan** would become ME **yulpen** or **yilpen** whereas non-West Saxon **ȝelpan** would become ME **yelpen.**

The evidence on this point is meager and affords only a fragmentary line, but one which performs the function of distinguishing West Midland from Southern.

SUMMARY

The characteristic forms of the various dialects as indicated by the criteria enumerated in the preceding section may be summarized in the following table:[122]

Feature	Line	Northern	N. E. Midland
OE ā	A	[ɑː]	[ɔː]
OE a before nasals	D	[ɑ]	[ɑ]
OE ȳ, y, ēo, eo	F	[iː, ɪ, eː, ɛ]	[iː, ɪ, eː, ɛ]
i-umlaut of ēa, ea; diphthongization of e by initial ȝ, c, sc	J	[eː, ɛ]	[eː, ɛ]
Initial **f**	I	[f]	[f]
sal, shal, etc.	C	[s]	[s]
3d plural pers. pron.	E	**them**	**them**
3d sg. present indic.	G	**-es**	**-es**
3d pl. present indic.	B, H	**-es**	**-es, -e(n)**

107. Additional Dialect Features. In addition to the ten dialect characteristics, the distribution of which was sufficiently clear-cut, in the materials examined by Professor Moore and his associates, to warrant their inclusion among the criteria represented on their map, there are certain others which are of sufficient interest and importance to be included in any presentation of this subject. These will be referred to henceforth as auxiliary dialect features.

Why these auxiliary features should not have had so neat a distribution as the principal dialect characteristics may be variously explained. In some instances they simply did not occur in sufficient numbers in the materials examined, although they are to be found more often in less satisfactorily localized texts. Others are relatively earlier in date than the materials employed by Professor Moore, and by the late fourteenth and early fifteenth centuries, they had already been replaced by the intrusive

[122] It should be remembered, however, that since the isoglosses on the map of the Middle English dialects represent the farthest extension of recessive features, in certain instances forms other than those given in the boxed squares of the table *may* occur.

[123] See Section 109.5 below.

S. E. Midland	West Midland	Southern	Kentish
[ɔː]	[ɔː]	[ɔː]	[ɔː]
[ɑ]	[ɔ]	[ɑ]	[ɑ]
[iː, ɪ, eː, ɛ]	[yː, ʏ, œː, œ]	[yː, ʏ, œː, œ]	[iː, ɪ,[123] eː, ɛ]
[eː, ɛ]	[eː, ɛ]	[yː, iː, ʏ, ɪ]	[eː, ɛ]
[f]	[f, v]	[v]	[v]
[ʃ]	[ʃ]	[ʃ]	[ʃ]
hem	hem	hem	hem
-eth	-es, -eth	-eth	-eth
-e(n)	-e(n), -eth	-eth	-eth

forms of the developing standard language. Still others can be accounted for by the fact that though they do give general evidence of regional distribution, such distribution was sufficiently clear cut to justify inclusion among the principal characteristics of any one area.

108.   Auxiliary Characteristics of the Southern Dialect.

1. WS ǣ from West Germanic ā developed into Southern ME [æː], but Mercian ē from West Germanic ā developed into Midland ME [eː]. WS **dǣd,** Southern ME **deed** [dæːd]; WS **bǣron,** Southern ME **bere(n)** [bæːrən]; Mercian OE **dēd** [deːd], Midland ME **deed** [deːd]; Mercian OE **bēron,** Midland ME **bere(n)** [beːrən].

See Section **27.1.** In general these two sounds are not distinguishable in Middle English solely in terms of spelling

2. WS **ea** that developed out of æ followed by **ld** developed when lengthened (according to Section **27.**8) into **ēa** which became Southern ME [æː], but the Mercian **a** that developed out of æ followed by **ld** was lengthened to ā and developed into Midland ME [ɔː]. EWS **eald,** LWS **ēald,** Southern ME **eld** [æːld]; EWS **healdan,** LWS **hēaldan,** Southern Me **helde(n)** [hæːldən]; Mercian OE **ald,** later **āld,** Midland ME **old** [ɔːld]; Mercian OE **haldan,** later **hāldan,** Midland ME **holde(n)** [hɔːldən].

3. The diphthong [æɪ] (see Section **56** above) had a source in the Southern dialect which did not exist in the Midland dialect, namely West-Saxon ǣ followed by the [ɣ] sound that developed in Middle English into [j]; e.g., WS **lǣġon,** Southern ME **leie(n)** [læɪən]. The corresponding development in the Midland dialect was **lie(n)** [liːən] from Mercian OE **lēġon** (with ē for WS ǣ according to 1 in Section **27** above).

4. The results of the Mercian and Northumbrian smoothing (see Section **27.**9) were for the most part obliterated by later developments that occurred either in OE or in ME. The most conspicuous trace of this OE dialect characteristic that remains in ME is that EWS **ea** followed by **h** became LWS **e,** according to Section **27.**9, b, and then developed according to Section **56.**3 above into Southern ME [æɪ], whereas the Mercian æ which came from earlier **ea** followed by **h** developed according to Section **59.**3 into Midland ME [ɑu]: EWS **feaht,** LWS **feht,** South-

ern ME **feight** [fæɪxt]; Mercian **feaht,** later **fæht,** Midland ME **faught** [fɑuxt].

5. Final **e** was retained in pronunciation throughout the fourteenth century.

6. The historical forms of the noun declensions (see Section **71** ff. above) were displaced only slowly by analogical forms. Genitive and dative singulars in **e,** nominative, genitive, and accusative plurals in **e,** dative plurals in **e(n),** etc., are common in texts of the thirteenth century and occur occasionally in texts of the fourteenth century. The distinctions of grammatical gender were maintained with a considerable degree of consistency throughout the first half of the thirteenth century, and relics of grammatical gender are found even in texts of the first half of the fourteenth century.

7. The historical forms of the genitive, dative, and accusative in the strong adjective declension (see Section **85** ff. above) were displaced only slowly by analogical forms; the historical forms occur frequently in texts of the first half of the thirteenth century.

8. The historical forms of the genitive, dative, and accusative of the definite article and demonstrative **þe (se),** **þeo (seo),** **þat**[124] (see Section **93** above) were displaced only slowly by analogical forms; historical forms are common in the first half of the thirteenth century and occasional until at least the end of that century.

9. The historical forms of the accusative of the third personal pronoun (see Section **92** above) were not wholly displaced by analogical forms until the second half of the thirteenth century.

10. The pronouns **ha, a** (*he, she, they, them*), **hare** (*her, their*), and **ham** (*them*) were in frequent use.

11. Weak verbs like **erien** and **luvien** (see Section **96** above) preserved their historical endings, **-ie, -ieþ, -ie(n),** etc., throughout the thirteenth century with little substitution of analogical forms.

12. The ending of the present participle of strong verbs was **-inde,** later **-inge;** the ending of the present participle of weak verbs was **-inde,** later **-inge,** or **-iinde,** later **-inge.**

---

[124] In the Southern dialect **þat** is used as the definite article as well as the demonstrative; in the Midland and Northern dialects **þat** is used only as the demonstrative.

109. Auxiliary Characteristics of the Kentish Dialect. The auxiliary features by virtue of which Kentish differs from the Southern dialect on the one hand and from the Midland dialects on the other are set forth here. In this connection it should be borne in mind that the counties of Sussex and Surrey are included within the Kentish dialect area.

1. WS ǣ from West Germanic ā developed into Southern ME [æ:], but Kentish ē from West Germanic ā developed into Kentish ME [eː]; WS dǣd, Southern ME deed [dæːd]; WS bǣron, Southern ME bere(n) [bæːrən]; Kentish OE dēd [deːd], Kentish ME deed [deːd]; Kentish OE bēron, Kentish ME bere(n) [beːrən].

2. Kentish Old English e from earlier æ (<WGmc a) developed into Middle English [ɛ], but East Mercian Old English æ developed into East Midland a; e. g. Kentish OE gled, weter, Kentish ME gled, weter; East Mercian OE glæd, wæter, East Midland ME glad, water. So also Kentish Old English e from earlier æ followed by ġ developed into Middle English ei, but the corresponding East Mercian æ followed by ġ developed into East Midland ai; e.g. Kentish OE deġ, Kentish ME dei; East Mercian OE dæġ, East Midland ME dai.

3. Kentish Old English [eː] which resulted from the i-umlaut of ā (<WGmc ai) became Middle English [eː], but in the other dialects the ǣ which resulted from this umlaut became [æː]: Kentish OE dēl, Kentish ME deel [deːl]; West Saxon, Mercian, and Northumbrian OE dǣl, Southern Midland, and Northern ME deel [dæːl].

4. Kentish Middle English [eː] preceded by h or cl developed into a diphthong written ie or ye, which is believed to have been originally a rising diphthong but to have developed later into a falling diphthong. Kentish OE hēr, Kentish ME hier or hyer; Kentish OE clēne, Mercian, West-Saxon clǣne, Kentish ME cliene.

5. Kentish e and ē which resulted from the i-umlaut of u and ū became Middle English [ɛ] and [eː]: Kentish OE gelt, fēr, Kentish ME gelt, ver. Surprisingly enough the evidence on this point in the materials examined by Professor Moore was not sufficiently clear to warrant its inclusion on the map.

6. Kentish Old English ēa did not become [æː] but developed into a sound written ea, ia, ya, yea, and (sometimes) a or e. This sound is believed to have been a diphthong approximating

[ea] whose two elements originally had equal stress. Later this diphthong is believed to have developed into either a rising or a falling diphthong. The former development led to [jɑ] and sometimes eventually to [ɑɪ]; the latter to [eə] and sometimes eventually to [eɪ]. Kentish OE ḡrēat, Kentish ME great, gṛiat, grat; Kentish OE lēaf, Kentish ME leaf, lyaf, lyeaf; Kentish OE strēam, Kentish ME stream, strem.

a. Kentish ea which developed out of æ followed by ld developed when lengthened according to Section 27.8 into late Kentish ēa, which underwent the usual Kentish development in Middle English: Kentish OE eald, later ēald, Kentish ME eald, iald, yeald, ald; Mercian OE ald, later āld, Midland ME old [ɔːld].

b. Kentish Old English ēa followed by w developed into [ɛʊ] or [eʊ] if the diphthong which developed from the ēa was a falling diphthong, but into [eɑu] or [jɑu] if it was a rising diphthong; e.g., Kentish OE fēawe, Kentish ME vewe or veawe. The corresponding Midland development was [ɛʊ].

7. Kentish Old English īo developed into a sound written ie, ye, i, y, and e. This sound is believed to have been a diphthong approximating [ie] whose two elements originally had equal stress. Later this diphthong is believed to have developed into either a rising or a falling diphthong. The former development led to [je] and sometimes eventually to [eɪ]; the latter to [iə] and sometimes (especially when final) to [iː]. Kentish OE diore, Kentish ME diere, dyere; Kentish OE bīon, Kentish ME bie, bi, by; Kentish OE clīofan, Kentish ME cleve(n).

a. Early Kentish Old English ēo became late Kentish īo which underwent the usual Kentish development in Middle English, but Mercian Old English ēo developed into Midland Middle English [eɪ]; e.g. late Kentish OE dīop (from earlier dēop) Kentish ME diep, dyep; Mercian OE dēop, Midland ME deep, [deːp].

b. Kentish Old English īo followed by the [j] sound that developed in Middle English out of Old English [ɣ] underwent the normal Kentish development of īo. OE līogan, Kentish ME lieʒe(n).

8. The differences that resulted from the Mercian (and Northumbrian) smoothing were for the most part obliterated by later developments in Old English or in Middle English; the most

conspicuous trace in Middle English of this difference between Kentish and Mercian Old English is that late Kentish **eh** from earlier **eah** (according to Section **27.**9c) developed into Middle English **ei**, whereas Mercian **æh** from earlier **eah** developed into Middle English **au**: late Kentish **feht** (from earlier **feaht**), Kentish ME **feight**; Mercian OE **fæht** (from earlier **feaht**), Midland ME **faught.**

9. Kentish Middle English [oɪ] and [ɔɪ] preceded by **g** or **b** developed into a diphthong which is believed to have been originally a rising diphthong but to have developed later into a falling diphthong. Kentish OE **gōd,** Kentish ME **guod;** Kentish OE **bān,** Kentish ME **buon.**

10. Final **e.** As in the Southern dialect see Section **108.**5 above.

11. Consonant Sounds. As in the Southern dialect, Section **108.**6 above.

12. The morphology of the Kentish dialect was like that of the Southern dialect except that the historical forms of the noun declensions, of the strong adjective declension, of the definite article and demonstrative, of the accusative of the third personal pronoun, and of weak verbs like **erie(n)** and **luvie(n)** were displaced by analogical forms even more slowly in the Kentish than in the Southern dialect. The morphology of the *Ayenbite of Inwit*, written in Canterbury in 1340, is more conservative than Southern texts written at least seventy-five years earlier.

110. The Midland Dialect. The most important characteristics of the Midland dialect are the following:

1. Vowel Sounds. The normal development and the special developments of the Mercian Old English vowel sounds in the East Midland dialect of Middle English have been given above in Sections **52-61.** The following points deserve special mention:

a. The development of West Germanic **ā** in Midland Middle English corresponds to the development that took place in Mercian Old English, as stated above in Section **27.**1, Mercian **ē** becoming Middle English [eɪ] in the western and northeastern portions of the Midland territory and southeast Mercian **æ** becoming Middle English [æɪ] in the southeast; e.g. Mercian OE **dēd, bēron,** West and Northeast Midland ME **deed** [deɪd], **bere(n)** [beɪrən]; southeast Mercian **dǣd, bǣron,** Southeast Midland ME **deed** [dæɪd], **bere(n)** [bæɪrən].

b. Southwest Mercian Old English **e** from earlier **æ** according to **27.**4 above developed into Southwest Midland Middle English [ε], but Northwest and East Mercian Old English **æ** developed into Northwest and East Midland Middle English [ɑ]: southwest Mercian OE **ġled, weter,** Southwest Midland ME **ġled, weter;** northwest and east Mercian OE **ġlæd, wæter,** Northwest and East Midland ME **ġlad, water.** So also southwest Mercian **e** from earlier **æ** followed by **ġ** developed into Southwest Midland Middle English [εɪ], but the corresponding northwest and east Mercian **æ** followed by **ġ** developed into Northwest and East Midland Middle English [ɑɪ]; e.g. southwest Mercian OE **deġ,** Southwest Midland ME **dei;** northwest and east Mercian OE **dæġ,** Northwest and East Midland ME **dai.**[125]

2. Final **e.** Final **e** was to a great extent retained in pronunciation throughout the fourteenth century, but apocope of final **e** began before the end of the thirteenth century.

3. The analogical changes that took place in the inflection of nouns (see **71** ff. above) and adjectives (see **85** ff.) were carried out before the end of the twelfth century.

4. The distinctions of grammatical gender were lost before the end of the twelfth century.

5. The historical forms of the genitive, dative, and accusative of the definite article and demonstrative **þe (sē), þeo (sēo), þat** (see Section **93** above) were displaced by analogical forms before the end of the twelfth century.

6. The historical forms of the accusative of the third personal pronoun (see Section **92** above) were displaced by dative forms before the end of the twelfth century.

7. An important morphological criterion for distinguishing between the East Midland and the West Midland dialects is that the feminine nominative singular pronoun **ho** is frequently used in West Midland texts but does not appear to be used in East Midland texts.

8. The ending of the present indicative plural of strong and weak verbs was **-e(n).** The Midland dialect used both **are(n)** and **been** or **be** as the present indicative plural of the verb **bee(n);** **are(n)** was characteristic of the northern part of the Midland territory.

[125] See Section **56.**1, and note 66.

9. The historical endings (ie, ie(n), etc.) of weak verbs like erien and luvien (see Section 96 above) were for the most part displaced by analogical forms before the end of the twelfth century.

10. The ending of the present participle of strong and weak verbs was -ende, later -inge or -ing. (The ending -and also occurs, especially in the North Midland.)

111. Auxiliary Characteristics of the Northern Dialect.

1. Although not included in the principal dialect features of Northern Middle English as listed in Section 106, the late Old English ā which developed before a homorganic consonant cluster (see Section 27.8) remained unchanged in the Northern dialect: Northumbrian and Mercian OE āld, Northern ME ald, Midland ME old; OE lānd, Northern ME land, East Midland ME lond.

2. [aʊ] developed instead of Midland and Southern [ɔːʊ]:

a. Out of Old English ā followed by w. OE cnāwan, Northern ME knaw(e) [knaʊə], Midland and Southern ME knowe(n) [knɔːʊən].

b. Out of Old English ā followed by [ɣ]; e.g. OE āgan, Northern ME aw(e) [aʊə], Midland and Southern ME owe(n) [ɔːʊən].

c. Out of Old English ā followed by h; e.g. OE āh, Northern ME augh [aʊx], Midland and Southern ME ough [ɔːʊx].

3. Before the end of the fourteenth century the diphthong which had developed out of early Middle English [aɪ] and [ɛɪ][126] lost its second element in part of the Northern territory (except when final) and became identical with [aː]; e.g. Northern ME vanys, Midland ME veines; Northern ME avale, Midland ME availe(n).

4. Northern Middle English [ɔː] developed, about the beginning of the fourteenth century, into a sound which is believed to have been similar to or identical with [yː] and which was represented at first by o or u and later by o, oi, u, or ui. OE stōd, early Northern ME stod [stoːd], later Northern ME stod, stud, stuid. This sound rimes with the u of French loan words that had [yɪ] in French.

5. Old English ō followed by ʒ underwent a similar development and became first [yu] and then [ɪu] instead of developing

126 See Section 56, and note 66.

into [uː] as in the Midland dialect according to Section **60.5** above. OE **bōgas;** Northern ME **bewes** [bɪuəs], Midland ME **bowes** [buːəs].

6. Final **e** and **e(n)**. Final **e** was entirely lost by the middle of the fourteenth century or even earlier. Final **n** of the ending **e(n)** was lost before the beginning of the fourteenth century, except in the past participles of strong verbs.

7. Old English **hw** was spelled in the North **qu.** OE **hwæt,** Northern ME **quat,** Southern and Midland ME **what, wat.** The sound represented by the **qu** was probably that of [x] followed by [w].

8. With regard to the displacement of historical forms by analogical forms in the inflection of nouns, adjectives, pronouns, and verbs, and with regard to the loss of grammatical gender, the Northern dialect was even less conservative than the Midland dialect.

9. Adjectives. With the loss of final **e** all inflection of the adjective was lost.

10. Pronouns. The plural of **þis** (*this*) is **þir** or **þer.**

11. The ending of the present indicative first person singular and of the present indicative plural of verbs was **-es** unless the subject of the verb was a personal pronoun which immediately preceded or followed the verb, in which case the verb was without ending or had the ending **-e.** The present indicative forms of the verb **find(e),** for example, were

	I		II
SING.	1 I find(e)	SING.	1 I that (i.e. *who*) findes
	2 thou findes		2 thou that findes
	3 he findes		3 he that findes
PLUR.	we, ye, they find(e)	PLUR.	we, ye, they that findes

a. The present indicative plural of the verb **bee(n)** was **are(n).**

b. The ending of the imperative plural was **-es.**

12. The preterit singular and preterit plural of strong verbs had the same vowel, the difference of ablaut which had existed in most of the strong verbs (see Section **98** above) being done away with by analogy; in most verbs the preterit plural took the vowel of the preterit singular. Thus, with the loss of the ending **-e(n)**, the preterit singular and the preterit plural be-

came identical in form; e.g., Northern **he sang, we sang,** Southern and Midland **he sang, we sunge(n).**

a. The ending of the past participle of strong verbs was **-en** (never **-e).**

13. The ending of the present participle was **-and(e).**

14. The preposition used with the gerund is either **to** or **at;** e.g. Midland ME **to singe(n),** Northern ME **to sing(e)** or **at sing(e).**

112. Specimens of the Middle English Dialects. Since most students are generally more familiar with East Midland than with the other dialects of Middle English, the following illustrative selections have been included. Each selection will be found to demonstrate some, but not all of the characteristics peculiar to the dialect it has been chosen to represent. All of the selections are from the early part of the fourteenth century.

I (Southern)

South English Legendary

Josep eode vrom Galilee,   out of þe cite
Þat is i-cleped Nazareth,   into þe lond of Jude,
To þe cite of Bedleem,   as king David was i-bore,
Vor he was of Daviþes hous   and of is meine i-core.
He wende with is wif i-spoused,   þat wiþ childe was.
So þat þe time was folfulled,   as God ȝaf þe cas,
Þat heo scholde hire child bere;   and hire furste sone heo ber
And biwond him in cloþes   and a-doun leide him þer
In a schupene, vor þer nas   non oþer stude þere,
Bote þulke þat men to-drowe   whan hei inles were.
And in þilke selve kinges lond   schepeherdes þer woke
Over heore bestes al þe niȝt   þat heo hedden to loke.
And lo! oure Lordes angel   bi hem stod bi niȝte,
And þe clernesse of oure Lord   a-bouten him al a-liȝte.
Þo douteden þe schepherdes   and in gret drede weren i-brouȝt.
Þo seide þe angel to hem: "Ne dredeþ ow riȝt nouȝt!
Vor lo! ic bringe ou tidinge   of grete joie and blis,
Þat schal beo to uch volk,   vor i-bore he is i-wis
To ow to-day, þe saveour,   þat Crist Lord is,
In þe cite of David;   and þe token to ow worþ þis:
Ȝe schulen finde þat ȝonge child   in cloþes i-wounde
And in a cracche iþleid."

II (Kentish)

William of Shoreham: The Five Joys of the Virgin Mary

Meche hys þat me syngeþ and redeþ
Of hyre þat al mankende gladeþ
   I-bore was here on erthe;
And þey alle speke, þat spekeþ wyd tonge,
Of hyre worschype, and murye sounge,
   Ʒet more he were worthe.

Þyse aungeles heryeþ here wyþ stevene,
Ase he hys hare quene of hevene
   And eke hare blysse;
Over al erþe levedy hys here,
And þorʒout helle geþ here power,
   Ase he hys emperysse.

Cause of alle þyse dignyte,
Þorʒ clennesse and hymylyte,
   Was Godes owene grace;
Werþorʒ he ber þan hevenekyng:
Worschype hys worþy in alle þyng,
   In evereche place.

Al þat hys bove and under molde,
Hou myʒt hyt bote hyt bowe scholde
   To hyre owene mede?
Wanne he þat al þys wordle schel welde
To hyre worschipe hys y-helde
   For here moderhede.

Al þyse maydenes, wyþout bost,
Hy bereþ God in here goste,
   In hare holy þouʒte;
Ac hy wyþoute mannes y-mone
In body, and nauʒt in gost al one,
   To manne hyne broute.

III (West Midland)

Song on the Execution of Sir Simon Fraser, 1306

Lystneþ, lordynges, a newe song ichulle bigynne
Of þe traytours of Scotlond þat take beþ wyþ gynne;
Mon þat loveþ falsnesse ant nule never blynne,
Sore may him drede þe lyf þat he is ynne,
  Ich understonde:
Selde wes he glad   þat never nes a-sad
  Of myþe ant of onde.

Þat y sugge by þis Scottes þat bueþ nou todrawe,
Þe hevedes o Londone-brugge whose con y-knawe:
He wenden han buen kynges, ant seiden so in sawe;
Betere hem were han y-be barouns ant libbe in Godes lawe
  Wiþ love.
Whose hateþ soþ ant ryht,   Lutel he douteþ Godes myht,
  Þe heye kyng a-bove.

To warny alle þe gentilmen þat bueþ in Scotlonde,
Þe Waleis wes todrawe, seþþe he was anhonge,
Al quic biheveded, ys boweles y-brend,
Þe heved to Londone-brugge wes send
  To a-byde.
After Simond Frysel,   þat wes traytour ant fykel
  And y-cud ful wyde.

IV (Northern)

Metrical Homilies

In Rom was, als fel auntour,
A wonder myghti emperour,
That hiht Cesar and Augustus,
Als our bibel telles us,
And in his tim ger he telle,
Als sais sayn Louc in our godspelle,
Of all this werld the cuntres
And of cuntres the cites
And al the men that was wonand

Bathe in borwis and apon land,
Sua that ilk man of eld
Suld cum til his boru and gif yeld
For him self and for his menye
And graunt that he suld buxum be,
Efter his miht in al thing,
Til Cesar, that of Rom was king;
And over al this werld thoru and thoru
Com men and wymmen til thair boru
To do the king comandement
For quasa did noht, he war schent.
And than was Josep Mari spouse,
For he havid broht hir than til house,
And forthi led he hir him with
Til Bedlehem i-mang his kith
To held thar that to thaim felle,
Als said to-day our first godspelle.

CHAPTER VIII

THE DEVELOPMENT OF MODERN ENGLISH SOUNDS

113. Relation of Middle English to Modern English. The term Middle English is a convenient way of speaking of a number of local dialects of English which were used during a period lasting roughly from about 1050 or 1100 to about 1450 or 1500. These local dialects, as may be seen from a study of Chapter VII of this book, differed greatly from each other both in sounds and grammatical forms.

The local dialects of Middle English were not merely spoken varieties of English, but each local dialect had its corresponding written form which was intended to represent the spoken forms of that dialect and which did represent the spoken forms of the dialect as accurately as the varying skill of the writers and the inadequacy of their alphabet permitted. And the written forms of these various local dialects were used not only for records and memoranda of merely local, temporary, or utilitarian value, but were also the media in which the literary works of the Middle English period were written until about 1450. Until after this date no one written form of English was used over the whole or even over the greater part of England, just as no one spoken form of English was used outside of its own particular region.

We find, however, that the written form of the literary works and documents composed in the Southern, Kentish, West Midland, and Northern regions after about 1450 (or even a little earlier) becomes increasingly less representative of the spoken forms of the regions in which these writings originated and approximates more and more closely to a common standard. By about 1500 this written form of English, which we may now call Standard Written English, had come into such general use that even informal writings such as private letters and family papers seldom contain linguistic evidence of their local origin. The written form of English which thus displaced the written forms of the other dialects was that which was used by those whose spoken language was the dialect of London.

The dialect of London appears to have been originally of a type which might be called Southeastern,[127] but between about 1250 and 1350

[127] See Section **105** above.

most of the more specifically Southeastern and Southern characteristics of the London dialect were displaced by the forms of the Southeast Midland dialect. Between about 1350 and 1500 the London dialect underwent further modification and approximated more closely at the end of the Middle English period to the Northeast Midland dialect type. And even after 1500 at least one change took place in the spoken English of London which assimilated it still more closely to the Northeast Midland dialect type, namely the substitution of -(e)s for -eth as the ending of the present indicative third person singular of verbs.[128]

Standard Written English did not retain throughout the sixteenth and seventeenth centuries the form which it had between 1450 and 1500 when the written form of the London dialect first became the standard written form of English, but underwent a development that reflected changes that were taking place during the sixteenth and early seventeenth centuries in the spoken English of London.

114. Standard Written English and Standard Spoken English.
The establishment of a standard written form of English must be distinguished from the establishment of a standard form of spoken English. After the written form of the London dialect had been accepted as Standard Written English, the other local dialects still continued to be spoken and their derivatives are still spoken by certain classes in England, Scotland, and Ireland today. The London type of spoken English must, however, have become very much more widely diffused among certain classes during the sixteenth and seventeenth centuries than it was at an earlier period, for all the types of spoken English now used throughout the English-speaking world except the local dialects of England, Scotland, and Ireland are derivable from sixteenth century or seventeenth century London English. At least none of these varieties of spoken English exhibits either in its sounds or its inflections characteristics that indicate derivation from any other local dialect than the dialect of London. But there is no one variety of spoken English that is common even to the educated classes throughout the English-speaking world. In England itself there are important differences between the speech of southern and northern Englishmen of the same degree of social acceptability and cultivation. And when we consider all the varieties of English spoken by those who are

---

[128] This change began in the latter part of the fifteenth century but was not completed until after 1500.

admitted to speak "good English" in the different British colonies and in different parts of the United States, we must recognise that there is still no Standard Spoken English in any strict sense of the term. In every part of the English-speaking world some type of spoken English, that which is used by those who carry on the affairs of the cómmunity, is considered "good English," as contrasted with the non-standard English and local dialects spoken by other classes of the community. If we use the term Standard Spoken English at all we must recognize that it is merely a convenient way of speaking of the various kinds of "good English" that are current in various parts of the English-speaking world.

115. The Great Vowel Shift. In Section **52,** which dealt with the normal development of Old English sounds into Middle English, it was pointed out that fewer than half of the Old English vowel sounds and diphthong combinations underwent any change at all. Moreover, the changes which did occur were limited for the most part to the unrounding of rounded vowels and the simplification of diphthongs.

The development of Middle English sounds into Modern English is a quite different story. During the period between 1400 and 1600, all but two of the twenty significantly distinctive vowel sounds and diphthongal combinations of Chaucer's time underwent some sort of alteration, often involving shifts in jaw height and tongue position. In fact, so radical was the change in the whole phonetic structure of English during this period that it is often spoken of as the Great Vowel Shift. The results of it are reflected even in the names we give to the vowel characters in the English alphabet. Only in English is the first letter of the alphabet called [e]; in virtually every other Western European language it is [ɑ]. English is the only language in which the fifth letter (e) is [i] instead of [e] and in which the ninth letter (i) is called [ɑɪ]. The extent of the changes in the Middle English vowels and diphthongs will be observed in the following table, which indicates their Modern English equivalents.

MIDDLE ENGLISH			MODERN ENGLISH		
[ɑː]	name	[nɑːmə]	[e][129]	name	[nem]
[ɑ]	crabbe	[krɑbʲə]	[æ]	crab	[kræb]
[æː]	cleene	[klæːnə]	[i][130]	clean	[klin]
[eː]	sweete	[sweːtə]	[i]	sweet	[swit]
[ɛ]	helpe(n)	[hɛlpə(n)]	[ɛ]	help	[hɛlp]
[iː]	ride(n)	[riːdə(n)]	[ɑɪ]	ride	[rɑɪd]
[ɪ]	drinke(n)	[drɪŋkə(n)]	[ɪ]	drink	[drɪŋk]
[oː]	fode	[foːdə]	[u]	food	[fud]
[ɔː]	stoon	[stɔːn]	[o]	stone	[ston]
[ɔ]	oxe	[ɔks]	[ɑ][131]	ox	[ɑks]
[uː]	hous	[huːs]	[ɑʊ]	house	[hɑʊs]
[ʊ]	sone	[sʊnə]	[ʌ]	son	[sʌn]
[ɑʊ]	faught	[fɑʊxt]	[ɔ]	fought	[fɔt]
[æɪ]	seil	[sæɪl]	[e]	sail	[sel]
[ɪu]	fewe, rude	[fɪuə, rɪudə]	[ɪu], [u][132]	few, rude	[fɪu, rud]
[ɔɪ]	boy	[bɔɪ]	[ɔɪ]	boy	[bɔɪ]
[ɔːʊ]	soule	[sɔːʊlə]	[o]	soul	[sol]
[ɔʊ]	thought	[θɔʊxt]	[ɔ]	thought	[θɔt]

A glance at certain of the developments in the above table will illustrate the appropriateness of the term "vowel shift." Observe, for example, that the Middle English low back vowel [ɔː] developed into mid back [o] in Modern English. But Middle English [oː] in turn developed into the Modern English high back rounded vowel [u]. In both of these instances the jaw position for the sound was elevated one notch or degree—the low vowel became mid; the mid was raised to a high. When we next turn our attention to the ME high back vowel [uː], we see that it has become the

[129] It should be recalled that the MnE vowels [e], [i], [o], and [u] usually tend to be diphthongs in actual pronunciation (see Section **17**), whereas the vowels of the Old and Middle English periods are considered to have been "pure," i.e. undiphthongized, in character. Note also that with the MnE vowels the use of [ː] to indicate length is not employed. This arises from the circumstance that in MnE there are no pairs of sounds alike in quality in which length or duration is phonemic, i.e., makes the difference between one word and another, as in ME *cote* [kɔt] 'cot' and *cote* [kɔːt], 'coat.'

[130] ME [æː] first became [e] in Early Modern English and later (between the sixteenth and the eighteenth centuries) developed into MnE [i].

[131] ME [ɔ], or a vowel much like it, has been preserved in the speech of England and along the Atlantic seaboard in this country, particularly in New England, but it has become [ɑ] in most parts of the United States. See Section **158** below.

[132] See Section **119** below.

diphthong [ɑʋ], with its first element now a low back vowel. The circle is completed by ME [ɑʋ], which has become Modern English [ɔ]. This series of changes may be diagrammatically illustrated as follows:

[huːs] > [hɑʋs]

[foːd] > [fʋd]

[stɔːn] > [ston]

[fɔt] ←————————[fɑʋxt]

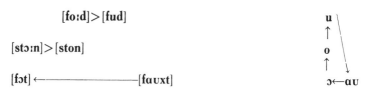

116. Shortening of Middle English Vowels. In the following instances certain of the sounds of Middle English did not develop according to the matter indicated in the table (Section **115**) because of considerations affecting their length.

1. Shortening of Middle English [æː].

Middle English [æː] became early Modern English [eː] and developed later into [iː], but before it became [iː] it was often shortened when it was followed by **d, t,** or [θ]. ME **deed** [dæːd], MnE [dɛd]; ME **swete(n)** [swæːtən], MnE [swɛt]; ME **deeth** [dæːθ], MnE [dɛθ].

2. Shortening of [uː] from Middle English [oː].

After Middle English [oː] had become [uː], the [uː] was in a great many words shortened when it was followed by **d, t,** or **k.** In some words the result of this shortening is [ʋ], but in others the [ʋ] has undergone the further change of [ʋ] to [ʌ]. ME **good** [goːd], MnE [gʋd]; ME **blood** [bloːd], MnE [blʌd]; ME **foot** [foːt], MnE [fʋt]; ME **book** [boːk], MnE [bʋk].

3. Another group of words which had early Modern English [uː], usually from Middle English [oː], shows a tendency to the shortening of [uː] to [ʋ] before **f, k, t, p, m,** and **n,** which was apparently of later date than the shortening mentioned in the preceding paragraph. This tendency has not been completely carried out, for the present pronunciation of these words both in England and in the United States varies between [uː] and [ʋ]. The most important words belonging to this group are: **roof, hoof; spook; hoop, cooper; root, soot; broom, room; soon, spoon.** Of these words **cooper** and **room** had early Modern English [uː] preserved before labial consonants according to **122** below.

117. Lengthening of Middle English Vowels.

1. Lengthening of [ɪ] before [x].

When [x] in the combination [xt] was lost, a preceding [ɪ] was lengthened to [iː] and was afterwards changed to [ɑɪ]. ME **right** [rɪxt], MnE [rɑɪt].

2. Middle English [a] became [æ] in early Modern English. In Northern British English and the speech of the greater part of the United States this sound has remained unchanged except for those situations dealt with in Sections **121-22.** In southern British English and in the speech of southern New England and eastern Virginia the [æ] was lengthened to [æː] and then retracted to [ɑː] when followed by the voiceless fricatives [f, θ, s] and the nasal combinations [mp, nt, nd, sn, ntʃ]. General American [kæf, tʃæf, æftɚ, pæθ, glæs, klæsp, pæst, æsk, ɛgzæmpl, tʃænt, kəmænd, dæns, bræntʃ]; Southern British and eastern seaboard American English [kɑːf, tʃɑːf, ɑːftɚ, pɑːθ, glɑːs, klɑːsp, pɑːst, ɑːsk, ɛgzɑːmpl, tʃɑːnt, kəmɑːnd, dɑːns, brɑːntʃ].

118. The Development of Middle English [ɔ]. It was pointed out in note 130 above that whereas ME [ɔ] has for the most part remained unchanged in British English, it has generally unrounded to [ɑ] in the United States. This observation, however, does not apply in every instance. Before the voiceless fricatives [f, θ, s] rounding has generally persisted in American English as well: ME **of** [ɔf], MnE [ɔf]; ME **motthe** [mɔθːə], MnE [mɔθ]; ME **los** [lɔs], MnE [lɔs].

Before **r** the rounded vowel has been regularly retained in monosyllables, although there is in the United States some variation in plurisyllables: ME **hors** [hɔrs], MnE [hɔɚs], ME **north** [nɔrθ], MnE [nɔɚθ], ME **forke** [fɔrk], MnE [fɔɚk]. Observe however American English **foreign** [fɔrən, fɑrən], **sorrow** [sɔro, sɑro].

In American English also similar variations in rounding occur before the stops [d, g, k]: ME **God** [gɔd], American English [gɔd, gɑd]; ME **frogge** [frɔgːə], American English [frɔg, frɑg]; ME **mokke(n)** [mɔkːə(n)], American English [mɔk, mɑk].

119. The Development of Middle English [ɪu]. ME [ɪu] remained a diphthong when it was preceded by a labial or labiodental consonant. ME **beauty** [bɪutɪ], MnE [bɪutɪ]; ME **puwe, pewe** [pɪuə], MnE [pɪu]; ME **fewe** [fɪuə], MnE [fɪu]; ME **vewe** [vɪuə], MnE [vɪu].

In initial position and after [h] and [k] the sound has developed into

Modern English [ju]: ME **use** [ɪus], MnE [jus]; ME **humour** [ɪumuːr], MnE [hjumɚ]; ME **cure** [kɪurə], MnE [kjuɚ].

After **r**, Middle English [ɪu] has regularly become [u]: ME **rude** [ɪudə], MnE [rud]; ME **rule** [ɪulə], MnE [rul].

After the alveolar consonants **n, l, d, t,** and **s,** present-day pronunciation varies between [ɪu] and [u], the latter being relatively more prevalent in American than in British English. ME **newe** [nɪuə], MnE [nɪu, nu]; ME **blew** [blɪu], MnE [blu, blɪu]; ME **due** [dɪuə], MnE [dɪu, du]; ME **Tuesday** [tɪuəsdæɪ], MnE [tɪuzdɪ, tuzdɪ]; ME **Susanne** [sɪuzanːə], MnE [suzən, sɪuzən]. The pronunciation [ju] may also occur as a variant in any of these words. See also Section 124.3 c.

120.   Special Developments Before r.

1. Middle English [ɛ] followed by **r** often changed to [æ] in very early Modern English and later developed into [ɑ]: ME **sterve(n)** [stɛrve(n)], early MnE [stærv], MnE [stɑɚv]. Middle English [ɑ] followed by **r** remained [ɑ] in Modern English: ME **hard** [hɑrd], MnE [hɑɚd].

2. Middle English [ɪr] and [ʊr] have regularly, and Middle English [ɛr] has frequently, become [ɝ] in Modern English: ME **first** [fɪrst], MnE [fɝst]; ME **curse(n)** [kʊrsə(n)], MnE [kɝs]; ME **lerned** [lɛrnəd], MnE [lɝnəd].

3. Middle English [æɪ] has sometimes become [æɪ] in Modern English and sometimes [ɛ]. Often the same word will vary considerably in pronunciation, particularly in the United States. ME **bere(n)** [bæːrə(n)], MnE [bæɪɚ, bɛɚ]. Middle English [ɑɪ] and [æɪ] have also become Modern English [æɪ] or [ɛ]: ME **spare(n)** [spɑɪrə(n)], MnE [spæɪɚ, spɛɚ]; ME **fair** [fæɪr], MnE [fæɪɚ, fɛɚ]. See note 9 above.

4. The Modern English development of Middle English [ɔɪ] and [oɪ] followed by **r** is a vowel which varies between [ɔɪ] and [oɪ]: ME **more** [mɔɪrə], MnE [mɔɚ, moɚ]; ME **swor** [swoːr], MnE [swɔɚ, swoɚ].

5. Early Modern English [iː], [uː], and [ɪu] followed by **r** were usually replaced by [ɪ], [ʊ], and [ɪʊ]. MnE [hɪɚ], [pʊɚ], [pɪʊɚ].

6. Middle English [ɑ], [ɛ], [ɪ], and [ʊ] often developed normally (i.e. followed the regular patterns of development as shown in the chart in Section 115) in words in which the **r** is still followed by another vowel in Modern English: ME **carie(n)** [kɑrːə(n)], MnE [kærɪ]; ME **very** [vɛrɪ], MnE [vɛrɪ]; ME **sirop** [sɪrɔp], MnE [sɪrəp]; MnE **corage** [kʊradʒə], MnE [kʌrɪdʒ] in some dialects. But in some varieties of English the special development of ME [ɛ], [ɪ], and [ʊ] has occurred even in these words, re-

sulting in [vɜ·rɪ], [sɜ·rəp], and the usual American form [kɜ·rɪdʒ]. In this connection see also the treatment of [ɔ] before r in Section 118.

These special developments of vowels before r have been stated in terms of their results in the speech of those who pronounce a retroflex r before consonants as well as before vowels (see notes 12 and 15 above). In the speech of those who do not pronounce r when it is followed by a consonant, the same vowels have developed except that [ɝ] is replaced in some varieties of English by [ɜ], and that there is a tendency to the development of a glide [ə] sound after the vowel, or to compensatory lengthening, resulting in [ɑə], [ɑː], [ɛə], etc. The words used above to illustrate the development of vowels before r would therefore be transcribed as follows by those who pronounce r only before vowels: [stɑːv] or [stɑəv], [hɑːd] or [hɑəd], [fɜst], [kɜs], [lɜnəd], [spæə] or [spɛə], [fæə] or [fɛə], [bæː] or [bɛə], [hɪː] or [hɪə], [pʊː] or [pʊə], [pɪuː] or [pɪuə], [pɔːt] or [pɔət], [mɔɪ] or [mɔə], [swɔː] or [swɔə].

121. Special Developments before l.

1. Middle English [a] followed by l plus another consonant or final l did not become [æ] but was diphthongised to [ɑu] in early Modern English. This diphthong then developed, like Middle English [ɑu], into [ɔɪ]; ME **smal** [smal], early MnE [smɑul], MnE [smɔl]; ME **talke(n)** [talkə(n)], early MnE [tɑulk], MnE [tɔk].[133]

2. Middle English [ɔ] followed by l was diphthongized to [ɔːu] in early Modern English; this diphthong then developed, like Middle English [ɔːu], into Modern English [o]: ME **folk** [fɔlk], early MnE [fɔːulk], MnE [fok].

122. The Influences of Labial Sounds.

1. Special developments after [w].

When preceded by w Middle English [a] did not become [æ] but developed in the seventeenth century into [ɔ]. In British English [ɔ] has either remained or has become a slightly higher and more rounded vowel (see note 6). In American English [ɔ] has remained in some localities and in others has developed into [ɑ]: ME **water** [watər], MnE [wɔtɚ], [watɚ]; ME **washe(n)** [waʃə(n), MnE [wɔʃ], [waʃ]; ME **warm** [warm], MnE [wɔɚm].

2. Preservation of Middle English [uː] and [u].

[133] But before **lm, lf,** and **lv** Middle English [a] has developed into [ɑ] or [æː]

Middle English [uː] has been preserved in Modern English before lip consonants (b, p, m, f, v); ME **stoupe(n)** [stuːp(ə)n], MnE [stup]; ME **toumbe** [tuːmbə], MnE [tum]. In some words this [uː] before lip consonants was shortened to [ʊ] and afterwards changed to [ʌ]; ME **shouve(n)** [ʃuːvə(n)], MnE [ʃʌv]; ME **double** [duːbəl], MnE [dʌbl].

Middle English [ʊ] has been preserved in Modern English under the following circumstances: regularly between lip consonants and l; ME **bole** [bʊlə], MnE [bʊl]; ME **ful** [fʊl], MnE [fʊl]; ME **wolf** [wʊlf], MnE [wʊlf]; and frequently between lip consonants and consonants other than l: ME **wode** [wʊdə], MnE [wʊd]; ME **putte(n)** [pʊtːə(n)], MnE [pʊt].

123. Vowels in Unaccented Syllables.

1. Final **e**, i.e. [ə], was universally lost at the end of the Middle English period. But final [ɪ] remained and the final [e] or [eː] which occurred in numerous French loan-words became [ɪ] in Modern English. ME **holy** [hɔːlɪ], MnE holy [holɪ]; ME **pitee** [pɪte] or [pɪteː], MnE **pity** [pɪtɪ].

2. Syncopation of the [ə] in the ending **-es** has occurred universally except after [s], [z], [ʃ], [tʃ], and [dʒ]; ME **thinges** [θɪŋɡəs], **bokes** [boːkəs], **fishes** [fɪʃəs]; MnE [θɪŋz], [bʊks], [fɪʃəz].

Syncopation of the [ə] in the verbal ending **-ed** has occurred universally except after [d] and [t]; e.g., ME **loved, loked, wedded;** MnE [lʌvd], [lʊkt], [wɛdəd].

Middle English [ər] has become [ɚ], Middle English [əl] has usually become [l], and Middle English [ən] has to a large extent become [n]; ME **better, gospel, ride(n)**; MnE [betɚ], [ɡɑspl], [rɪdn]. In the speech of those who pronounce [r] only before vowels, [ɚ] is replaced by [ə], MnE [bɛtə].

3. Extensive qualitative changes took place in the vowels of syllables which were either unstressed in Middle English or which, through loss of the primary or secondary stress which they had in Middle English, became unstressed syllables in Modern English. The final result of these changes has been (to speak in the most general terms) that nearly all vowel sounds in syllables which have neither primary nor secondary stress have been reduced in colloquial Modern English to [ə] or [ɪ]. The distribution of unstressed [ə] and [ɪ] is very far from uniform. The following examples are intended merely to illustrate the nature of these qualitative changes but not to be representative in the sense of exemplifying all the changes that occurred:

Middle English	Modern English
acordant [akɔrdant]	[əkɔɚdənt]
confessioun [kɔnfɛsːɪuːn]	[kənfɛʃən]
corage [kuraːdʒə]	[kɜ·rɪdʒ]
curteisie [kurtæiziːə]	[kɜ·təsɪ]
felawshipe [fɛlauʃɪpə]	[fɛləʃɪp]
honour [ɔnuːr]	[anɚ]
welcome [wɛlkumə]	[wɛlkəm]
wisdom [wɪzdoːm]	[wɪzdəm]

For a fuller treatment of the Modern English changes that took place in the vowels of unstressed syllables see Jespersen's *Modern English Grammar*, Part I, Chapter IX.

124. The Development of Consonants in Modern English.

1. Voicing of fricatives.

a. Initial [θ] changed to [ð] in a number of pronouns and particles which were commonly pronounced without stress: **the, they, them, thou, thee, thy, that, those, this, these, then, than, there.**

b. Final [f], [s] and [θ] became [v], [z], and [ð] if they were preceded by a vowel that was without stress or if they occurred in words that were commonly pronounced without stress in the sentence; ME **actif,** MnE [æktɪv]; ME **of** [ɔf], MnE [əv];[134] ME **faces** [faːsəs], MnE [feːsəz]; ME **his** [hɪs], MnE [hɪz]; ME **with** [wɪθ], MnE [wɪð].

2. Loss of consonants.

a. [x] has been lost in Modern English: ME **saugh** [saux], MnE [sɔ]; ME **night** [nɪxt], MnE [naɪt].[135]

b. l has been lost before k and the lip consonants m and f when the vowel that preceded it was Middle English [a] or [ɔ]; ME **talke(n)** [talk(ə)n], MnE [tɔk]; ME **folk** [fɔlk], MnE [fok]; ME **palm** [palm], MnE [pam]; ME **half** [half], MnE [hæf] or [haf].

c. r in Modern English has lost its trilled quality and has become a

---

[134] Modern English **off** [ɔːf] is historically the stressed form of **of**; in **of** the [f] changed to [v] because of lack of stress, but in **off** the [f] remained unchanged.

[135] In some words Middle English [x] has become [f] in Modern English; e.g., ME **laughe(n)** [lauxən], MnE [læf] or [laf]; ME **tough** [tuːx], MnE [tʌf]; in these words the vowel has also been modified in a special way; in the examples just given ME [au] has become [æ] or [a] instead of [ɔ], and ME [uː] has been shortened to [ʌ].

vowel-like sound which in some varieties of English is pronounced only before vowels.

3. Simplification.

a. Middle English double consonants became single in Modern English: ME **sonne** [sʊnːə], MnE [sʌn]; ME **sitte(n)** [sɪtːə(n)], MnE [sɪt].

b. Initial **gn** and **kn** have become **n** and initial **wr** has become **r**; ME **gnawe(n)** [gnɑʊən], MnE [nɔ]; ME **knight** [knɪxt], MnE [nɑɪt]; ME **write(n)** [wriːtə(n)], MnE [rɑɪt].

c. Final **mb** has been reduced to **m**; ME **domb** [dʊmb], MnE [dʌm].

d. Final [ŋg] has been reduced to [ŋ]; ME **thing** [θɪŋg], MnE [θɪŋ].

e. [sj] and [zj] have become [ʃ] and [ʒ]; early MnE **special** [spɛsjɑl], MnE [spɛʃl]; early MnE **mission** [mɪsjʊn], MnE [mɪʃən]; early MnE **portion** [pɔrsjʊn], MnE [pɔɚʃən];[136] early MnE **vision** [vɪzjʊn], MnE [vɪʒən].

[tj] and [dj] have become [tʃ] and [dʒ]; early MnE **fortune** [fɔrtjʊn], MnE [fɔɚtʃən]; early MnE **cordial** [kɔrdjɑl]; MnE [kɔɚdʒl].

---

[136] The suffix **-tion** is merely a Latinized spelling of the suffix which was spelled **-cioun** or **-cion** in Middle English.

CHAPTER IX

THE DEVELOPMENT OF MODERN ENGLISH INFLECTIONS

125. Middle English and Modern English Inflections. The Modern English development of the Middle English inflectional forms was very different both in its results and in its causes from the Middle English development of the inflectional forms of Old English. When we compare the inflectional forms of Modern English with those of late Middle English (e.g. the dialect of Chaucer), we find no such radical differences as we find when we compare the inflectional forms of late Middle English with those of Old English. The Middle English development of the Old English inflectional forms resulted in a complete transformation of the inflectional pattern of nouns, adjectives, and pronouns and changed it from a rather highly inflected language to one having relatively few and simple inflections (see **68** above). The Modern English development of the Middle English inflectional forms resulted in a complete loss of inflection in the adjective and in some simplification of the inflectional forms of verbs, but in very little simplification of the inflectional forms of nouns and pronouns. Speaking very generally, we may say that the Modern English development resulted in numerous *changes* of inflectional forms but not in any great *reduction* of inflectional forms or in any great modification of the *system* or pattern of inflectional forms.

The Middle English development of the Old English• inflectional forms was chiefly the result of two causes, **sound-change** and **analogy** (see **69, 70** above). The Modern English development was chiefly the result of sound-change; some analogical changes took place, but the analogical changes were very much less numerous and less important than those that took place in the earlier period.

The language of Chaucer is the form of Middle English that has been most thoroughly investigated and is most generally known; Chaucer's language, moreover, was the dialect of London, which was the source of both the written and the spoken form of Modern English. For these two reasons it is appropriate to take Chaucer's language as the norm of Middle English in a comparison of the inflectional forms of Middle English with those of Modern English. But the source of

141

Modern English was not the London dialect of the second half of the fourteenth century, in which Chaucer lived, but the London dialect of the sixteenth and early seventeenth centuries, for we have seen (Section 113) that the London dialect developed after 1350 from a Southeast Midland to a Northeast Midland type of speech. The basis of our comparison of Middle English with Modern English will therefore be the Southeast Midland forms of Chaucer's dialect supplemented when necessary by the Northeast Midland forms that established themselves in the London dialect in the 250 years following Chaucer's death. It is the purpose of the following sections to trace the processes by which these Middle English forms developed into the forms of Modern English.

NOUNS

126. Regular Noun Inflection. Both in Late Middle English and in Modern English the regular inflection of nouns has two singular forms and a common plural form; one of the singular forms is genitive, the other is the common form used wherever the genitive is not used. There were two types of regular nouns in Middle English: (1) those whose common singular form ended in [ə]; (2) those whose common singular form ended in a consonant or in some other vowel than [ə]. The Modern English development of the Middle English forms is shown in the following tables.

		Middle English[137]	Modern English[138]	Middle English	Modern English
SING.	COMMON	tre [treː]	[tri]	sone [sunə]	[sʌn]
	GEN.	trees [treːəs]	[triz]	sones [sunəs]	[sʌnz]
PLUR.	COMMON	trees [treːəs]	[triz]	sones [sunəs]	[sʌnz]
SING.	COMMON	book [boːk]	[bʊk]	roote [roːtə]	[rut]
	GEN.	bokes [boːkəs]	[bʊks]	rootes [roːtəs]	[ruts]
PLUR.	COMMON	bokes [boːkəs]	[bʊks]	rootes [roːtəs]	[ruts]

[137] Unless otherwise stated, the Middle English forms used in this and the following sections are those of Chaucer's dialect, taken as the representative of the London dialect of the second half of the fourteenth century.

[138] The Modern English forms used in this and the following sections are the *spoken* forms of English widely prevalent in general American. In certain other types of speech the endings [ɪz] and [ɪd] are used in place of [əz] and [əd]. In Middle English also the corresponding endings probably varied between [əs], [əd] and [ɪs], [ɪd]; see note 78 above.

		Middle English[137]	Modern English[138]	Middle English	Modern English
SING.	COMMON	bush [buʃ]	[buʃ]	chirche [tʃɪrtʃə]	[tʃɜʳtʃ]
	GEN.	bushes [buʃəs]	[buʃəz]	chirches [tʃɪrtʃəs]	[tʃɜʳtʃəz]
PLUR.	COMMON	bushes [buʃəs]	[buʃəz]	chirches [tʃɪrtʃəs]	[tʃɜʳtʃəz]

This development of the Middle English forms was the result of the following sound-changes that occurred in late Middle English or early Modern English in the order in which they are given here:

1. Voicing of Final Fricative. Final [əs] changed in late Middle English (according to 124.1 b above) to [əz], so that [treːəs], [boːkəs], and [tʃɪrtʃəs] became [treːəz], [boːkəz], and [tʃɪrtʃəz];

2. Loss of Final e. Final [ə] was lost at the end of the Middle English period (according to 123.1 above), so that [sʊnə], [roːtə], and [tʃɪrtʃə] have become [sʌn], [rut], and [tʃɜʳtʃ];

3. Syncopation. The [ə] of the ending [əz] was syncopated at the very end of the Middle English period or the beginning of the Modern English period, except after [s], [z], [ʃ], [tʃ], and [dʒ] (according to 123.2 above), so that late Middle English [treːəz] and [sʊnəz] became Modern English [triz] and [sʌnz], but the full ending remains in Modern English [buʃəz] and [tʃɜʳtʃəz];

4. Assimilation. The final voiced sound [z] was assimilated, after syncopation of the [ə] had occurred, to preceding voiceless consonants and became the corresponding voiceless sound [s], so that late Middle English [boːkəz] and [roːtəz] developed, after syncopation of [ə] and assimilation of [z], into Modern English [bʊks] and [ruːts]; the late Middle English [z] remained, however, when it was preceded by a voiced sound, either vowel or consonant, as in Modern English [triz], [sʌnz], [buʃəz], [tʃɜʳtʃəz].

The result of this development has been that there are three types of regular nouns in Modern English:

(1) Those whose common singular form ends in some voiced sound other than [z], [ʒ], or [dʒ] and whose genitive singular and common plural form ends in [z].

(2) Those whose singular common form ends in some voiceless consonant other than [s], [ʃ], or [tʃ] and whose genitive singular and common plural form ends in [s].

(3) Those whose common singular form ends in [z], [ʒ],[139] [dʒ], [s], [ʃ], or [tʃ] and whose genitive singular and plural common form ends in [əz].

127. Irregular Noun Inflection. The following groups of nouns have inflectional forms which do not conform to any of the three types defined in the preceding section:

1. A few nouns (including *wife, life, calf; mouth, bath, path, lath; house*) whose singular common form ends in [f], [θ], or [s] have a genitive singular form of the regular type, i.e., ending in [fs], [θs], or [səz], but plural common forms ending in [vz], [ðz], or [zəz]; the Modern English development of the Middle English forms of a typical word of this group is shown below.

	MIDDLE ENGLISH	MODERN ENGLISH
SING. COMMON	wif [wiːf]	[waɪf]
GEN.	wives [wiːvəs]	[waɪfs] *wife's*
PLUR. COMMON	wives [wiːvəs]	[waɪvz]

Modern English [waɪf] and [waɪvz] developed out of Middle English [wiːf] and [wiːvəs] by sound-change; that is, they are the Middle English forms pronounced in the Modern English way.[140] Such forms we may call historical forms. Modern English [waɪfs], on the other hand, is not the product of sound-change but is a new formation that developed in early Modern English on the analogy of the regular noun inflection. The fact that it is an analogical form is indicated in the table by printing *wife's* in italic type.

2. A small group of nouns (*man, woman, foot, tooth, goose, mouse, louse*) have a genitive singular of the regular type, a plural common

---

[139] At the time of the changes discussed here, no English nouns ended in [ʒ]. Since then a few French borrowings such as **rouge** and **garage** have been introduced into the language. These also have the unsyncopated final inflection [əz].

[140] The interchange between [f] and [v], [θ] and [ð], [s] and [z] which appear in [waɪf]-[waɪvz], [mauθ]-[mauðz], [haus]-[hauzəz], etc., goes back to the Old English period, and the "irregularity" of the Modern English forms is due ultimately to the fact that in Old English the fricative consonants spelled **f, þ** or **ð,** and **s** were always voiceless when they were initial or final but voiced (unless they were doubled) when they occurred between voiced sounds. See Section 24 above. Other Modern English illustrations of this interchange are **thief** from OE **þēof** and **thieve** (from OE **þēofian**); **south** (from OE **sūþ**) and **southern** (from OE **sūðerne**); **grass** (from OE **grǣs**) and **graze** (from OE **grasian**).

form with vowel change but with no ending, and also a genitive plural with both vowel change and the ending [z], [s], or [əz]. The Modern English development of a typical word of this group is shown below.

		MIDDLE ENGLISH	MODERN ENGLISH
SING.	COMMON	man [mɑn]	[mæn]
	GEN.	mannes [mɑnːəs]	[mænz]
PLUR.	COMMON	men [mɛn]	[mɛn]
	GEN.	mennes [mɛnːəs]	[mɛnz]

The Modern English forms are all historical forms, developed from the Middle English forms by sound-change alone.   Middle English [mɑn]-[mɛn], [foːt]-[feːt], [toːθ]-[teːθ], [goːs]-[geːs], [muːs]-[miːs], and [luːs]-[liːs] were just as much irregularities in Middle English as their Modern English developments [mæn]-[mɛn], [fʊt]-[fit], [tuθ]-[tiθ], [gus]-[gis], [mɑʊs]-[mɑɪs], and [lɑʊs]-[lɑɪs] are irregularities in Modern English.   And the Middle English forms were the historical development of Old English plural forms that constituted a rather isolated group even in Old English.[141]

Modern English [wʊmən]-[wɪmən], however, though it has a plural common form with vowel change but no ending, has not developed from the Middle English forms by sound change alone.   In Middle English the word had two sets of forms, [wʊmːɑn]-[wʊmːɛn] and [wɪmːɑn]-[wɪmːɛn], both sets derived from Old English wifman-wifmen, a compound wif and mɑn.   But either in very late Middle English or early Modern English a redistribution of forms occurred which resulted in restricting the [ʊ] forms to the singular and the [ɪ] forms to the plural. The vowel change that appears in Modern English [wʊmən]-[wɪmən], therefore, has an entirely different origin from the vowel change that appears in [mæn]-[mɛn], [fʊt]-[fit], etc.

3.   Three nouns have a genitive singular of the regular type, a plural common form with the ending [ən], and a genitive plural form with the ending [ənz].   The Modern English development of these three nouns is shown below.

[141] The Middle English genitive plural forms of these nouns, however, were analogical forms that developed in late Middle English.

	MIDDLE ENGLISH	MODERN ENGLISH
SING. COMMON	oxe [ɔksə]	[ɑks]
GEN.	oxes [ɔksəs]	[ɑksəz]
PLUR. COMMON	oxen [ɔksən]	[ɑksən]
GEN.	oxen [ɔksən]	[ɑksənz] *oxen's*
SING. COMMON	child [tʃiːld]	[tʃaɪld]
GEN.	childes [tʃiːldəs]	[tʃaɪldz]
PLUR. COMMON	children [tʃɪldrən}	[tʃɪldrən]
GEN.	children [tʃɪldrən]	[tʃɪldrənz] *children's*
SING. COMMON	brother [broːðər]	[brʌðr]
GEN.	brother [broːðər][142]	
	brothres [broːðrəs]	[brʌðrz]
PLUR. COMMON	brethren [brɛðrən]	[brɛðrən]
	brothres [broːðrəs]	[brʌðrz]
GEN.	brethren [brɛðrən]	[brɛðrənz] *brethren's*
	brothres [broːðrəs]	[brʌðrz]

The Modern English forms are all historical forms except the genitive plurals *oxen's*, *children's*, and *brethren's*. These forms (which are printed in italics to distinguish them from the historical forms that developed by sound-change) are analogical forms that developed in early Modern English.

These words with **-en** plurals were exceptional even in late Middle English, but the "weak" type of inflection which they represent was very common in Old English (for the Old English forms and the Middle English development see Sections **26** and **80-82** above). The only word of the group which originally had this type of inflection is *ox-oxen*, but the weak type of plural inflection was extended in early Middle English (see Section **84** above) to many nouns which in Old English had other types of inflection; *children* and *brethren* are the Modern English survivals of these Middle English analogical plurals in **-en**. The Old English nominative plural forms were **ċildru** [tʃɪldrʊ] and **brēðru** [breːðrʊ],[143] which developed into Middle English **childre** [tʃɪldrə], and **brethre** [brɛðrə], later **children** and **brethren**.

---

[142] The genitive singular was originally uninflected in Old English and the inflected form was an analogical development.

[143] The form **brēðru** is not recorded in Old English but is inferred from the Middle English forms; the plural **ċildru** represents an inflectional type that was rare even in Old English.

4. Two nouns, *sheep* and *deer*, have a genitive singular of the regular type, a plural common form which is identical with the singular common form, and a genitive plural form which is identical with the genitive singular. The Modern English development of the typical word *sheep* is shown below.

		MIDDLE ENGLISH	MODERN ENGLISH
SING.	COMMON	sheep [ʃeːp]	[ʃip]
	GEN.	sheepes [ʃeːpəs]	[ʃips]
PLUR.	COMMON	sheep [ʃe(p]	[ʃip]
	GEN.		[ʃips] *sheeps'*

The Modern English genitive singular and plural common are historical forms, but the genitive plural *sheeps'* is an early Modern English analogical formation, as is indicated by printing it in italics.[144]

Both these nouns were neuter nouns in Old English, and the inflectional type which they represent, though exceptional even in late Middle English (see Section **36.**7 above), was very common in Old English (for the Old English forms see Sections **26** and **78** above).[145]

We may sum up this historical account of Modern English noun inflections[146] by saying that the regular noun inflections are wholly

[144] The genitive plural of these nouns is rarely used even in Modern English and it has not been possible to find late Middle English examples; it is possible that an analogical form developed in Middle English.

[145] A somewhat large and rather indefinite number of Modern English nouns (mostly names of fishes, birds, or units of measurement) have either an uninflected plural common form or the regular plural in [z], [s], or [əz], but the use of one or other of the two plural forms is determined by differences of meaning or of syntax; examples are *trout, snipe, year, pound, dozen*. Modern English *fish*, though it was inflected according to the regular noun declension in Middle English and early Modern English, now has an uninflected plural when used in one sense and a regular plural when used in another; it was masculine, not neuter, in Old English. Some of these nouns (e.g. *year* and *pound*) are derived from Old English genitive plurals used partitively after numbers and other expressions of quantity. The genitive plural inflection, ending in -a in Old English, became [ə] in Middle English and was lost in Modern English.

[146] All the changes of word form that strictly belong to an account of the development of Modern English noun inflections are included in Sections **126** and **127**. Such other matters as the use of the apostrophe and of *s* or *se* in the spelling of the plural, nouns with double plurals like *pennies* and *pence*, foreign plurals, and words used only in the plural, are partly matters of orthography, which does not belong to grammar at all, partly matters that belong to the dictionary rather than the grammar, and partly matters that belong to syntax rather than morphology.

and the irregular noun inflections predominantly the product of sound-change alone; analogical developments were few and unimportant. In this respect the Modern English development presents a striking contrast to the Middle English development of the Old English noun inflections, as may be seen from the summary of the Middle English analogical changes given in Section **83** above.

ADJECTIVES

128. Inflection of Adjectives. There were two types of adjectives in late Middle English. The dissyllabic adjectives that ended in [ə] were invariable in form.[147] Monosyllabic adjectives like **good** had a plural form that ended in [ə] and two singular forms, the **strong** and the **weak**. The weak form, which ended in [ə], was used if the adjective was preceded by the definite article **the,** by a demonstrative (**this** or **that**), by a possessive pronoun, or by a noun in the genitive case, or if it modified a noun used in direct address. The strong form, which had no ending, was used except under the conditions which called for the use of the weak form. (For examples from Chaucer see Sections **37, 45** above.) The Modern English development of the Middle English forms of the typical adjectives **good** and **swete** is shown in the following table.

		MIDDLE ENGLISH		MODERN ENGLISH
SINGULAR STRONG	**good** [goːd]	**swete** [sweːtə]	[gʊd]	[swit]
WEAK	**goode** [goːdə]	**swete** [sweːtə]	[gʊd]	[swit]
PLURAL	**goode** [goːdə]	**swete** [sweːtə]	[gʊd]	[swit]

It is obvious that the Modern English development was the result wholly of a sound-change, the loss of the final [ə] in the presence or absence of which consisted the sole difference between the two types of adjectives and between the inflected and the uninflected forms of adjectives like **good.**[148]

[147] Adjectives that had two or more syllables and that ended in some other sound than [ə] were sometimes inflected like the monosyllabic adjectives but were usually not inflected at all. See Section **37.2** above.

[148] The comparative and superlative adjectives ending in [ɚ] and [əst] are derivatives rather than inflectional forms, and the comparatives and superlatives formed by prefixing *more* and *most* are neither inflectional forms nor derivatives but syntactical groups. Strictly speaking, therefore, the comparison of adjectives is not a part of morphology.

Pronouns

129. The Modern English forms of pronominal words are for the most part historical forms, developed from the Middle English forms by the regular processes of sound-change, but **its** is an analogical formation and the nominative and singular uses of **you** may roughly be called syntactical developments. When we consider the development in detail, however, we find that the relations between the Middle English and the Modern English forms is less simple than would seem to be implied by the generalization just made. The development of pronominal words is always complicated by the fact that most words of this class have strong forms which are used when the pronoun is stressed, and weak forms which are used when the pronoun is not stressed (see Section **20** above). These strong and weak forms are never phonetically identical. If the strong form has a long or tense vowel, the weak form may have a short or lax vowel which may often be of somewhat different quality (cf. Modern English [wi] and [wɪ]). If the strong form has a short or lax vowel, the vowel of the weak form will be somewhat shorter and possibly "obscured" (cf. Modern English [ʌs] and [əs]). Now when we consider that the strong forms are stressed syllables and that the weak forms are unstressed syllables; that the sound changes that take place in stressed syllables are seldom identical with those that take place in unstressed syllables (cf. Section **62** above); and that the sound-changes undergone by long vowels are frequently different from those undergone by short vowels, we see that when pronouns are affected by sound-change the resulting strong and weak forms are apt to be less similar than they were before the sound-change took place. But if the dissimilarity is very great, either the strong or weak form is likely to be modified by becoming assimilated to the other, so that similarity between the two is restored.

For example, the strong form of the objective case of the second person plural pronoun in Middle English was **you** [juː] and the corresponding weak form was probably [ju]. The regular phonetic development of the Middle English strong form would have been [jɑu], and there existed in very early Modern English a form which had the diphthong [ɑu] or some similar diphthong. The Middle English weak form [ju], however, remained in very early Modern English, for the change of [u] to [ʌ] was not completed until the seventeenth century. The Modern English strong form [ju] is the result of restressing the weak form [ju], the process of restressing naturally resulting in lengthening the vowel to some extent and changing its quality. The opposite process is illustrated in Modern English [əs], the weak form of [ʌs]. The late Middle English strong form was [us], which has developed regularly into [ʌs]. The late Middle English weak form was probably [uz], (final [s] becoming [z] in the unstressed syllable according to Section 124.1 above), which would have developed into Modern English [əz]. The Modern English weak form [əs], therefore, is probably not derived from the late Middle English weak form but is the result of destressing the Modern English strong form [ʌs].[149]

The historical relations between the Modern English strong forms of the pronouns and the Middle English strong forms is shown in the following sections.[150]   Unless it is otherwise stated, the Modern English forms developed from the Middle English forms by the regular processes of sound-change.

130.   First Personal Pronoun.

		MIDDLE ENGLISH	MODERN ENGLISH
SING.	NOM.	I [iː]	[aɪ]
	GEN.	my [miː] myn [miːn][151]	[maɪ]
	OBJ.	me [meː]	[mi]

[149] The term *restressing* was applied to this process by Prof. J. S. Kenyon (*American Pronunciation*, §139). Professor Moore improvised the term *destressing* to designate the reverse process.

[150] A detailed account of the historical development of the Modern English weak forms would involve space-consuming complexities that would be inconsistent with the plan of this book, and the weak forms are therefore dealt with only when they are of special interest. In many cases they are probably the result of destressing the Modern English strong forms; e.g. Modern English [əi], the weak form of [ɑi], cannot possibly have developed from the Middle English weak form, which was [i] or [ɪ]. In other cases the Modern English weak form that would have developed from the Middle English weak form is the same as that which would have resulted from destressing the Modern English strong form; e.g. [ʃɪ], the weak form of [ʃi], would be the regular development of the Middle English weak form [ʃe] according to 123.1 above and would also be the result of destressing the Modern English strong form. In still other cases, one of the Modern English weak forms might have developed from the Middle English weak form and another be a destressed form; e.g. Modern English [ɚ], a weak form of [ɑʊɚ], might have developed from Middle English [ur] or [ʊr], but the weak form [ɑɚ] must have resulted from destressing the Modern English strong form. A convenient list of strong and weak forms of pronouns, auxiliaries, prepositions, etc., may be found in Webster's New International Dictionary, *Guide to Pronunciation*, pp. xxxviii–ix.

[151] There was a tendency to use [miːn] and [θiːn] before words beginning with

		MIDDLE ENGLISH	MODERN ENGLISH
PLUR.	NOM.	we [weː]	[wi]
	GEN.	oure [uːrə], our [uːr]	[ɑʊɚ], [ɑɚ][152]
	OBJ.	us [ʊs]	[ʌs][153]

131. Second Personal Pronoun.

		MIDDLE ENGLISH	EARLY MODERN ENGLISH	MODERN ENGLISH
SING.	NOM.	thou [θuː]	[ðɑʊ], [jiː], [juː]	⌜ju]
	GEN.	thy [θiː], thyn [θiːn][151]	[ðɑɪ], [ðɑɪn], [juːr]	[jʊɚ]
	OBJ.	thee [θeː]	[ðiː], [juː]	[ju]
PLUR.	NOM.	ye [jeː]	[jiː], [juː]	[ju]
	GEN.	your [juːr]	[juːr]	[jʊɚ]
	OBJ.	you [juː]	[juː]	[ju]

The Modern English development here is by no means simple. The occurrence in Modern English [ju] and [jʊɚ] of a simple vowel in place of the diphthong that developed from Middle English [uː] has already been accounted for in Section 129, but three other points require explanation.

1. Modern English [ð] in place of Middle English [θ] is probably the result of the influence of the weak forms, which (being unstressed syllables) would have [ð] according to Section 124.1 above.

2. The use of ye, your, you as singular pronouns was at first a ceremonious use employed only by persons of the upper class in addressing those who were their superiors in rank. This practice began at least as early as the thirteenth century. Later the singular use of the plural pronouns was employed with less and less discrimination until, in the latter part of the sixteenth century, the old singular pronouns were ordinarily used only in addressing those who were admittedly inferiors and in addressing familiarly equals with whom one was on intimate terms. After 1600 the colloquial use of the old

vowels or h and [miː] and [θːi] before words beginning with a consonant when these words were used attributively (immediately before or after the word they modified).

[152] The special development of [ɑʊr] into [ɑɚ] occurs not only in this word but in some regional varieties of English is extended to many of the words in which the combination exists; flower [flɑʊɚ] may become [flɑː]. For the development of ours, see Section 133.

[153] For the development of the Modern English weak form, see Section 129 above.

singular pronouns became less and less frequent and finally obsolete.[154]

3. The use of **you** instead of **ye** as the nominative form of the second personal pronoun occurs occasionally as early as the fourteenth century and increased until before the end of the seventeenth century the colloquial use of **ye** was obsolete. In Shakespeare's works **you** occurs more often than **ye** as the nominative form. This development appears to have been the result of a complex of causes in which sound-changes, analogy, and syntactic developments all had a part. The investigation of this phenomenon is complicated by the fact that the nominative use of **you** is not an isolated phenomenon, for certain nominative uses of objective forms of the pronouns (and, though less frequently, objective uses of the nominative forms) have been common since the sixteenth century and occur in spoken English today.[155]

132. Third Personal Pronoun. All of the strong forms of the third personal pronoun except **its** are historical forms. The earliest example of **its** that has so far been discovered is dated 1596; the form occurs 10 times in the First Folio of Shakespeare but not in any earlier editions, and did not come into general literary use until the second half of the seventeenth century, though it must have been in colloquial use at least as early as the latter part of the sixteenth century. The development of **its** was perhaps facilitated by the fact that **it** was used as a neuter genitive singular form from the fourteenth century on. The genitive form **its** was based on the analogy of the regular genitive singular of nouns (*its* : it : : cat's : cat).

The genitive and objective plural forms of the third personal pronoun illustrate the change that took place in London English between 1350 and 1500 (see **113** above), for the Modern English forms are derived from the Northeast Midland forms which belonged to the London dialect in 1500, not from the Southeast Midland forms which were used in the fourteenth century London English of Chaucer.

The Modern English development is shown in the following tables.

[154] Even now the old singular pronouns of the second person have a quasi-colloquial use in prayer. This use of the singular pronouns seems to have no relation to their ordinary sixteenth century use but to be the result of a conservative tendency which has maintained in this one field the strictly singular function which these pronouns had previous to the fourteenth century.

[155] The fullest discussion of these case-shiftings in pronouns is in Jespersen's *Progress in Language, with Special Reference to English*, chapter VII. The nominative use of *you* is dealt with particularly in Section **152** and on pp. 188 ff., 197–208. See also Fries, *American English Grammar*, pp. 88–96.

	MIDDLE ENGLISH			MODERN ENGLISH
	Southeast Midland	Northeast Midland	Early Modern English	

MASCULINE

SING. NOM.	he [heː]			[hi]
GEN.	his [hɪs]			[hɪz][156]
OBJ.	him [hɪm]			[hɪm]

FEMININE

SING. NOM.	she [ʃeː]			[ʃi]
GEN.	hir(e) [hɪrə], [hɪr]			[hɝ]
	her(e) [hɛrə], [hɛr]			
OBJ.	hir(e), [hɪrə], [hɪr]			[hɝ]
	her(e) [hɛrə], [hɛr]			

NEUTER

SING. NOM.	hit [hɪt], it [ɪt]			[ɪt]
GEN.	his [hɪs]	hit [hɪt], it [ɪt]	[hɪz], [hɪt], [ɪt]	[ɪts]
OBJ.	hit [hɪt], it [ɪt]			[ɪt]

PLURAL

NOM.	they [θæɪ]			[ðe][157]
GEN.	hir(e) [hɪrə], [hɪr]			
	her(e) [hɛrə], [hɛr]	their [θæɪr]		[ðɛɝ]
OBJ.	hem [hɛm]	them [θɛm]		[ðɛm], [əm][158]

133. Absolute Forms of Possessive. The Modern English absolute forms of the genitive (or possessive), *mine, ours, thine, yours, his, hers, theirs,* are derived from Middle English myn [miːn], oures [uːrəs], thyn [θiːn], youres [juːrəs], his [hɪs], hires [hɪrəs], heres [hɛrəs], theires [θæɪrəs]. The Middle English forms in [əs] underwent the regular change of [s] to [z] in unstressed syllables and the subsequent syncopation of [ə], according to **126** above. Otherwise their development is precisely similar to that of the attributive forms *my, our, thine, your, his, her,* and *their,* and the initial [ð] of *thine* and *theirs* and the final [z] of *his*

---

[156] The final [z] of [hɪz] is probably the result of restressing the weak form, which had [z] according to Section **124.1** above.

[157] The initial [ð] of [ðæɪ], [ðɛɝ], [ðɛm] is probably the result of restressing weak forms which had [ð] according to Section **124.1** above.

[158] [əm] is a weak form (spelled *'em*) from Middle English [hɛm].

are due to the influence of the attributive forms. These absolute forms
are always stressed.

134. Demonstrative Pronouns. The Modern English development of the demonstrative pronouns **this** and **that** is shown in the following tables.

	MIDDLE ENGLISH		MODERN ENGLISH
	Southeast Midland	Northeast Midland	
SING.	that [θɑt]		[ðæt]
PLUR.	tho [θɔː]	thos [θɔːs]	[ðoz]
SING.	thes [θeːs], this [θɪs]		[ðɪs]
PLUR.	thes [θeːs], these [θæːzə]		[ðiz]

The Modern English forms are derived trom Middle English [θɑt],
[θɔːs], [θɪs], and [θæːzə] respectively. Since the demonstratives are
always stressed and have no weak forms, we might expect that the
initial [θ] of the Middle English forms would be preserved in Modern
English. The change of [θ] to [ð] is probably due to the fact that
these words, though never entirely unstressed, are usually not pronounced
with full stress and may therefore have been subject to this sound-
change. The final [s] of Middle English **this** has been preserved in
Modern English just as in stressed words, and the [z] of Modern
English **those** must go back to a late Middle English form with final
[z].[159]

135. Relative and Interrogative Pronouns. Of the relative and
interrogative pronouns, only *who* is inflected. The Modern English
development is shown below.

	MIDDLE ENGLISH	MODERN ENGLISH
SING., PLUR. NOM.	who [hwoː][160]	[hu]
GEN.	whos [hwoːs]	[huz][161]
OBJ.	whom [hwoːm]	[hum][162]

[159] The origin of Middle English **thos** is uncertain. It seems quite possible that it
may have developed from the form tho⸱on the analogy of the plural inflection of nouns.
Such a development would be readily intelligible in the substantive use of the word
and would explain the occurrence of final [z] in Modern English.

[160] There are very few examples in Chaucer of the use of *who* as a pure relative,
though there are numerous examples of relative *whos* and *whom*.

[161] Modern English [hu] and [hum] are used only of persons, but [huz] is used

The interrogative forms are always stressed, but the relative forms are usually unstressed. Final [z] is therefore the regular product of sound-change in the relative *whose*, but not in the interrogative. Final [z] in the interrogative is possibly the result of the influence of the relative but more probably it is from the analogy of the genitive singular of nouns.[163]

The historical development of the other pronominal words of Modern English (reflexive, intensive, determinative, etc.) belongs to the syntactical rather than the morphological development of English. The inflectional changes which occur in these words (most of them are uninflected) conform to inflectional types whose development has been explained in previous sections.

VERBS

136. Classification of Modern English Verbs. Modern English verbs may be classified as **normal** and **anomalous**. The inflectional forms of the present indicative third person singular are the basis for distinguishing between the normal verbs and the anomalous verbs (**say, have, do; shall, can, may, must, ought, dare, need; will; be**). The **normal** verbs may be further classified as **regular** and **irregular**. The inflectional forms of the preterit (or past) tense are the basis for distinguishing between the regular and the irregular verbs.

137. Present Forms of Normal Verbs. Modern English has three present forms: (1) the simple or common form used as present indicative first and second persons singular, present indicative plural, present subjunctive, imperative and infinitive; (2) the present indicative third person singular; and (3) the present participle. The historical development of these forms is shown in the following tables. The development of the present indicative and the imperative will be illustrated by three verbs, **hear, hunt,** and **rise,** the development of the other forms by **rise** only. It is to be understood, however, that the other present tense forms of **hear** and **hunt** are analogous to those of **rise.**

---

also as a singular and plural neuter genitive form; this use goes back to the Middle English period, though it does not occur in Chaucer.

[162] The use of [hu] as the objective form of the interrogative is frequent in colloquial English.

[163] The change of Middle English [hw] into Modern English [h] is a special development which probably occurred after the change of Middle English [oː] into Modern English [u]. The [oː] of Middle English *who* from Old English **hwā** [hwɑː] is a special development that occurred also in Middle English *two* [twoː] from Old English **twā** [twɑ̄ː].

		MIDDLE ENGLISH		MODERN ENGLISH
		Southeast Midland	Northeast Midland	
PRES. IND. SING.	1	here [heɪrə]		[hɪɚ]
	2	herest [heɪrəst]		[hɪɚ]
	3	hereth [heɪrəθ]	heres [heɪrəs]	[hɪɚz]
PLUR.		here(n) [heɪrən][164]		[hɪɚ]
IMPERATIVE SING.		her [heɪr]		[hɪɚ]
PLUR.		hereth [heɪrəθ], here [heɪrə][165]		[hɪɚ]
PRES. IND. SING.	1	hunte [hʊntə]		[hʌnt]
	2	huntest [hʊntəst]		[hʌnt]
	3	hunteth [hʊntəθ]	huntes [hʊntəs]	[hʌnts]
PLUR.		hunte(n) [hʊntən]		[hʌnt]
IMPERATIVE SING.		hunte [hʊntə][166]		[hʌnt]
PLUR.		hunteth [hʊntəθ] hunte [hʊntə]		[hʌnt]
PRES. IND. SING.	1	rise [riːzə]		[raɪz]
	2	risest [riːzəst]		[raɪz]
	3	riseth [riːzəθ]	rises [riːzəs]	[raɪzəz]
PLUR.		rise(n) [riːzən]		[raɪz]
PRES. SUBJ. SING.		rise [riːzə]		[raɪz]
PLUR.		rise(n) [riːzən][164]		[raɪz]
IMPERATIVE SING.		ris [riːs]		[raɪz]
PLUR.		riseth [rizəθ], rise [riːzə]		[raɪz]
PRES. INFINITIVE		rise(n) [riːzən][167]		[raɪz]
GERUND		to rise(n) [toː riːzən][167]		[tə raɪz]

[164] e(n) indicates that the ending [ən] interchanges with [ə]. See note 112 above. The Modern English development of the Middle English forms that ended in e(n) is always based on the form without n, except that the Modern English past participle of strong verbs (see Sections 139, 141, below) is sometimes based on the Middle English form with [ən] and sometimes on the form with [ə].

[165] The Modern English forms of the imperative plural are based on the Middle English forms with the ending [ə], not on those with the ending [əθ].

[166] Some verbs had the ending [ə] in the imperative singular and some had no ending.

[167] The gerund originally consisted in Old English of the preposition tō followed by

	MIDDLE ENGLISH	MODERN ENGLISH
	Southeast Midland	
VERBAL NOUN	risinge [riːzɪŋgə], rising [riːzɪŋg][168]	[rɑɪzɪŋ]
PRES. PARTICIPLE	risinge [riːzɪŋgə], rising [riːzɪŋg][168]	[rɑɪzɪŋ]

The Modern English forms of the present tense are the product of sound-change, with no interference from analogical formations. Apart from sound-changes that occurred within the body of the word, most of them are the Middle English forms minus the final [ə] that was regularly lost at the end of the Middle English period. Three forms, however, require special mention.

1. The Modern English present indicative second singular and imperative singular have developed from the Middle English present indicative plural and imperative plural. This was the result of the use of the plural pronoun **ye** or **you** as a substitute for the singular pronoun **thou** (see Section **131.**2 above). The use of the plural subject naturally entailed the use of the plural form of the verb, so that **ye here, ye hunte, ye rise** gradually displaced **thou herest, thou huntest, thou risest** in early Modern English. The imperative singular of most verbs became identical in form with the imperative plural by mere process of sound-change, as in Modern English [hɪɚr] and [hʌnt]; but when (as in the case of Middle English [riːs] and [riːzə], which would have developed into Modern English [rɑis] and [rɑiz]), the two forms were not levelled by sound-change, the plural form displaced the singular.

an inflected form of the infinitive and the Old English infinitive form of this verb was **rīsan** and the gerund was **tō rīsenne.** Even in Old English, however, the gerund was sometimes composed of the preposition followed by the uninflected infinitive, so that the gerund of this verb could assume the form **tō rīsan.** In Middle English the inflected form of the infinitive became less and less common in the gerund, so that the gerund regularly ended in [ən] or (with loss of the final **n**) in [ə]. The Modern English forms of both infinitive and gerund are based on the Middle English forms in [ə]. In addition there was, of course, a considerable amount of confusion and interchange among the infinitive, gerund, and verbal noun with respect to their various syntactical functions.

[168] For the distinction between verbal noun and present participle see note 119 above. The forms without final **e** were much commoner in late Middle English than those with final **e**; for the loss of final **e** in trisyllabic words see Section **62.**3 above.

2. The Modern English present indicative third person singular has developed from the Northeast Midland form ending in -es. The development of [heɪrəs], [hʊntəs], [riːzes] into Modern English [hɪɚz], [hʌnts], [rɑɪzəz] is the same as that which has already been explained in connection with the regular noun inflection (Section 126 above), and the three types of present indicative third person singular forms are identical with the three types of the regular genitive singular and plural common of nouns. The Southeast Midland forms [heɪrəθ], [hʊntəθ], [riːzəθ] developed into early Modern English [hiːrəð], [hʊntəð], [rɑɪzəð], (see Section 124.1 above) but were gradually displaced in the London dialect by the forms ending in [z], [s], [əz] and became obsolete as spoken forms early in the seventeenth century. (See Section 113 above.) In Shakespeare's works the s-forms are much more frequent than the th-forms; the latter occur mostly in verse. Milton always uses the s-forms except in *hath* and *doth*, in which the th-forms survived longer than in other verbs.

138. Preterit Form of Regular Verbs. The regular verbs of Modern English have a common preterit form which is used as preterit indicative, preterit subjunctive, and past participle. All regular verbs conform to one of the three following types:

1. The common present form ends in a voiced sound other than [d] and the preterit form consists of the common present form plus [d]: common present [fɪl], [stɝ]; preterit [fɪld], [stɝd].

2. The common present form ends in a voiceless sound other than [t] and the preterit form consists of the common present form plus [t]: common present [kɪs], [lʊk]; preterit [kɪst], [lʊkt].

3. The common present form ends in [d] or [t] and the preterit form consists of the common present form plus [əd]: e.g. common present [hʌnt] [wɛd], preterit [hʌntəd], [wɛdəd].

These three types of inflection are all derived from that of the Middle English **weak** verbs. The preterit indicative first and third singular of weak verbs ended in Middle English in -ede or -ed on the one hand or in -de or -te on the other. The Modern English development of the representative verbs, **fill, stir, kiss, look, hunt** is shown in the following tables.

	MIDDLE ENGLISH	MODERN ENGLISH
PRET. IND. SING. 1	filde [fɪldə]	[fɪld]
2	fildest [fɪldəst]	ˈfɪld]
3	filde [fɪldə]	[fɪld]
PLUR.	filde(n) [fɪldən]¹⁶⁹	[fɪld]
PRET. SUBJ. SING.	filde [fɪldə]	[fɪld]
PLUR.	filde(n) [fɪldən]¹⁶⁹	[fɪld]
PAST PARTICIPLE	filled [fɪlːəd], fild [fɪld]	[fɪld]
PRET. IND. SING. 1	stirede [stɪrədə], stired [stɪrəd]¹⁷⁰	[stɜ˞d]
2	stiredest [stɪrədəst]	[stɜ˞d]
3	stirede [stɪrədə], stired [stɪrəd]¹⁷⁰	[stɜ˞d]
PLUR.	stirede(n) [stɪrədən], stired [stɪrəd]¹⁷¹	[stɜ˞d]
PRET. SUBJ. SING.	stirede [stɪrədə], stired [stɪrəd]¹⁷⁰	[stɜ˞d]
PLUR.	stirede(n) [stɪrədən], stired [stɪrəd]¹⁷¹	[stɜ˞d]
PAST PARTICIPLE	stired [stɪrəd]	[stɜ˞d]
PRET. IND. SING. 1	kiste [kɪstə]	[kɪst]
2	kistest [kɪstəst]	[kɪst]
3	kiste [kɪstə]	[kɪst]
PLUR.	kiste(n) [kɪstən]	[kɪst]
PRET. SUBJ. SING.	kiste [kɪstə]	[kɪst]
PLUR.	kiste(n) [kɪstən]	[kɪst]
PAST PARTICIPLE	kist [kɪst]	[kɪst]
PRET. IND. SING. 1	lokede [loːkədə], loked [loːkəd]¹⁷⁰	[lʊkt]
2	lokedest [loːkədest]	[lʊkt]
3	lokede [loːkədə], loked [loːkəd]¹⁷⁰	[lʊkt]
PLUR.	lokede(n) [loːkədən], loked [loːkəd]¹⁷¹	[lʊkt]
PRET. SUBJ. SING.	lokede [loːkədə]¹⁷⁰	[lʊkt]
PLUR.	lokede(n) [loːkədən], loked [loːkəd]¹⁷¹	[lʊkt]
PAST PARTICIPLE	loked [loːkəd]	[lʊkt]

---

¹⁶⁹ See note 164 above.

¹⁷⁰ The ending **-ed** was much commoner in late Middle English than the ending **-ede.** For the Middle English loss of final **e** in words of three syllables see Section **62.3** above. The Modern English forms are based on the Middle English forms with **-ed.**

¹⁷¹ The plural forms in **-ed** developed (according to Section **62.3** above) out of those in **-ede.** The Modern English forms are based on the Middle English forms in **-ed.**

		MIDDLE ENGLISH	MODERN ENGLISH
Pret. Ind. Sing.	1	huntede [hʊntədə], hunted [hʊntəd][170]	[hʌntəd]
	2	huntedest [hʊntədəst]	[hʌntəd]
	3	huntede [hʊntədə], hunted [hʊntəd][170]	[hʌntəd]
Plur.		huntede(n) [hʊntədən], hunted [hʊntəd][171]	[hʌntəd]
Pret. Subj. Sing.		huntede [hʊntədə], hunted [hʊntəd][170]	[hʌntəd]
Plur.		huntede(n) [hʊntədən], hunted [hʊntəd][171]	[hʌntəd]
Past Participle		hunted [hʊntəd]	[hʌntəd]

The Modern English forms are the product of sound-change, with no interference from analogy, allowing of course for the fact that the preterit indicative second singular has developed from the Middle English preterit plural as the result of using the plural pronoun ye or you as a substitute for the singular pronoun thou (cf. Section 137.1 above). Middle English [fɪldə] and [kɪstə] developed into Modern English [fɪld] and [kɪst] through loss of final [ə] according to Section 123.1 above. Middle English [stɪrəd] developed into Modern English [stɝd] after syncopation of the unaccented vowel [ə] according to Section 123.2 above. In Middle English [loːkəd], however, the syncopation of the unaccented [ə] was followed by an assimilation of the voiced [d] to the voiceless [k] that preceded it, so that the Modern English development is [lʊkt]. In [stɪrəd], however, no assimilation would occur because the [r] that preceded the [d] after syncopation was a voiced sound. In Middle English [hʊntəd] no syncopation took place, so that the Modern English development [hʌntəd] is still dissyllabic. So also (according to Section 123) in Middle English [wɛdːəd] no syncopation took place and the Modern English form is [wɛdəd].

139. Classification of Irregular Verbs. All Modern English verbs (except the anomalous verbs) whose preterit does not conform to one of the three types defined in Section 138 are called irregular verbs. The irregular verbs may be classified from the Modern English point of view as **irregular weak** verbs, **strong** verbs, and **indeterminate** verbs.

1. The irregular weak verbs are those **irregular** verbs whose preterit form ends in [d] or [t] and whose common present form ends

in some other sound than [d] or [t]: **creep, deal, hear, buy, make, bring.**

2. The strong verbs are those verbs whose preterit form ends in some other sound than [d] or [t]: **drive, freeze, drink, steal, give, draw, blow, fall.**

3. The indeterminate verbs are those **irregular** verbs whose common present and preterit forms both end in [d] or [t]: **lead, burst, hurt, set, sit, ride, hide.**

140. Preterit Form of Irregular Weak Verbs. In Middle English, as in Old English and all other Germanic languages, there were two conjugations of verbs, the strong and the weak. There were two types of weak verbs in Middle English. Weak verbs of Type I had preterits ending in **-ede,** later **-ed,** and past participles ending in **-ed.** Weak verbs of Type II had preterits ending in **-de** or **-te** and past participles ending in **-ed, -d,** or **-t.**[172] The principal parts (i.e. infinitive, preterit indicative first and third singular, and past participle) of representative weak verbs are as follows:

Type I	hunte(n) [hʊntən]	hunted [hʊntəd]	hunted [hʊntəd]
	loke(n) [loːkən]	loked [loːkəd]	loked [loːkəd]
	stıre(n) [stɪrən]	stıred [stɪrəd]	stired [stɪrəd]
	wedːe(n) [wɛdːən]	wedded [wɛdːəd]	wedded [wɛdːəd]
Type II	fille(n) [fɪlːən]	filde [fɪldə]	fild [fɪld]
	kisse(n) [kɪsːən]	kiste [kɪstə]	kist [kɪst]
	caste(n) [kastən]	caste [kastə]	cast [kast]
	bende(n) [bɛndən]	bente [bɛntə]	bent [bɛnt]
	dwelle(n) [dwɛlːən]	dwelte [dwɛltə][173]	dwelled [dwɛlːəd], dwelt [dwɛlt]
	fede(n) [feːdən]	fedde [fɛdːə]	fed [fɛd]
	here(n) [heːrən]	herde [hɛrdə]	herd [hɛrd]
	kepe(n) [keːpən]	kepte [kɛptə]	kept [kɛpt]
	mete(n) [meːtən]	mette [mɛtːə]	met [mɛt]
	fele(n) [feːlən]	felte [fɛltə]	feled [feːləd], felt [fɛlt]
	bye(n) [biːən]	boughte [bɔuxtə]	bought [bɔuxt]

[172] See Section **96** above.

[173] In earliest Middle English this verb belonged to Type I; the preterit was **dwelede** and the past participle **dweled.**

bringe(n) [brɪngən]   broughte [brɔuxtə]   brought [brɔuxt]
seke(n) [seːkən]   soughte [sɔuxtə]   sought [sɔuxt]
selle(n) [sɛlːən]   solde [sɔːldə]   sold [sɔːld]

The Middle English weak verbs of Type I have become regular verbs in Modern English, developing according to the processes explained in Section 138 above. Of the Middle English weak verbs of Type II, however, some have become regular verbs, some have become irregular verbs, and some have become indeterminate verbs; that is:

1.   Weak verbs of Type II whose present stems ended in [d] or [t][174] have become indeterminate verbs; e.g. M.E. caste(n), fede(n) mete(n).

But of the weak verbs of Type II whose present stems did not end in [d] or [t]:

2.   Those whose preterits ended in -de preceded by a voiced sound or in -te preceded by a voiceless sound and which had the same vowel in the infinitive and preterit have become regular verbs: fille(n), kisse(n).

3.   Those whose preterits ended in -te preceded by a voiced sound and those which had a different vowel in the infinitive and preterit have become irregular weak verbs:[175] ME dwelle(n), here(n), kepe(n), fele(n), bye(n), selle(n).

It can be seen even from the examples just given that the Middle English weak verbs which have become irregular weak verbs in Modern English were already (from a descriptive point of view) irregular in Middle English. The chief sources of irregularity were the following:

a.   In Old English and early Middle English the preterit ending -de always occurred after voiced sounds and the preterit ending -te after voiceless sounds, so that the preterits of bende(n), dwelle(n), and fele(n) were bende [bɛndə], dwelde [dwɛldə], and felde [fɛldə]. Later, however, the -de changed to -te in those verbs in which it was preceded by n and in many verbs in which it was preceded by l, so that the late Middle English preterits were bente, dwelte, and felte.[176]

---

[174] By the present stem of a verb is meant the present infinitive form minus the infinitive ending e(n).

[175] The Modern English development of the irregular weak verbs was like that of fille(n) and kisse(n) as shown above in 138.

[176] The ending -te was preceded by a voiced consonant also in Middle English dremte [drɛmtə], preterit of dreme(n) [dræːmən], and in Middle English girte [gɪrtə],

The past participles were originally **bended, dweled,** and **feled,** and became **bent, dwelt,** and **felt.**

b.   In Old English and in very early Middle English the preterits of verbs like **fede(n), here(n), kepe(n), mete(n),** and **fele(n)** had the same vowel as the infinitive. But long vowels were usually shortened in early Middle English (according to Section 54.1, above) when they were followed by a double consonant or by two or more consonants, so that very early Middle English **fedde** [feːdɪə], **herde** [heːrdə], [keːptə], **cepte mette** [meːtɪə], and **felde** [feːldə] became [fɛdɪə], [hɛrdə], [kɛptə], mɛtɪə], and [fɛldə].

c.   The vowel change that appears in the preterits of verbs like **bye(n), bringe(n), seke(n),** and **selle(n),** however, was not a Middle English development but existed already in Old English as the result of developments that occurred very early in the history of the Germanic languages and which are reflected in modern High German, Low German, Dutch, and the Scandinavian languages as well as in English.[177]

141.   Preterit Forms of Strong Verbs.   The Middle English strong verbs are most simply defined as those whose preterit indicative first and third singular does not end in **-ede, -ed, -de,** or **-te.** The principal parts (infinitive, preterit indicative first and third singular, preterit indicative plural, and past participle) of representative strong verbs are as follows:

---

preterit of **girde(n)** [gɪrdən], which have developed into the Modern English preterits [drɛmt] and [gɜːrt]. And in Middle English **lefte** [lɛftə], preterit of **leve(n)** [læːvən], and **loste** [lɔstə], used as the preterit of the strong verb **lese(n)** [leːzən], the change of **-de** to **-te** also occurred; the early Middle English forms were **levde** [lɛvdə] and lɔsde [lɔzdə], but the voiced [v] and [z] were assimilated to the ending that followed after the change of **-de** to **-te.** The past participles of these verbs were **dremed** [drɛːməd], **girt** [gɪrt], **left** [lɛft], and **lost** [lɔst]. The change of [d] to [t] that occurred in the preterit and past participle of weak verbs was due in part to analogy with the syncopated and assimilated third person singular, present indicative of such verbs as **sendan** (*sent*) and **girdan** (*girt*) and in part to the West Midland unvoicing of final [d] when preceded by a liquid or nasal consonant, resulting in the development of forms like **bent** from **bend, bilt** from **bild.** The first evidences of the development of these forms are found in the twelfth century.

[177] See Moore and Knott, *Elements of Old English*, §146.

rise(n)	[**riːzən**]	**roos**	[**rɔːs**]	**rise(n)**	[**rɪzən**]	**rise(n)**	[**rɪzən**]
frese(n)	[**freːzən**]	**frees**	[**fræːs**]	**frose(n)**	[**frɔːzən**][178]	**frose(n)**	[**frɔːzən**][178]
drinke(n)	[**drɪŋkən**]	**drank**	[**drɑŋk**]	**drunke(n)**	[**drʊŋkən**]	**drunke(n)**	[**drʊŋkən**]
stele(n)	[**stæːlən**]	**stal**	[**stɑl**]	**stole(n)**	[**stɔːlən**][178]	**stole(n)**	[**stɔːlən**]
bere(n)	[**bæːrən**]	**bar**	[**bɑr**][179]	**bore(n)**	[**bɔːrən**][179]	**bore(n)**	[**bɔːrən**]
breke(n)	[**bræːkən**]	**brak**	[**brɑk**]	**broke(n)**	[**brɔːkən**][178]	**broke(n)**	[**brɔːkən**]
speke(n)	[**spæːkən**]	**spak**	[**spɑk**]	**spoke(n)**	[**spɔːkən**][180]	**spoke(n)**	[**spɔːkən**]
shake(n)	[**ʃɑːkən**]	**shook**	[**ʃoːk**]	**shoke(n)**	[**ʃoːkən**]	**shake(n)**	[**ʃɑːkən**]
falle(n)	[**fɑlːən**]	**fell**	[**fɛlː**]	**felle(n)**	[**fɛlːən**]	**falle(n)**	[**fɑlːən**]
knowe(n)	[**knɔːʊən**]	**knew**	[**knɪu**]	**knewe(n)**	[**knɪuən**]	**knowe(n)**	[**knɔːʊən**]

The Modern English development of the preterit forms of **rise(n)**, **drinke(n)**, **speke(n)**, and **shake(n)** is shown in the following tables.

		MIDDLE ENGLISH	MODERN ENGLISH
PRET. IND. SING.	1	**roos** [**rɔːs**]	[**roːz**] *rose*
	2	**rise** [**rɪzə**], **roos** [**rɔːs**]	[**roːz**] *rose*
	3	**roos** [**rɔːs**]	[**roːz**] *rose*
PLUR.		**rise(n)** [**rɪzən**]	[**roːz**] *rose*
PRET. SUBJ. SING.		**rise** [**rɪzə**]	[**roːz**] *rose*
PLUR.		**rise(n)** [**rɪzən**]	[**roːz**] *rose*
PAST PARTICIPLE		**rise(n)** [**rɪzən**]	[**rɪzən**]
PRET IND. SING.	1	**drank** [**drɑŋk**]	[**dræŋk**]
	2	**drunke** [**drʊnkə**], **drank** [**drɑŋk**]	[**dræŋk**]
	3	**drank** [**drɑŋk**]	[**dræŋk**]
PLUR.		**drunke(n)** [**drʊŋkən**]	[**dræŋk**] *drank*

178 These forms are Northeast Midland forms; the forms that occurred in early Midland Middle English were **frure(n)** [**frʊrən**], **frore(n)** [**frɔrən**]; **stele(n)** [**steːlən**] or [**stæːlən**]; **breke(n)** [**breːkən**] or [**bræːkən**], and the forms given in the tables developed on the analogy of the past participle. Whether fourteenth century London English had the earlier Midland forms or the later is uncertain.

179 The forms that occurred in Chaucer's fourteenth century London English were **bar** [**bɑr**], **baar** [**bɑːr**], **beer** [**beːr**] and **bere(n)** [**beːrən**], **bare(n)** [**bɑːrən**]. The preterit plural **bore(n)** was a Northeast Midland form that developed from the analogy of the past participle.

180 The preterit plural forms that occurred in Chaucer's fourteenth century London English were **speke(n)** [**speːkən**] and **spake(n)** [**spɑːkən**]; **spoke(n)** was a Northeast Midland form that developed from the analogy of the past participle.

		MIDDLE ENGLISH	MODERN ENGLISH
PRET. SUBJ. SING.		drunke [druŋkə]	[dræŋk] *drank*
	PLUR.	drunke(n) [druŋkən]	[dræŋk] *drank*
PAST PARTICIPLE		drunke(n) [druŋkən]	[drʌŋk]
PRET. IND. SING.	1	spak [spɑk]	[spoːk] *spoke*
	2	spoke [spɔːkə], spak [spɑk]	[spoːk]
	3	spak [spɑk]	[spoːk] *spoke*
	PLUR.	spoke(n) [spɔːkən]	[spoːk]
PRET. SUBJ. SING.		spoke [spɔːkə]	[spoːk]
	PLUR.	spoke(n) [spɔːkən]	[spoːk]
PAST PARTICIPLE		spoke(n) [spɔːkən]	[spoːkən]
PRET. IND. SING.	1	shook [ʃoːk]	[ʃuk]
	2	shoke [ʃoːkə], shook [ʃoːk]	[ʃuk]
	3	shook [ʃoːk]	[ʃuk]
	PLUR.	shoke(n) [ʃoːkən]	[ʃuk]
PRET. SUBJ. SING.		shoke [ʃoːkə]	[ʃuk]
	PLUR.	shoke(n) [ʃoːkən]	[ʃuk]
PAST PARTICIPLE		shake(n) [ʃɑːkən]	[ʃeːkən]

All of the Modern English forms except those printed in italics are the unmodified product of sound change, the indicative and subjunctive plural forms developing from the Middle English forms without final n and the past participles developing usually from the forms with final n but sometimes (as in **drunk**) from forms without final n. The italicized forms require special comment.

1. The Middle English preterit indicative first and third singular [rɔːs] would have developed into Modern English [roːs]; it therefore seems probable that Modern English [roːz] is really a late Middle English plural form [rɔːz] which developed as explained in (3) below. Modern English preterit indicative first and third singular [spoːk] is also a plural form. After the loss of final [ə] the preterit indicative singular and plural of many strong verbs became identical; e.g. [ʃoːk] and [ʃoːkə] developed into [ʃoːk], [fɛlː] and [fɛlːə] into [fɛl], and [knɪu]

and [knɪuə] into [knɪu]. And after the loss of final [ə] the preterit indicative singular and plural of the other verbs—except those whose singular ended in a voiceless consonant and whose plural ended in a voiced consonant, as in [fræːs] and [frɔːz] from [fræːs] and [frɔːzə]—differed only in the quality of their vowel; e.g. [drɑŋk] and [drʊŋkə] became [drɑŋk] and [drʊŋk], [spɑk] and [spɔːkə] became [spɑk] and [spɔːk], etc. Then new analogical preterit singulars or preterit plurals were made; e.g. the new singular [spɔːk] which developed on the analogy: *preterit singular* [spɔːk] : preterit plural [spɔːk] : : preterit singular [ʃoːk] : preterit plural [ʃoːk], etc.[181]

2. The early Middle English preterit indicative second singular always differed from the first and third singular in having the ending -e which the first and third persons lacked and usually also in having a different vowel in the accented syllable (e.g. **rise, drunke,** etc.). In late Middle English, however, the preterit indicative second singular came to be identical with the first and third persons (e.g. **roos, drank**). But before the end of the fifteenth century there developed analogical forms of the preterit indicative second singular with the ending -est, e.g. **rosest, shokest,** etc. The Modern English preterit indicative second singular forms are derived from the early Modern English preterit indicative **plural** forms as a result of using the plural pronoun **ye** or **you** instead of the singular pronoun **thou** (cf. Section **137.1** above).

3. The preterit plural forms **rose** and **drank** are based on analogical preterit plural forms that developed, probably after the loss of final [ə], as explained above under (1). When the originally singular form [rɔːs] came to be used as a plural form the final consonant continued to be voiced, as it had been in the earlier forms of the preterit plural, e.g. Middle English [rɪzən], [frɔːzən].

4. The preterit subjunctive forms **rose** and **drank** did not develop from the Middle English forms [rɪzə], [rɪzən], and [drʊnkə], [drʊnkən], but are based on later forms that developed by analogy after [rɔːz] and [drɑnk] had become the preterit indicative plural.

The Modern English development of the preterit forms of the other strong verbs whose principal parts are given at the beginning of this section has been similar to that of the four verbs whose develop-

---

[181] Analogical formations of this kind were made also before the loss of final [ə]; e.g. the preterit singular forms [beːr] and [bɑːr] referred to in note 165 above were analogical formations made on the basis of the preterit indicative plural forms [beːrən] and [bɑːrən], but the loss of final [ə] gave a very strong impetus to the tendency.

ment has been traced in detail. The development was not completed, however, in Standard Written English until at least the middle or the latter part of the seventeenth century. The forms of the strong verbs that occur in Shakespeare's works are frequently different from those of present English. Shakespeare used as the preterits of **bear, break,** and **speak,** for example, not only the forms that occur in present English but also **bare, brake,** and **spake,** which are based on a different set of Middle English forms from those given in the tables above. As the past participles of **steal, bear, break, speak, shake,** and **fall** he used not only the forms that occur in present English but also **stole; bore; shook** and **shaked; fell.** And as the preterit of **drink** he used both **drank** and **drunk.** In fact, even in present English there is not *complete* uniformity of usage with regard to the principal parts of the strong verbs.

142. Preterit Form of Indeterminate Verbs. The weak and strong verbs constituted in Middle English clear-cut, mutually exclusive morphological types, the weak verbs being those whose preterit indicative first and third singular ended in **-ed, -de,** or **-te** and the strong verbs being those whose preterit indicative first and third singular did not end in **-ed, -de,** or **-te.** There can be no question as to which of the following Middle English verbs are weak and which are strong:

bete(n)	[bæːtən]	beet	[beːt]	bete(n)	[beːtən]	bete(n)	[bæːtən]
binde(n)	[biːndən]	bond	[bɔːnd]	bounde(n)	[buːndən]	bounde(n)	[buːndən]
bite(n)	[biːtən]	bot	[bɔːt]	bite(n)	[bɪtən]	bite(n)	[bɪtən]
caste(n)	[kastən]	caste	[kastə]	caste(n)	[kastən]	cast	[kast]
fede(n)	[feːdən]	fedde	[fɛdːə]	fedde(n)	[fɛdːən]	fed	[fɛd]
fighte(n)	[fɪxtən]	faught	[fauxt]	foughte(n)	[fɔuxtən]	foughte(n)	[fɔuxtən]
hide(n)	[hiːdən]	hidde	[hɪdːə]	hidde(n)	[hɪdːən]	hid	[hɪd]
holde(n)	[hɔːldən]	held	[hɛld][182]	helde(n)	[hɛldən][182]	holde(n)	[hɔːldən]
mete(n)	[meːtən]	mette	[mɛtːə]	mette(n)	[mɛtːən]	met	[mɛt]
ride(n)	[riːdən]	rood	[rɔːd]	ride(n)	[rɪdən]	ride(n)	[rɪdən]
sette(n)	[sɛttən]	sette	[sɛtːə]	sette(n)	[sɛtːən]	set	[sɛt]
sitte(n)	[sɪtːən]	sat	[sat]	sete(n)	[seːtən]	sete(n)	[sæːtən]
stande(n)	[standən][183]	stood	[stoːd]	stode(n)	[stoːdən]	stande(n)	[standən][183]

[182] Chaucer's forms appear to have been [heːld] and [heːldən].
[183] Chaucer's form appears to have been [stɔːndən].

In Modern English, however, these verbs (*beat, bind, bite, cast, feed, fight, hide, hold, meet, ride, set, sit, stand*) can be classified as irregular verbs but not as either strong or weak verbs. Because of the loss of final [ə] at the end of the Middle English period it is no longer possible for us to recognise that **beat** is a strong verb but **cast** is a weak verb; that **bite** is a strong verb but **hide** is a weak verb;[184] that **sit** is a strong verb but **set** is a weak verb. Like all irregular verbs whose common present form ends in [d] or [t], they are **indeterminate** verbs.

The Modern English development of the strong verbs given in the list above was like that of the strong verbs whose development is traced in the preceding section.[185] The Modern English development of the weak verbs in the list was like that of **fille(n)** and **kisse(n)** as shown above in Section 138, and Middle English **fedde, fed; hidde, hid;** and **mette, met** have the shortened vowel as explained in-Section 140.b.[186]

143. Classification of Anomalous Verbs. The anomalous verbs may be classified as follows:

1. The anomalous weak verbs **say, have, do.**
2. The preteritive-present verbs **shall, can, may, must, ought, dare** and the verbs **need** and **will,** which though not preteritive-present verbs historically have developed in Modern English certain formal characteristics of the preteritive-present verbs.
3. The verb **be.**

All of these verbs except **ought, dare,** and **need** have both stressed and unstressed forms, and the unstressed forms of all but **say** (and possibly **have**) are used very much more frequently than the stressed forms. The following account of the Modern English development of the anomalous verbs will confine itself to showing the relation between the Middle English stressed forms and the Modern English stressed forms. The Middle English and the Modern English unstressed forms will be mentioned only when there is special occasion for

---

[184] The Modern English past participle [hɪdn] is an analogical development.

[185] The Modern English past participles [held], [sæt], and [stʊd] are analogical formations of a type that is not illustrated in any of the verbs given in 141.

[186] Many Middle English strong verbs have become regular verbs or irregular weak verbs in Modern English; the Middle English principal parts of **help** were **helpe(n) halp, holpe(n), holpe(n)** and even Shakespeare used both the strong preterit and past participle **holp** and the weak form **helped.** A few Middle English weak verbs have become strong; e.g. **dig** is still a weak verb in Shakespeare but has become strong in later English. An account of these shiftings, however, belongs rather to the history of words than to the history of morphological types.

doing so.[187]   Unless it is otherwise stated, the Modern English stressed forms are derived from the Middle English stressed forms by the regular processes of sound-change.

All of the anomalous verbs except **say** have, in addition to their morphological characteristics, important syntactical characteristics and functions that are outside the scope of the present book.[188]

144. Anomalous Weak Verbs.   The anomalous weak verbs differ from the normal verbs in the formation of their present indicative third person singular.   The present indicative third person singular of these verbs has the ending [z], but the ending is not added to the present common form.   The Modern English development of the Middle English forms of the present indicative is shown in the following tables.

	MIDDLE ENGLISH		MODERN ENGLISH
	Southeast Midland	Northeast Midland	
PRES. IND. SING. 1	seye [sæɪə]		[seː]
2	seyest [sæɪəst]		[seː]
3	seyeth [sæɪəθ]	seyes [sæɪəs]	[sɛz]
PLUR.	seye(n) [sæɪən]		[seː]
PRES. IND. SING. 1	have [hɑvə]		[hæv]
2	hast [hɑst]		[hæv]
3	hath [hɑθ]	has [hɑs]	[hæz]
PLUR.	have(n) [hɑvən]		[hæv]
PRES. IND. SING. 1	do [doː]		[duː]
2	dost [doːst]		[duː]
3	doth [doːθ]	dos [doːs]	[dʌz]
PLUR.	do(n) [doːn]		[duː]

All of the present indicative forms except the third person singular are the result of the regular sound-changes, allowing for the fact that the plural form has developed from the Middle English form without

---

[187] The development of the unstressed forms of these verbs has been similar to the development of the unstressed forms of the pronouns; see note 150 above.

[188] All of these verbs have special negative forms, e.g. [hæznt], [dont], [ʃænt], etc. Their interrogative form is also different from that of other verbs. The commonest use of *have, do, shall, can, may, must, will,* and *be* is in the various periphrastic forms of the verb.

n and that the second person singular form has developed from the
Middle English plural. The present indicative third singular forms
have developed from the Northeast Midland forms, and Modern
English [hæz] is phonetically regular except in having the voiced final
[z], which developed only in unstressed syllables (see Section 124.1b
above). The voiced ending has developed either from the analogy of the
verbs in which the final [z] is phonetically regular or else is the result of
restressing the weak form, which (being an unstressed syllable) had
final [z] by regular phonetic development. The voiced ending occurs
for the same reason in [dʌz], but it is phonetically regular in [sɛz]
from the late Northeast Midland form [sæɪəz]. The vowel sound of [dʌz]
is also the result of restressing the early Modern English weak form,
which had the short vowel [u] in place of the [u] which was the regular development of Middle English [oː] in the strong form.[189]   The
vowel of [sɛz] was also probably the result of restressing, for in early
Modern English the strong form was probably [seːz] and the weak form
[sɛz].

These three verbs have irregular weak preterits. The Modern English
development of the Middle English principal parts (infinitive, preterit
indicative first and third singular, and past participle) was as follows:

MIDDLE ENGLISH	MODERN ENGLISH
seye(n) [sæɪən]	[seː]
seyde [sæɪdə]	[sɛd]
seyd [sæɪd]	[sɛd]
have(n) [havən]	[hæv]
hadde [hadːə]	[hæd]
had [had]	[hæd]
do(n) [doːn]	[du]
dide [dɪdə]	[dɪd]
don [doːn]	[dʌn]

The Modern English forms are the product of sound-change, except
that the preterit singular [sɛd] is a restressed weak form, that the past
participle [sɛd] is an analogical form based on the preterit, and that

---

[189] [dʌz] might also have resulted from restressing the Modern English weak form
[dəz]. The explanation of the negative form [doːnt] is difficult and uncertain.

the past participle [dʌn] is probably an analogical form which has the vowel of the present third singular [dʌz]. (The past participles cannot be explained as restressed weak forms because they are always stressed and have no weak forms.)

145. Preteritive-Present Verbs. The preteritive-present verbs (a group of verbs common to all the Germanic languages) are so called because their Old English **present** indicative forms were originally the **preterit** indicative forms of strong verbs. These old **preterit** forms acquired a **present** meaning and new **weak** preterits were then formed on the basis of the present stems.[190]   Even in Modern English these verbs can be recognised as a distinct morphological group by the fact that their present indicative third singular has no ending, but the peculiarities of their formation can be more clearly recognised in Middle English than in Modern English.   The Modern English development of the Middle English forms of **shall, can, may,** and **dare** was as follows.

		MIDDLE ENGLISH	MODERN ENGLISH
Pres. Ind. Sing.	1	shal [ʃal]	[ʃæl]
	2	shalt [ʃalt]	[ʃæl]
	3	shal [ʃal]	[ʃæl]
Plur.		shulle(n) [ʃulːən], shul [ʃul], shal [ʃal]	[ʃæl]
Pret. Ind. Sing.	1	sholde [ʃoːldə]	[ʃud]
	2	sholdest [ʃoːldəst]	[ʃud]
	3	sholde [ʃoːldə]	[ʃud]
Plur.		sholde(n) [ʃoːldən]	[ʃud]
Pres. Ind. Sing.	1	can [kan]	[kæn]
	2	canst [kanst]	[kæn]
	3	can [kan]	[kæn]
Plur.		conne(n) [kunːən], can [kan]	[kæn]
Pret. Ind. Sing.	1	couthe [kuːðə], coude [kuːdə]	[kud]
	2	couthest [kuːðəst], coudest [kuːdəst]	[kud]
	3	couthe [kuːðə], coude [kuːdə]	[kud]
Plur.		couthe(n) [kuːðən], coude(n) [kuːdən]	[kud]

[190] See Section **100** and note **105** above.

		MIDDLE ENGLISH	MODERN ENGLISH
PRES. IND. SING.	1	may [mæɪ]	[me]
	2	mayst [mæɪst]	[me]
	3	may [mæɪ]	[me]
PLUR.		mowe(n) [muːən], may [mæi]	[me]
PRET. IND. SING.	1	mighte [mɪxtə]	[maɪt]
	2	mightest [mɪxtəst]	[maɪt]
	3	mighte [mɪxtə]	[maɪt]
PLUR.		mighte(n) [mɪxtən]	[maɪt]
PRES. IND. SING.	1	dar [dɑr]	[dæːɚ]
	2	darst [dɑrst]	[dæːɚ]
	3	dar [dɑr]	[dæːɚ][191]
PLUR.		dorre(n) [durːən], dar [dɑr]	[dæːɚ]
PRET. IND. SING.	1	dorste [durstə]	[dæːɚd] dared[192]
	2	dorstest [durstəst]	[dæːɚd] dared
	3	dorste [durstə]	[dæːɚd] dared
Plur.		dorste(n) [durstən]	[dæːɚd] dared

All the Modern English forms except *should* and *could* are the product of sound-change, the second person singular developing from the early Modern English plural forms, the present plural from the monosyllabic Middle English forms, and the preterit plural from the Middle English forms without n.   The Middle English preterit form [ʃoːldə] developed regularly into early Modern [ʃuːld], the corresponding Early Modern English weak form being [ʃʊld], later [ʃʊd]; the Modern English strong form [ʃʊd] is probably the early Modern English weak form restressed.   The development of Modern English [kʊd] is less clear.   The early Modern English strong form was [kuːld]; this form was not derived from Middle English [kuːdə] but developed under the influence of early Modern English [ʃuːld] and [wuːld] (for the latter see under **will** below).   The early Modern English weak form was [kʊld], later [kʊd], and the Modern English strong form [kʊd] appears to have resulted from restressing the weak form.   The preservation of the early Modern English vowel [ʊ] in [ʃʊd] and [kʊd]

---

[191] There is also an analogical form [dæːɚz].

[192] The analogical preterit [dæːɚd] has displaced the older [dɝst] both in colloquial and literary use.

may be due to the influence of Modern English [wʊd] (for which see below).

Modern English **must** is derived from Middle English **moste** [moɪstə], **mostest** [moɪstest], **moste** [moɪstə], plural **moste(n)** [moɪstən], the preterit form of the preteritive-present verb **moot** [moɪt], which originally meant *be permitted* but which in Chaucer's time was used also in the sense of *be under obligation*. Even in Chaucer's period **moste,** originally preterit, was beginning to be used in a present sense. In Modern English *must* regularly has the sense of *be under obligation*, but it still has the older meaning *be permitted* in negative sentences like "You mustn't go." It is always used as a present form except in sentences like "He said he must go." Modern English [mʌst] is not derived directly from Middle English [moɪstə], which became early Modern English [muɪst] but is a restressed weak form.

Modern English **ought** is derived from Middle English **oughte** [ɔuxtə], **oughtest** [ɔuxtəst], **oughte** [ɔuxtə], plural **oughte(n)** [ɔuxtən], which was originally the preterit of a preteritive-present verb that meant *possess* (for the Old English forms and the Middle English development see Section **101** above). In Chaucer's time the present tense of this verb had lost its preteritive-present characteristics and had the regular present endings; it has developed into the Modern English regular verb **owe** (which in Shakespeare was still very frequently used in the older sense of *possess*). The originally preterit form **oughte** was used by Chaucer both as a preterit and a present form in the sense of *be under obligation*. Modern English [ɔt] is always used as a present form except in sentences like "He said he ought to go." It is the regular phonetic development of Middle English [ɔuxtə] and is always stressed.

Modern English **need** is derived from the Middle English weak verb **nede(n)** [neɪdən] and has a regular preterit in Modern English. In very late Middle English or early Modern English it developed an uninflected present indicative third singular which still survives in present English. The uninflected form is chiefly used in questions and negative sentences (e.g. "Need he go?", "He needn't go."); in other situations the regular form [nidz] is generally used. It is by no means clear why this verb developed the uninflected form, but it seems to have been (at least in part) from the analogy of the preteritive-present verbs; there was a Middle English preteritive-present verb thar [θɑr], preterit **thurte** [θʊrtə], from the Old English preteritive-present verb **þurfan,** which meant *need.*

The development of Modern English **will** is shown in the following table.

		MIDDLE ENGLISH	MODERN ENGLISH
PRES. IND. SING.	1	**wil** [wɪl], **wol** [wʊl]	[wɪl]
	2	**wilt** [wɪlt], **wolt** [wʊlt]	[wɪl]
	3	**wil** [wɪl], **wol** [wʊl]	[wɪl]
PLUR.		**wille(n)** [wɪlːən], **wil** [wɪl], **wol** [wʊl]	[wɪl]
PRET. IND. SING.	1	**wolde** [woːldə]	[wʊd]
	2	**woldest** [woːldəst]	[wʊd]
	3	**wolde** [woːldə]	[wʊd]
PLUR.		**wolde(n)** [woːldən]	[wʊd]

The Modern English present form is the regular product of sound-change. Middle English [woːldə] developed regularly into early Modern English [wuːld]; the early Modern English weak form was [wʊld, later [wʊd]. The strong form [wʊd] is a restressed form.[193] This verb was not originally a preteritive-present verb but an anomalous verb of entirely different formation (for the Old English and early Middle English forms see Section **102.2** above).

146. The Verb *be.* The Modern English development of the Middle English forms of the verb **be** is shown in the following table.

		MIDDLE ENGLISH		MODERN ENGLISH
		Southeast Midland	Northeast Midland	
PRET. IND. SING.	1	**am** [ɑm]		[æm]
	2	**art** [ɑrt]		[ɑɚ]
	3	**is** [ɪs]		[ɪz]
PLUR.		**be(n)** [beːn]	**are(n)** [ɑːrən]	[ɑɚ]
PRET. SUBJ. SING.		**be** [beː]		[biː]
PLUR.		**be(n)** [beːn]		[biː]

[193] The explanation of the negative form [woːnt] is difficult and uncertain.

	MIDDLE ENGLISH		MODERN ENGLISH
	Southeast Midland	Northeast Midland	
PRET. IND. SING. 1	was [wɑs]		[wɔz], [wɑz], [wʌz]
2	were [wæːrə]		[wɜ·], [wæːɚ][194]
3	was [wɑs]		[wɔz], [wɑz], [wʌz]
PLUR.	were(n) [wɛːrən]		[wɜ·], [wæːɚ][195]
PRES. SUBJ. SING.	were [wæːrə]		[wɜ·], [wæːɚ]
PLUR.	were(n) [wæːrən]		[wɜ·], [wæːɚ]
IMPERATIVE SING.	be [beː]		[biː]
PLUR.	beth [beːθ], be [beː]		[biː]
PRES. INFINITIVE	be(n) [beːn]		[biː]
GERUND	to be(n) [toː beːn]		[tə biː]
VERBAL NOUN	being [beːɪŋg]		[biːɪŋ]
PRES. PARTICIPLE	being [beːɪŋg]		[biːɪŋ]
PAST PARTICIPLE	be(n) [beːn]		[bɪn], [biːn], [bɛn]

All the Modern English forms except *is*, *was*, *were*, and *been* are historical forms derived from the Middle English form by the regular process of sound change, the Modern English plural forms and the infinitive and gerund being derived from the Middle English forms without **n**.

The present indicative third singular [ɪz] is a restressed weak form, for though its vowel shows the regular development of Middle English [ɪ] its final consonant could only have developed in an unstressed syllable. The present indicative plural form [ɑɚ] is the restressed form of the early Modern English weak form [ɑr], for the regular development of the Northeast Midland Middle English [ɑːrə] would have been [æːr], a form which existed in earlier Modern English but which is now obsolete.

All of the preterit indicative singular forms are restressed, for they have the final [z] that developed only in unaccented syllables; [wɔz]

---

[194] The second person singular form is of course developed from the early Modern English plural form. The second person singular forms **wert** and **wast** developed apparently in early Modern English from the analogy of the preteritive present verbs (e.g. **shalt, canst**).

[195] Middle English **was** and **were(n)** were originally the preterit forms of a strong verb.

and [wɑz] have developed from a restressing of the early Modern English weak form [wɑz] (see Section **122.1** above), [wɔz] being the usual form in British English and [wɑz] the usual form in American English; [wʌz] is a later form which has developed from a restressing of the later Modern English weak form [wəz].

The plural form [wæːɚ] is the regular development of Middle English [wæː rə]; the form [wɝ] would have developed from restressing either the early Modern English weak form [wɛr] or the later weak form [wɚ].

The past participle [biːn] is the regular development of Middle English [beːn]; [bɛn] is the result of restressing the early Modern English weak form [bɛn]; [bɪn] is the result of restressing a later Modern English weak form, probably [bɪn], which developed from the destressing of the strong form [biːn].

INDEX

References are to page numbers
Accentuation 12–13
Adjectives, comparison 148
Adjectives, declension
  Chaucer 51–52
  Middle English 51–52, 88–90
  Modern English 148
  Old English 22
Affricates 2, 17
Alphabet, phonetic v, vi, 8–11
American English 9, 10, 135–137
Analogy 80–82, 87, 91, 103, 119, 122–23,
  125, 141, 144–147, 163–167
Anomalous verbs 58, 108, 109, 168–176
Apocope 37, 62–63
Article, definite
  Middle English 95–97
  Old English 23
Assimilation 143–160

Back vowels 4
Breaking 25, 118, 121, 124
British English 8, 10, 137

Chaucer
  Inflections 50–63
  Phonetic transcription 38–45
  Pronunciation 36–50
  Spelling 46–49
Consonant chart 17
Consonants
  Affricates 2
  Classification of 2–3, 17–18
  Fricatives 2, 17, 139, 143
  Glides 17–18
  Laterals 17
  Middle English 50, 73–74, 77–78
  Modern English 1–3, 17–18, 139–140
  Nasals 3, 17
  Old English 20
  Oral 3, 17
  Stops 2, 17
  Syllabic 13

Voiced 1, 17
Voiceless 1, 17

Definite article
  Middle English 95–97
  Old English 23
Demonstrative pronoun
  Middle English 95–97
  Modern English 154
  Old English 22–23
Destressing 149–150
Dialects
  London 130–132
  Middle English vi, 72, 84, 110–130
  Old English 24–35
Diphthongization
  Modern English 11
  Old English 25, 27
  Middle English 115–117
Diphthongs
  Middle English 69–72
  Modern English 7, 10–11
  Old English 19, 66
Doubled consonants
  Middle English 50, 140
  Old English 20

Elision 37, 62–63
English language, periods 17

Final *e*
  In Chaucer 37, 59–62
  Loss of 138, 143
Fricative consonants 2, 17, 139, 143
Front vowels 4

Glides 17, 18
Gradation 13, 91–92

Homorganic consonants in OE 28–29

Indeterminate verbs 162
Inflections

Chaucer 50–63
Development of 79–82
Middle English, 79–110
Modern English 141–176
Old English 22–24, 79
Interrogative pronoun 154
Irregular nouns 144–148
Irregular weak verbs 161–163

Kentish 24, 34–35, 116–117, 120–122, 127

Larynx 1
Lateral consonants 17
Lengthening
Of Middle English vowels 135
Of Old English vowels 68–69, 71
London, dialect of 130–132
Long vowels 6–7

Mercian 25, 32–33
Middle English
Adjectives 51–52, 88–90
Consonants 50, 73–74, 77–78
Dialects vi, 72, 84, 110–130
Diphthongs 69–72, 76–77
Inflections 50–63, 79–110
Nouns 50–52, 83–88
Pronouns 53–54, 91–97
Sounds of 36–45, 65–74
Spelling 46, 74–78
Unstressed vowels 72–74
Verbs 54–58, 98–109
Vowels 75–69, 76–77
Midland dialect 116–117, 122–124, 128
Modern English
Adjectives 148
Consonants 1–3, 17–18, 139–140
Diphthongs 7, 10–11
Gradation 13, 91–92
Inflections 141–176
Nouns 142–148
Pronouns 149–155
Sounds 8–18, 133–140
Stress 12–13
Verbs 155–176
Vowels 3–7, 11–13, 16, 133–139

Nasal consonants 3

New diphthongs in Middle English 69–72
Northern dialect, 116–117, 124–126, 128–129
Northumbrian 24, 32–33
Noun declensions
Chaucer 50–51
Middle English 50–51, 83–88
Modern English 142–148
Old English 22–24

Old English
Development of vowels 65–74
Dialects 24–35
Inflections 22–24, 79
Pronunciation 19–24
Sounds 19–24
Specimen passages 20–21, 32–35
Spelling 19–20, 74
Oral consonants 3

Personal pronoun
Middle English 53–54, 19–95
Modern English 149–154
Old English 22
Phonetic alphabet v–vi, 8–11
Phonetic transcription
Chaucer 38–45
Middle English 38–45
Modern English 14–15
Old English 19–24
Preteritive present verbs 57, 105–108, 171–174
Pronoun declensions
Chaucer 53–54
Middle English 53–54, 91–97
Modern English 149–155
Old English 22–23

Quantity, of vowels 6–7

Relative pronoun 154
Restressing 149–150, 153, 170, 175–176
Retroflex vowels 16, 136–137
Rounding in Late West Saxon 30

Shortening
Of Middle English vowels 134
Of Old English vowels 67–68

Smoothing 29–30
Sound change 46, 48. 64–65, 79–80, 147–
   148, 157, 160
Sounds
   Chaucer's English 46–50
   Middle English 36–45, 65–74
   Modern English 8–18, 133–140
   Old English 19–24
   Oral 3
   Nasal 3
   Voiced 1
   Voiceless 1
Southern dialect 116–119, 126
Speech organs 1
Spelling
   Chaucerian 46
   Middle English 46, 74–78
   Old English 19–20, 74
   Old French 75–76
Standard English, development of 130–
   132
Stops 2
Stress 12–13
   In pronouns 91–92
Stress shift 139
Strong adjectives 22, 51–52, 88–89
Strong verbs 23, 55–57, 102–105, 163–167
Syllables, open and closed 68
Syncopation 37, 62–63, 138, 143

Umlaut 27, 28, 115–116
Unrounding in Late West Saxon 30
Unstressed vowels
   Middle English 72–74, 79–80, 91–92
   Modern English 138–139

Verb conjugation
   Chaucer 54–58
   Middle English 54–58, 98–109

Modern English 155–176
Old English 23
Verbs
   Anomalous 58, 108–109, 174–176
   Irregular weak 161–163
   Preteritive present 57, 105–108
   Strong 23, 55–57, 102–105, 163–167
   Weak 23, 54–55, 97–101, 158–163
Vocal lips 1
Voiced sounds 1
Voiceless sounds 1
Vowel chart 16
Vowel shift 132–134
Vowels
   Classification of 4–6, 16
   Gradation 13
   Height 4
   Lax 5
   Lengthening in Old English 28–29
   Long 6
   Middle English 46–49, 64–69
   Modern English 3–7, 11–13, 16, 133–
      139
   Old English 19, 48–49, 65–67
   Quantitative changes 67–69, 134–136
   Quantity 6, 11–12
   Retroflex 16, 136–137
   Rounded 4
   Short 6
   Tense 5, 11
   Tongue position 4
   Unround 4
   Unstressed 72–74, 79–80

Weak adjectives 22, 51–52, 90
Weak nouns 22, 86–88
Weak verbs 23, 54–55, 97–101, 158–163
West Saxon 24
Whisper 1